Ellen Glasgow and
a Woman's Traditions

John O. Tyler, Jr. JD PhD
October 1, 2017

Ellen Glasgow and a Woman's Traditions

Pamela R. Matthews

University Press of Virginia

Charlottesville and

London

This is a title in the series
Feminist Issues: Practice, Politics, Theory

The University Press of Virginia
Copyright © 1994
by the Rector and Visitors
of the University of Virginia

First Published 1994

Frontispiece: Ellen Glasgow in 1897. (Ellen Glasgow
Papers, Acc. no. 5060, courtesy Special Collections
Department, Manuscripts Division, University of Virginia
Library)

Library of Congress Cataloging-in-Publication Data

Matthews, Pamela R.
Ellen Glasgow and a woman's traditions / Pamela R.
Matthews.
p.   cm. — (Feminist issues)
Includes bibliographical references and index.
ISBN 0-8139-1539-2 (cloth)
1. Glasgow, Ellen Anderson Gholson, 1873–1945—
Criticism and interpretation. 2. Feminism and literature—
Southern States—History—20th century. 3. Women
and literature—Southern States—History—20th
century.   I. Title.   II. Series: Feminist issues
(Charlottesville, Va.)
PS3513.L34Z718   1994
813'.52—dc20   94-28531
CIP

Printed in the United States of America

To Dennis

Contents

Preface

Through others' eyes, Ellen Glasgow (1873–1945) has been the rapacious devourer of negative critics, the demanding and unsatisfied friend or lover, the disembodied intellectual, even, to H. L. Mencken, the deaf "old girl" who gossips but is nonetheless "pretty good company."[1] Often she has been "Miss Ellen," the feisty but gracious little lady from the South; occasionally, she has been Glasgow the self-pitying romanticizer of women's passivity. All of these views have shared stereotypical and biased views of Glasgow as a woman writer. She was criticized for being too strong/weak, too public/private, too professional/personal, too Southern/not Southern enough, too masculine/feminine. She was criticized by mostly male critics for reasons that didn't fit with my expectations of a woman writer. For wanting recognition she was seen as a usurper, an intruder, a threat (James Branch Cabell compared her to Circe enchanting swinish reviewers); if she demanded fair terms with her publishers, she was seen as pushy and self-aggrandizing. All such criticisms denigrated her in familiar ways for being a woman and trying to find a place in a man's world, for trying to speak for herself within what Domna C. Stanton has called "a particular discursive context, an (ideo)logical boundary that always already confines the speaking subject."[2]

Bearing my own "particular discursive context" in mind, I have tried as much as possible to describe not my own attitudes toward such subjects as women's traditions or women's community but Glasgow's. Inhabiting a cultural limbo between a world of "women's culture" in the nineteenth century and that of New Women who followed, Glasgow, with many of her contemporaries, faced highly charged conflicts about female identity.

To Glasgow, "female identity" would not have suggested, as it does today, the double-faced specter of essentialism, used often in the service of both women's power and women's inferiority. I rely, heavily at times, on the insights of historians and psychological theorists such as Nancy Cott, Carol Gilligan, and Carroll Smith-Rosenberg, while realizing that their work at times can suggest essential qualities of femaleness. For me, their work on separate spheres for women, on female psychosocial and psychosexual development, and on women's community, also can argue just as convincingly for the power of cultural constructions to delimit women's (and others') self-representations. Glasgow was clearly engaged in questions of women's relationships to other women; scholars such as those I have just named have helped me to sort through her responses. While I might question the terms of Glasgow's search for something called her self, might question even the idea of a female self at all, I must grant Glasgow her effort and attempt to describe it in her terms.

Likewise, Glasgow's attitudes toward "traditions" do not necessarily correspond to my own. At the time Glasgow began her writing career in the late nineteenth century (as early as 1880, when she was seven, if we accept her own account), she had very different ideas about a woman's place in any kind of tradition, literary or personal. Thus, while I live in a critical and cultural climate that recognizes the problems with establishing any tradition—indeed, a climate in which I can agree with Mary Helen Washington's notion of the "*fiction* of tradition"[3]—Glasgow lived and worked in an atmosphere that kept her largely ignorant about many women's traditions that would have been, and in fact ultimately did become, useful to her.

I persist, even at the risk of charges of separatism or critical naïveté, in seeing the recovery of many traditions, if not a single one, as a valid pursuit for feminist scholars today. What Margo Culley in speaking of autobiography has referred to as a "*mondo bizzarro*" of different traditions of women's textual productions seems vitally important to describe and discuss. Florence Howe proposes that perhaps we need to consider traditions as "smaller in size than monuments," more like quilt or tapestry patterns. Elaine Showalter, enacting in the conclusion to *Sister's Choice* her own version of one kind of tradition—that of quilting—echoes Howe's sentiments and language: "To recognize that the tradition of American women's writing is exploding, multi-cultural, contradictory, and dispersed is yet not to abandon the critical effort to piece it together, not into a monument, but into a literary quilt that offers a new map of a changing America."[4] Glasgow's coming to embrace (in a re-created form) her mother's generation's world of separate spheres is a gesture we might lament as reactionary, separatist, and essentialist. For her, it was a personal step forward. My title is intended to acknowledge my recognition that I am speaking about a single woman and a few of many possible traditions, and to serve as a reminder that many worlds exist other than the one I happen to be describing here.

A final word about race and class. Some readers will regret my decision to confine most of this book to Glasgow's own limited perspective as an economically comfortable white woman ("*a* woman," in my title) who lived most of her life in her native Richmond, Virginia. A careful consideration of Glasgow and her work in the interstices of race and class will itself require a full-length study. Among recent studies, Elizabeth Ammons's *Conflicting Stories* has suggested helpful directions for such a work; I hope my own book will suggest others. Glasgow's limitations in sensitivity to the imbalances of racism and classism are not difficult to imagine or to find evidence of, but I have chosen to celebrate her moments of insight rather than to stress her perhaps more frequent moments of blindness. I live in a climate of heightened awareness of the inescapability of cultural and historical context; it has seemed to me unfair to ask Glasgow somehow to transcend her own culture and history.

Glasgow's attention to the problems of women and the traditions that have borne them along testifies to her belief in the project of recovering the lives and stories of women, including her own. Even when she disagreed with these women, denied them, lashed out at them, imitated or loved them, Glasgow remained aware of the women who went before her, of those who sustained her during her life, and, I'll bet, of those of us who've shared her concerns since then. With Carolyn Heilbrun, then—and like her, "not without trepidation"—I begin my study of a "privileged" white woman [5] whose story, I maintain, nevertheless can teach us all something.

Many others have contributed to the making of this book. The staff at the University of Virginia's Alderman Library facilitated my work during two research trips there. Carmen Hurff at the University of Florida, Gainesville, helped me with the Marjorie Kinnan Rawlings Papers housed there. Alice Birney of the Library of Congress is responsible for locating the Glasgow-Moulton correspondence, for which I am most grateful. For permission to quote copyrighted material, I sincerely thank Margaret Williams and the Society for the Prevention of Cruelty to Animals in Richmond, Virginia (Ellen Glasgow's papers);

Frances (Mrs. James Asa) Shield (Henry Anderson's letters); Norton Baskin (Marjorie Kinnan Rawlings's papers). Without the generosity of these individuals, this book would not have been possible.

Louis J. Budd provided encouragement in the project's earliest stages and has continued to be supportive. Merrill and Diane Whitburn of Pride and Prejudice-Books and Rich Fusco sent first editions of Glasgow's works; Rich has remained a willing listener and contributor of ideas. The series editors and the anonymous readers at the University Press of Virginia sharpened my thinking and improved the manuscript; and I sincerely thank Nancy C. Essig, the director, for her unflagging support of this project.

This book would not exist without the critical insights of other Glasgow scholars, too numerous to mention by name, even when our interpretations differ. My thanks to them, and in particular to E. Stanly Godbold, Jr., Julius Rowan Raper, and Linda Wagner-Martin. I am especially grateful to another Glasgow scholar, Dorothy Scura, whose enthusiastic support has gone far beyond any professional duty to a fledgling critic.

Colleagues and friends at Texas A&M University have demonstrated warm collegiality and generous professional support. The Interdisciplinary Group for Historical Literary Study has fostered an intellectual atmosphere that nurtures scholarly activity. Harriette Andreadis lent early support. Larry J. Reynolds read perceptively an early draft. Margaret J. M. Ezell has read the entire manuscript twice at crucial stages, and her critical skills and encouragement have been invaluable. Janis Stout, Mary Ann O'Farrell, and Lynne Vallone read and improved portions of the manuscript; Lynne, during our regular lunches and walks, also has listened faithfully, asked the right questions, and helped me keep a sense of humor. The Texas A&M University mini-grant program provided the funds for a research trip to Gainesville, Florida. In 1991, Dean Daniel Fallon and the College of Liberal Arts at Texas A&M awarded me a Summer Research Grant that gave me uninterrupted work time at a crucial stage. The Department of English at A&M has granted two course reductions for research, and J. Lawrence Mitchell has been the kind of department head whose support goes far beyond routine encouragement.

Finally, my family deserves my utmost love and gratitude. My mother teaches me about women's traditions, and my sister reminds me of a different audience of women for whom I write. My young son, who has grown along with this project, is the kind of sensitive and loving boy a feminist mother dreams of. My husband, colleague, and number-one fan, Dennis Berthold, has provided a rare personal and professional support. His constant encouragement, unrelenting domestic help, and remarkable critical acumen have helped make this project manageable, and much better than it would have been without him. To Matthew and Dennis, my heartfelt thanks for showing me what is possible.

ONE

Introduction:
Re-viewing Ellen Glasgow

> The need of woman for woman was not written in the
> songs and the histories of men, but in the neglected
> and frustrated lives which the songs and the histories
> of men had ignored.
>
> Glasgow, *The Miller of Old Church*

> Women . . . have no past, no history, no religion of
> their own.
>
> Beauvoir, *The Second Sex*

THE IDEA THAT women must redefine their very selves apart
from the mediation of patriarchal expectations resonates with
particular urgency in the work of feminists since Simone de Beauvoir's *The Second Sex* asserted that "One is not born, but rather
becomes, a woman."[1] Our twentieth-century critical views of many
women writers have been changed completely by the eye-opening insistence of readers from Beauvoir to Adrienne Rich and others that,
in Rich's term, we "re-vision" women writers and their contexts. As a
consequence, feminist critics, concerned specifically with a variety of
subjects ranging from the sentimental novel to French feminist theory
have shared one general goal: an insistence on the centrality of revisionist reading and writing in the feminist critical and theoretical
project.[2]

But many writers have yet to be re-viewed. Ellen Glasgow—who
wrote and published nineteen novels (and a draft of a twentieth) as

well as poems, short stories, essays, reviews, and an autobiography in a career that spanned nearly fifty years in her native Richmond—has not been subject to change (to borrow Nancy K. Miller's phrase) from feminist reevaluation in the way that writers such as Charlotte Perkins Gilman or Willa Cather have been. Miller's perspicacious reminder that we must take into account not only the writer's gender but the reader's as well[3] helps to explain some of the puzzles in studying Ellen Glasgow and to highlight the necessity for an interpretive strategy that foregrounds Glasgow's perception of her role as a woman writer and her critics' (mis)understanding of that role. Critics have usually read Glasgow from stereotypical viewpoints that emphasize her elusive love life (real or imagined), her assiduous courting of influential male critics, or her excessive attention to her appearance, for example. They depend on an ideology of feminine dependence, passivity, triviality, or vanity. Using gender as it inescapably influences point of view, I propose alternative interpretations of the material of Glasgow's life and fiction. Looking anew at "facts" historically read in ways that slant critical perspectives on Glasgow often yields altogether different readings.

One example will serve. One of Glasgow's biographers, E. Stanly Godbold, Jr., cites correspondence between Glasgow and her close friend Virginia novelist Amélie Rives Troubetzkoy as evidence of what appears to be Glasgow's nearly obsessive attention to her appearance.[4] Indeed, Rives Troubetzkoy does respond to what clearly were questions about effective cosmetics and beauty secrets. But this series of letters between these close friends has an important and overlooked context: Rives Troubetzkoy at the time appeared dangerously close to severe depression after the death of her husband, Pierre. Her letter to Glasgow on the first anniversary of Pierre's death speaks at length of him and of her suicidal feelings.[5] Two weeks later she answers a letter from Glasgow (destroyed at Glasgow's request, as Rives Troubetzkoy makes clear in her letter) with fourteen pages of devotion and beauty advice, an epistolary trend that continues for at least a month longer.[6] The shift in tone from near panic and depression to lively advice argues that Glasgow's requests were sensitive responses to her friend's mood and mental condition more than sincere expressions of her own need. By channeling her friend's energy into a subject Glasgow correctly knew Rives Troubetzkoy would warm to, the depression dissipates. The series of letters ends with Rives Troubetzkoy thanking Glasgow for a Christmas gift of expensive cosmetics, ones she had recommended but either could not or would not buy for herself at the time. Glasgow had helped pull her friend safely through a near crisis. Rather than indicating Glasgow's vanity, the letters can thus be reread as equally revealing illustrations of both her devotion to a dear friend and her psychological astuteness.

What makes this kind of gender-inflected rereading crucial with Glasgow? For one thing, readers' responses from the time of Glasgow's first published work reveal a subtle—and sometimes not so subtle—antifeminism underlying their critical judgments. The history of Glasgow's critical fate demonstrates remarkably well not only the difficulties she must have faced in determining her own place but also the subsequent difficulties we have had in placing her life and work accurately. The example most relevant to my study focuses on readers' responses to Glasgow as a woman writer. Her first published novel, *The Descendant*—written, according to Glasgow, after she had destroyed an earlier manuscript, *Sharp Realities* (c. 1891)—appeared anonymously in 1897, when Glasgow was just twenty-three. Anonymity itself (often in the form of pseudonymity) was particularly common in the history of nineteenth-century women novelists, and this may have been the only way—or at least the quickest—to get her book published, especially given the trouble Glasgow had had with earlier rejections.[7] According to her autobiography, one editor advised her to "stop writing, and go back to the South and have some babies." Another decided that the " 'new woman sort of thing' " was passé. Only when an editor chosen by a friend submitted her manuscript anonymously to Harpers was it accepted.[8]

Reviewers immediately began speculating about the novel's authorship. The protagonist, a fiery-tempered young socialist of unknown parentage named Michael Akershem, certainly seemed to argue in 1897 against a female author; Glasgow reports that an "elderly kinsman," who might have been speaking for many others, found it "incredible" that "a well-brought-up Southern girl should even know what a bastard is."[9] Before the novel's authorship was revealed, reviewers employed language associated with stereotypical masculinity: it had "uncommon vigor" and a feel for the "dramatic"; it was "distinctly, almost audaciously, virile and vigorous"; it was "forceful," "able," and "daring."[10] One rumor was that Harold Frederic, author of the best-selling tale of a man's moral and religious degeneration, *The Damnation of Theron Ware* (1896), had written *The Descendant*.[11] Though similar speculations and descriptions still appeared in reviews after Glasgow's identity was known, the shift in tone is marked. One review notes Glasgow's reading in science, social science, and philosophy that informs *The Descendant*—her "masculine" reading—and cautions the author not to identify too closely with George Eliot,[12] a woman writer with a man's name and, presumably, too much "masculine" knowledge.

In a gesture whose exaggerated attention to the novelty of the author's gender speaks volumes about the history of women's writing, a review of *The Descendant,* three months after the novel appeared in March 1897, published a photograph of Glasgow (see frontispiece) and identified her as "the author of *The Descendant*." The picture shows an attractive, petite, demure, and very young woman seated in an elaborately carved chair and wearing a dress, suitable for any debutante ball, made of yards of frilly white fabric. The photographic choice cannot but argue that yes, unbelievable as it seems, this pretty young thing actually wrote a novel about "bastards," socialism, and women artists who enjoy the privileges of marriage without the actual ceremony. Both this male reviewer and the female author of another review that reproduced a sketch of the same photo may have been aiming for an entirely different goal: women *can* publish serious philosophic fiction. But the effect of either interpretation is to isolate Glasgow, to make her efforts exceptional, to point out the idiosyncrasy of her achievement.[13]

This patronizing attitude toward Glasgow continued, though sometimes more subtly, as critics of her subsequent novels addressed the issue of Glasgow's gender directly. A review of *The Voice of the People* (1900), probably intending to compliment Glasgow, called her novel a "masterly study of social and political conditions" showing no sign of "the feminine hand."[14] Glasgow's admittedly feminist treatment of her title character in *Virginia* (1913)[15] may have irritated some reviewers, who responded with stereotypical attitudes toward women's writings and female characters. One ostensibly favorable review perceives a trend away from Glasgow's previous masculine vigor to presumably limp feminine concerns. According to this reviewer, *Virginia*, a "transition" in Glasgow's career, lacks the "robust vigour" of earlier novels, though it adds "subtle shadings and delicate intuitions." Another less-generous assessment says it "overflows with trivialities that can have no possible human interest." These "trivialities" reveal the reviewer's antifeminism; they are precisely the stuff of many women's lives: trivialities of Virginia's "mental attitude," of "household life and nursery cares," of "infantile illnesses and other details of the sick room," of "the anticipations of birth and the preparations for weddings and funerals." An anonymous reviewer described Glasgow's 1916 *Life and Gabriella* as "still another study of the modern woman and marriage" in which—rather tiresomely according to this reviewer—"man is on trial again, and once more is found wanting."[16]

Had Glasgow suffered from the responses of reviewers only in her own time, there might have been less misunderstanding of her and her career since then. But the critical biases have continued, though usually less overtly. Louis D. Rubin, Jr., in 1959, complains that Glasgow's novels are so driven by her "private feminine desires and needs that the reader may find it all but impossible to accept Miss Glasgow's version of experience."[17] Rubin's assessment, no less than the reviewer in 1913, is predicated on an assumption that "*the* reader" must lack "private feminine desires and needs." Perhaps most damaging have been the critical responses from the seemingly objective perspectives of biography, bibliography, and letters—though postmodern critical methods have enabled us to recognize more readily the biases revealed in these modes of criticism. Godbold's biography, *Ellen Glasgow and the Woman Within* (1972), painstakingly reconstructs the "facts" of Glasgow's life. Though without question an indispensable source of information, the book's implied interpretations too often have clouded our view of Glasgow—an objection also raised by Edgar E. MacDonald, though for different reasons.[18] Too frequently, for instance, Godbold reads the novels as undiluted responses to some real or presumed love affair—or the lack of one—in Glasgow's life. Nick Burr, the protagonist of *The Voice of the People,* for example, is unconvincing because he is "not the sexual creature which the male of the species is inclined to be," thus revealing that Glasgow's "knowledge of men" was "scarcely even academic."[19] *Barren Ground* (1925) is built upon a "philosophy of life so without feeling, so without emotion, that its adherent might as well be dead," a philosophy Glasgow presumably adopts "as a simple means of survival in the aftermath of the rupture of her painful relationship with Henry Anderson."[20] Too many of Godbold's readings—and too much of his biographical emphasis—place Glasgow in a position peripheral to some presumed male center in her life. Moreover, the portrait of Glasgow that emerges is of a woman overly dependent upon others—particularly male others—for love or critical recognition, and excessively concerned with how others perceive her. Though such dependency and concern sometimes seem to characterize Glasgow, Godbold's analyses too often overlook the complexities of socially constructed representation and self-representation.

Godbold's biography is not alone among the seemingly objective approaches that fail to consider gender biases in reading Glasgow. MacDonald and Inge's comprehensive annotated bibliography, *Ellen Glasgow: A Reference Guide,* published in 1986, at times reveals a lack of objectivity in its protective patronizing of Glasgow, a misplaced chivalry that tries to shield "Miss Ellen," as some have called Glasgow,[21] from any observations deemed unseemly or inappropriate. And too often *inappropriate* seems to mean "feminist." Anne Goodwyn Jones's award-winning feminist study *Tomorrow Is Another Day,* highly regarded since its publication in 1981, is criticized for "indulg[ing] in impressionistic assertions," though its discussion of Glasgow's "minor characters" "has some interest."[22] An early (1973) feminist dissertation on Glasgow is dismissed with near sarcasm. MacDonald and Inge describe it as "characterized by such statements as 'Most of [Glasgow's] male characters are bent on destroying their women'" and judge its bibliography "anemic." Another among the first feminist studies of Glasgow is labeled "a litle treatise" and described as "more of an appreciation than a scholarly study." Yet another feminist approach to Glasgow is pronounced "lacking in control so that overstatements alternate with strange lacunae."[23] I do not mean to suggest that feminist approaches can have no faults, or that they should be protected from critical scrutiny, or that all negative assessments in this standard bibliography are of feminist studies. Nevertheless, the preponderance of unearned condemnation of feminist approaches to Glasgow is disturbing.

One final example of a work whose very nature suggests critical distance but which nevertheless implies a subtle antifeminism is Blair Rouse's volume of selected letters. It is perhaps understandable why—especially in 1958 when Glasgow's posthumous critical reputation had yet to be determined—the letters "selected" would be predominately professional ones. It may have seemed more urgent to establish the public Ellen Glasgow who wrote to Allen Tate, H. L. Mencken, and James Branch Cabell than to reveal the private woman who wrote warm and affectionate personal letters, especially to female friends. No doubt it was easier too, as is often the case, to show the public woman of letters, for Glasgow often requested that her friends destroy her letters. This means that personal correspondence is frequently one-sided, and Glasgow's responses must be inferred from letters written to her. Nevertheless, by focusing so nearly exclusively on the professional letters of Glasgow, especially those later in her career, Rouse tends to portray a woman who spends most of her time courting the favor of prominent literary men and seeking their critical approval. This apparently self-serving Ellen Glasgow is one who responds in an understandable, if unappealing, way to her own desire for recognition, one who knows which critics must publicly admire her work if it is to be accepted in serious literary circles. In contrast to the published correspondence, the unpublished letters of Ellen Glasgow demonstrate how relatively small a part of the woman this public Glasgow is; most of her extant correspondence is with friends and family members, usually female. Rouse's selection also reveals an attitude subject to productive feminist reinterpretation, for it relies on an assumption that women writers must be judged as significant only on the basis of their public selves, in correspondence with other important (usually male) public selves. This notion depends on a view that well-known public selves are inherently superior to lesser-known private ones, and we are back to a central problem in feminist criticism of women's lives and work: how to integrate necessarily more private concerns into our definition of significance.

The critical biases in these three examples of ostensibly objective approaches to Glasgow—biography, bibliography, and letters—are familiar to feminist critics. Familiar, too, is their primary effect. Glasgow is positioned not at the center of her life but on the edges, defined not by herself but by others. Her contemporaries, tired of the "woman question" in fiction, were happiest with demonstrations of Glasgow's more "masculine" prose. Her biographer would have her find a man she could love so that she could, presumably, settle down to write fiction reflective of a woman more satisfied with her personal life. Her bibliographers want Glasgow to be safely respectable, genteelly Southern, and not overly concerned with feminist issues. The editor of her letters prefers the Glasgow who is public and professional—and disturbingly dependent upon male judgment—rather than personal and emotionally revealing. The task of rereading Glasgow requires sorting through influential critical biases—which sometimes, I will argue, as in the case of her autobiography, appear to include Glasgow's own—in order to construct an alternate story.

That female and even feminist critics have generally failed to envision other possibilities for reading Glasgow as a woman writer is a testimony to the power of the prevailing critical trends. We find, for example, a relatively early (1976) feminist approach to Glasgow, despite its many important observations, marred by the author's obvious distaste for what she sees as "radical" feminism's lack of respect for niceties such as physical attractiveness and, in literature, for strong male characters.[24] Linda W. Wagner's *Ellen Glasgow* (1982) probably has done more to encourage feminist approaches to Glasgow than any other single work, but even it subscribes to the common belief that Glasgow spent much of her life searching for the man she could love and even marry, a belief fostered by Glasgow herself. These studies share with many others the view, though refreshingly tempered and often countered in Wagner, that Glasgow's unmarried state represented a void in her life unfilled by a man.

Two influential feminist theoreticians, one early and one more recent, contributed to the reluctance of others to address with more complexity the feminist implications of Glasgow's life and work. In fact, Patricia Meyer Spacks's *The Female Imagination* in 1972 and Adrienne Rich's poem "Education of a Novelist" (1983) a decade later are daunting even to a reader committed to a feminist reassessment of Ellen Glasgow. Spacks criticizes Glasgow for being preoccupied, particularly in her 1935 novel *Vein of Iron*, with "the glories of wifehood and motherhood and the heroic vision of the woman who achieves them." Rich, whose headnote indicates that her judgment is based on Glasgow's autobiography, criticizes Glasgow for arrogance, self-centeredness, and, most damningly, for racism.[25] These two critics' responses are understandable; both primary texts, especially the auto-biography, are problematic in the Glasgow canon. But Spacks and Rich depend upon works taken out of context too, and upon assumptions that prove to be less valid upon closer scrutiny. Without question, though, dismissal by these two important readers of women writers has helped to discredit Glasgow as a worthwhile subject for feminist study.

Even more unfortunate—and perhaps more influential—than others' misunderstandings, too often Glasgow herself contributed to her own marginalization, a fact that helps to explain the frequent critical myopia in reading her life. Desiring professional acceptance and knowing its terms, she often lived the split existence familiar to many women, and certainly to those who desired partnership in the patriarchal world of professional careers in the late-nineteenth and early-twentieth centuries. She made her choices—at first to reject (or at least not to openly accept), then to subvert, then to recast certain women's traditions, for example—and she felt the tensions such choices engendered. But the fissures show. Pieces of other possible stories are discernible through the cracks those tensions expose. Glasgow's decisions, the tensions they created, and the alternate stories they mask provide a key to her significance as a representative woman writer of her transitional time.

In 1928, Glasgow at age fifty-five clearly articulated in "Some Literary Woman Myths" her views of the subservient position of women in a man's world and of women writers in a male-dominated literary tradition. By 1938, Glasgow's reputation was secure. That year, Scribners published a twelve-volume collection (the Virginia Edition), for which Glasgow wrote new prefaces, chose the frontispieces, and signed and numbered the 810 copies. Ten years after complaining of the "literary woman myths" perpetuated by a male literary establishment, Glasgow—secure in her reputation as a writer worthy of a gilt-and deckle-edged limited edition of her works—incorporated parts of her earlier essay into her Preface to *They Stooped to Folly,* making the problems that she and other women writers face when they adopt the profession of authorship an integral part of her novel. Perhaps Glasgow's age also emboldened her to write more openly of her feminism as a professional issue. She wrote in her autobiography of her "thrilling discovery" that "until one is over sixty one can never really learn the secret of living" (*WW* 282).[26] For whatever reasons, her 1938 Preface extends her earlier feminist statement. In writing her novel nine years earlier, she explains, she had decided at the time to write about "one of the immemorial woman myths" that "had survived as an integral part alike of pagan legend and Christian tradition."[27] Now, in her new Preface, she returns to her musings on "woman myths" to explain more than just the germ of her novel. The implications of accepted myths of womanhood that are "not only sanctioned but invented by man" (*TSF* xii) are far-reaching: the woman writer's very identity and her right to her project depend upon male traditions, male perspectives, male assessments of what is valuable and worth repeating in human experience. To write women's lives, whether actual or fictional, Glasgow acknowledges, requires outright defiance, a quietly rebellious subversion, or, less productively for the woman writer, deception that often comes dangerously near self-delusion and loss of identity.

Although her tone in her 1938 Preface is simultaneously amused and angry, comedic and doleful, Glasgow never doubts the seriousness of her statements. In male versions of women, she argues, one finds "many of the major prejudices and a few of the minor prerogatives of the male sex. Women have been too much occupied with the serious business of life, with planning, contriving, scheming to outwit an adverse fortune, and tilling the fertile soil of man's vanity, to bother about so primitive a science as mythology" (*TSF* xii). Humorously but with undisguised irony, Glasgow describes the origin of male appropriation of female identity. She conflates Judeo-Christian mythological (biblical) and modern scientific (Darwinian) traditions to suggest at the outset the ubiquitousness of male-centered myths: "In some green Neanderthal sunrise, soon after man had aspired to walk upright, no doubt he peered into a silver stream and decided that he had been created in the Divine image. On the same occasion . . . he concluded . . . that, in constructing his companion, the pattern of his Maker had not been followed quite so closely" (*TSF* xii). She thus begins her own myth by attributing the evolutionary development of walking upright to man's search for self-approval. Then, in alluding to the ancient narcissistic myth of male identity through self-absorption, Glasgow rather neatly implies that Adam's love for Eve probably was based not on his perception of her worth but on his ability to see his own potentiality reflected in her. Almost as knowledgeable about popular Freudianism as she was about Darwinian theories, Glasgow also no doubt intended to undercut Freud's assumption that women as a group are particularly susceptible to narcissism. Here, man defines his own image; just as easily as he here assumes the right to speak for "his Maker," he will shortly take upon himself the role of defining woman.

Glasgow adroitly intertwines this composite male myth of creation with the equally overpowering myth of male literary creativity by quoting *Paradise Lost*. Since man's original "decision" that while he was created in God's image, woman was not, she argues, "masculine reason has clung firmly to the primal commandment: 'He for God only, she for God in him'" (*TSF* xii), a line she also copied, with obvious disdain, into one of her notebooks.[28] Gilbert and Gubar argued in *The Madwoman in the Attic* that Milton embodied for many women writers the patriarchal myth of literary creation, a myth as difficult to overcome as the patriarchal Judeo-Christian myth of physical creation, perhaps because the two are so closely linked.

Glasgow moves from Milton to other significant male figures, most of them literary, in outlining the history of man's creation of two "preeminent woman myths": "woman as an inspiration" and "woman as an impediment" (*TSF* xiii). In one dense paragraph, she manages to imply that Samuel Richardson, John Galsworthy, James Branch Cabell, Sigmund Freud, and "all the brave young men" of modern fiction are responsible for "inventing" and then "sanctioning" these two myths. "Masculine inclination has varied" between the myths, she argues, and "a whole flock of minor myths" have flown over the "passive female principle in literature," but both myths have been "immovable" (xiii). And both, destructively, have depended not on real women but on masculine illusions. Richardson's Clarissa, the earliest instance of the myth of woman as inspiration and ideal, Glasgow argues, is "more remarkable as a reflection of man's sentimentality than as an analysis of woman's nature" (xiv). "An inspiration," Glasgow points out, "is scarcely more solid than an ideal; and an ideal, conforming to the law of atmospheric refraction, appears not only higher than it is in reality, but looms still larger and brighter in situations of danger" (xiii–xiv). After World War I, Freud and "male disillusionment with virtue" transformed woman from man's ideal to "the obstacle to all his higher activities" (xvi). Woman, now an impediment, became the "devourer of dreams and poets," all male. "Male authorities," Glasgow wryly points out, "all converge upon the modest axiom that while man desires more than woman, woman desires only more of man," an axiom so tenaciously held that so far "no man and few women have been rash enough to dispute it." Glasgow dares to be rash: "The capacity to pine for what is not is a privilege, or an infirmity, that is independent of sex" (xvii). A "desire for unattainable perfection," she asserts, is not, as Cabell seems to believe, "a masculine prerogative" (xvi). Her message is that, whatever their permutations, the male-created "woman myths" have defined women solely from masculine viewpoints.[29]

Glasgow realized something very important about a masculine mythos as it affects women, and particularly women writers: too often the result is not just self-effacement, which is surely bad enough, but a belief that self-effacement is justified. Conditioned to believe against her own instincts or desires in a male definition of the world and even of artistic creativity, Glasgow argues, the woman's response has been to accept her place as peripheral, even though she thereby accepts the self-deception that inevitably results when something externally imposed does not confirm internal dictates. Like an ill-fitting garment worn with dignity and composure, women have made the best of men's definitions of them and of their place in his world. And insidiously, the myths have made their way into women's own psyches, into the "practical mind of woman" that has allowed any woman "to believe anything that is useful, and to find anything useful that she believes," even when "uncomplimentary." "Much practice," Glasgow pointedly remarks, "has perfected her in the fine art of dissembling" (*TSF* xii–xiii). At times—and with no less dedication than the externally imposed marginalization of Glasgow by her critics, mentioned earlier—woman has pushed herself, Glasgow argues, to the periphery of her own existence.

But, of course, in the very act of retelling these male myths, recounting their origins, and reinterpreting them, Glasgow demonstrates her own defiant rejection of them and indicates a possible response for other women. At least here in her Preface, unlike the "practical" women who have historically accepted these myths, Glasgow exposes them for the self-destructive narratives that they are. By adroitly revising the male version of the myth of woman's literal and literary creation, she thereby reappropriates the story, reclaiming the woman's right to tell herself and to envision her own image rather than to seek external confirmation of her selfhood. Man may be created in the image of divinity, she suggests; woman is—or at least can and should be—created in her own. Like Muriel Rukeyser's Sphinx to Oedipus when the latter asserts that "man" means "women too," Glasgow in effect replies, " 'That's what you think.' "[30]

In many ways this complex and important Preface serves as a fitting paradigm for the narrative of Glasgow's own life. Less confident earlier in her life than she was by the time of her critical prefaces, Glasgow, like many women writers, felt torn between the wide critical acceptance that signaled inhabiting a male literary world and the personal choice that signaled rebellion against it. A split female self, wavering between public and private worlds and finding it difficult to inhabit both, is familiar in women's narratives. As Carolyn Heilbrun observes, women, comfortable in the private domain and encouraged to remain so, have had difficulty seeing their lives as "exemplary" in the public one. When Glasgow began her public writing career in 1895 with her first published short story, she accepted the challenge to fit herself, at least publicly, into a world dominated by men. She did not want a place in the "popular" literary tradition, which had long been more congenial for women writers than the critically correct world of "serious" literature. Indeed, in an unpublished statement probably meant for inclusion in her autobiography, she writes (not entirely accurately) that she is glad not to have had to "submit" herself or her "way of writing" to the demands for movies or sentimental fiction.[31] But this decision often meant frustration. It was difficult for Glasgow to find her niche in a male-dominated world and equally difficult to reject a desire for public recognition and respect—something, surely, most writers want.

Glasgow's decisions often involved trying to reject or appearing to reject what we now recognize as some women's personal and literary traditions in favor of dominant, more conventionally acceptable, male traditions. The use of two literary genres helps to demonstrate the complex issues involved. For example, in writing five Gothic short stories, atypical in her canon, Glasgow placed herself in a woman's tradition that Ellen Moers first called the "female Gothic."[32] In many ways Glasgow makes productive use of this tradition, as in her depiction of close female relationships to oppose a domineering male character. But she often stops short of taking full advantage of the subversive potential of a female Gothic tradition. Though she aligns herself with it long enough to posit female community, for example, she nevertheless fails to imagine such community as having any physical reality: it exists only spiritually, not materially. In autobiography, though Glasgow emphatically rejects elements of this traditionally male genre, her narrative surface conforms to it. Such apparent conformity, of course, can lend itself to misreading by burying too deeply the text's subversive elements. In retreating from full engagement with the radical stance implied by her alliance with the female Gothic literary tradition and by her rejection of male-centered models of autobiography, Glasgow demonstrates the limits of her attempts at gendered self-representation. At the same time, however—and, I think, ultimately more importantly—she shows herself willing to construct a female self against the dominant male paradigms.

It is not surprising, after all, to discover (in Glasgow and others of her generation) the problems of female self-definition and self-representation, whether personal or fictional or some mixture of the two. Women's search for identity—even when "identity" is admittedly multiple—has had few literary or psychological precursors, an absence that recent feminist theoreticians have begun to fill.[33] Even genre distinctions themselves, as feminist theory has suggested, can be agents for excluding those writers deemed marginal by virtue of gender, class, or other reasons.[34] By her willingness to follow generic prescriptions—or by her incapacity fully to replace them with her own—Glasgow may have unwittingly contributed to her own dis-ease with fully employing the conventions of female Gothic and autobiographical traditions.

Other choices were less strictly literary, fusing personal and professional in a way we now often view as typical of certain women's traditions. Glasgow's fiction, for example, often portrays close female friendships—close enough in many cases to reveal a strong homoerotic undercurrent that replaces the surface story's ostensibly conventional heterosexual focus and even usurps the traditional romantic plot. These friendships, though present in Glasgow's fiction from the beginning, have been largely ignored; even Wagner sees the female friendships in Glasgow's ninth novel, *The Miller of Old Church* (1911), as an "innovation." The implications of these friendships, both in Glasgow's fiction and in her life, have likewise been ignored, perhaps because—it is tempting to speculate—those who have controlled Glasgow's reputation have chosen not to explore them. But the narrator in *The Miller of Old Church,* quoted above as an epigraph to this chapter, probably speaks for Glasgow: "the need of woman for woman was not written in the songs and the histories of men, but in the neglected and frustrated lives which the songs and the histories of men had ignored." Glasgow obviously knew that a tradition of female companionship similar to that which Carroll Smith-Rosenberg has characterized as the "female world of love and ritual" common in the nineteenth century was available to her as an alternative to the patriarchal world and all that it represented. In her personal life these friendships played a far more significant part than has been realized, a fact that highlights the importance of plots of female companionship even in fiction that on the surface replays the traditional romantic story of woman's search for male companionship.[35]

On whatever level of consciousness her choices were made, Glasgow's recurring attempts to dissociate herself from women's traditions potentially represented more than a loss of personal or fictional patterns she probably would have found comforting and comfortable. Research in women's psychology has begun to elaborate ways in which many women (specifically white, economically secure women such as Glasgow), traditionally omitted from studies proposing models of human behavior and thought, may define themselves and their experience differently than men.[36] A common conclusion in these investigations is that women's experience revolves around a sense of connection to others, and relies less on autonomous decisions based on abstract rules than on relational responsibility.[37] If, indeed, female definitions of self typically rely on others for completion, then Glasgow, in her conflicted attempts to separate herself from women's traditions, may have participated in an alienation from her female past and present and, inevitably, even from her self.

However unattractive such aggressive, even belligerent, issues as power and control may have been to her,[38] Glasgow was aware that for women writers especially, the questions were: Who will be in charge? Who will be responsible for defining female selves? Who will take control of women's lives, of women writers' critical reputations? Gilbert and Gubar have examined the extent to which a "battle of the sexes" became a central concern for the modernist project, translating itself into the bellicose metaphors of its literature and its culture.[39] It might seem that Glasgow, armed with the inadequate legacy of restrictive attitudes toward Southern womanhood and sexuality and with an ambivalence about men, yet determined to succeed in a masculine literary world, would have been doomed to lose the war. But the critical battle is still one of control, and as feminist critics maintain, the balance of power can be tilted in a new direction. The question Glasgow's life asks today is still, Who is in control of a woman's life, a woman writer's place in a literary canon? Heilbrun argues that it is not lives but stories that serve as models for women's biography, and that new stories are hard to come by. All we can do, she believes, is "retell and live by the stories we have read or heard."[40] Perhaps, in the retelling, Glasgow's life will offer more stories to live by. By rereading—and rewriting—Glasgow's life, as others have tantalizingly suggested we can and should do with women's lives, we can appreciate anew the significance of her struggle and can re-place her in the women's traditions she herself at times appeared to have rejected.

TWO

Female Companionship I: Toward the Eden of Friendship

It is seldom in modern fiction that a friendship between two women . . . has assumed a prominent place.
Although such an association appears to be not uncommon in life, the novelist, since he is usually a man,
has found the relationship to be deficient alike in the
excitement of sex and the masculine drama of action.
But more and more, in the modern world, women are
coming to understand their interdependence as human
beings.

Glasgow, Preface to *They Stooped to Folly*

The point of value is that we [women] have realized
our plight and have set ourselves to abolish it, and
that we have stumbled on the important truth that
co-operation is strength. That will lead us out of the
wilderness.

Glasgow, "No Valid Reason against
Giving Votes to Women"

IN THE 1913 New York *Times* interview from which the second
epigraph above is quoted, Glasgow first explicitly linked two important ideas in her thinking about women: mutuality and tradition.
After asserting that the "most important thing for women to learn
is cooperation," she then elaborated on women's historical isolation
from one another: "Their lives have been absolutely aimless, and, for
that matter, actually cruel, and they have endured and endured simply
because they never stood shoulder to shoulder about anything. Each

woman has been a host unto herself, as far as she could go, but she was pitifully limited. She needed the help of her sisters, and she could not get it."[1] Looking back at the lives of Southern women in particular, Glasgow was, in her words, "horror-stricken" at what must have been their "loneliness and depression" (24). Historically, limited possibilities had meant that with one of a woman's customary options—marriage and the motherhood that ineluctably followed—her life was over as soon as husband and children ceased to need her. At that point her existence became, for Glasgow, "inexpressibly tragic" (25). With the other option—singleness without meaningful occupation—a woman's mind "lost its elasticity, and its urges to activity," leaving her "to settle into half-developed apathy and wait until she died" (25). With no alternative life stories and no recognition of the solidarity that might have confirmed her private sense of experience as shared experience, Glasgow believed, too many women had been unable to discover themselves and their potential and had been hindered from helping each other to do so.

Twenty-five years later in 1938, Glasgow identified as life's two most important "satisfactions" precisely the things she had seen missing in the lives of women before her: productive endeavor and friendship. She expresses gratitude that she was able to enjoy those "two equal and enduring satisfactions in life": "the association with one's fellow beings in friendship, in love, or in a community of interest, and the faithful pursuit of an art, a profession, or an aesthetic enjoyment."[2] Glasgow's observations in the 1913 interview and her retrospective statements in 1938 enunciate a lifelong concern with women's cooperative relationships and with certain traditions of women's lives, such as marriage, that often threaten them. Her two pronouncements also frame a narrative of ambivalence about the lives of women. Does the traditional structure of a woman's life isolate her, as Glasgow felt in her 1913 interview? Or can it encourage female cooperation and friendship, as it obviously came to do in her own life? And does the usual woman's story expand sufficiently to include a woman *writer*? These changing perspectives in Glasgow's interpretation of women's past lives help to pinpoint a major shift in Glasgow's attitude toward a woman's traditions: the aimlessness and alienation Glasgow sensed by 1913 gave way to her later recognition that the same tradition responsible for the "loneliness" of a woman's confinement to domesticity could be transformed into something positive, into the shared spirit of community that feminist critics have called "sisterhood" or "a female world of love and ritual,"[3] into a sense of "the important truth" that female "co-operation is strength."

But that transformation came later. In the early years of Glasgow's life and career, at least until about the time of her tenth novel, *Virginia,* in 1913, what she experienced was tension and ambivalence about the traditional plots of a woman's life story. Glasgow's image was of a tradition, defined by her culture and validated in the lives of her mother and other women, where women lived separated from the outside world in a virtual prison of domesticity. The ideology of separate spheres seemed firmly to fix the boundaries of male and female worlds. It was a woman's place to be nurturing and self-sacrificing within the world of the home, a man's place to seek activity outside in the public domain, where he gained the knowledge and authority that publicity conferred.[4] As a young woman who was also a writer, Glasgow experienced the tension that resulted from trying to find her own sphere that would encompass both public and private realms, a combination that historically had been denied to women of her race and class and region.

Glasgow's understandable ambivalence about these women's traditions and her place in them was shared by many women writers, particularly in this time period, as critics such as Elizabeth Ammons have observed.[5] Her intellectual confusion about women's traditions stemmed from a perception that to align herself with them meant accepting an unsatisfactory status quo rather than rebelling against it. *Tradition* dictated her role as debutante, wife, mother, and—as she came to believe—victim of a world fashioned by and for men. *Tradition* also meant her father's repressive and oppressive Calvinism, her region's obsession with past glories, her city's complacent satisfaction with its importance as the capital of the Confederacy, and an attitude toward women calculated, as Anne Goodwyn Jones and others have pointed out, to sustain the hegemony of white middle-class males.[6] For Glasgow as an aspiring young woman writer in turn-of-the-century Richmond, most often a woman's available traditions signaled submissiveness, passivity, frustration, and isolation from two communities: that of other women who might have confirmed her private sense of experience as shared experience; and that of a literary circle that might confirm her professional worth. Yet tradition as a literary concept could also mean admission into the world of "serious" literature, a world she wanted to inhabit.[7] As with many women writers, her dilemma was real: accept a woman's place and reject literary authority, or, alternatively, eschew a woman's traditions and compete with male writers for literary respectability and, hence, for a place in an honored and predominately white male tradition.

This question of alliances was, for Glasgow as for other women, more than academic. As her 1913 interview reveals, Glasgow sensed that her identity as a woman somehow needed to be formulated in relation to other women, whether her contemporaries or her predecessors or both. As she put it, the inexpressible tragedy of one woman's life and the "half-developed apathy" of another's sprang from isolation, from lack of cooperation. Contemporary feminist psychological theorists such as Carol Gilligan and Nancy Chodorow have suggested that women typically form their identity in relation to others, developing what Gilligan calls an "ethic of care" or a "morality of responsibility."[8] Such theories' tendency to universalize women's experience makes them problematic for many writers and questionable for their broad applicability. But they do help to explain some of the conflicts in Glasgow's search for female identity. Certainly for Glasgow, it seems, accepting or rejecting a woman's legacy meant accepting or rejecting a self as well. To deny a familiar female self whose definition was contextual and relational required replacing that self with another, elusive one that, presumably, asserted itself through separation from others, a developmental model that has been described as more typically masculine than feminine. But how does a woman (here white, middle-class, and Southern) find that contextual female self without losing an identity in the process? How does she make use of what Chodorow calls women's "permeable ego boundaries" without confusing self with other, without losing her own clearly delineated ego boundaries? How, in other words, as Elizabeth Abel adroitly phrases it, does she "merge" and "emerge" at the same time?[9]

The ambivalence Glasgow brought to questions of both professional and individual identity is figured in her feelings about her parents, feelings that she tended to frame in binary terms. Many scholars have noted the "conflict" she says she inherited from the different personalities of her mother and father;[10] it is something Glasgow often talks about, and it represents, among other things, her feelings of being torn between what she saw as typically male and typically female definitions of self. Her descriptions of her mother and father in *The Woman Within* underscore differences between male and female approaches to the world as described by feminist psychological theorists. Anne Jane Gholson Glasgow, Glasgow's mother, was the "center of my childhood's world, the sun in my universe"; as Glasgow says, she "made everything luminous" (*WW* 13). Glasgow most often describes her mother as one who defined herself relationally; it is part of her typically feminine appeal. Anne Glasgow's "whole nature was interwoven with sympathy. She would divide her last crust with a suffering stranger." Even when it meant self-sacrifice, "no one who had the slightest claim upon her ever went away empty handed" (14). And though Glasgow recognized the potential danger in embracing her mother's ethics of responsibility, she also appreciated its charms. Her mother, "magnanimous to a fault," "would have divided her last hope of Heaven with any spiritual beggar." Glasgow remembers her mother as not just the angel but the saint in the house, "eternally poised in an attitude of giving or blessing, as if time, or the past, or merely an illusion of memory, had crystallized around her lovely and beneficent image." [11] When she adopted her mother's family name, Gholson, as part of her own name in an act of matrilineal self-naming, Glasgow demonstrated the strength of the ties she felt to her mother and the urge to connect herself with the traditions of her foremothers.[12]

In contrast to her mother's "luminous" pliancy, her father's "unbending" (*WW* 16) nature made him independent and judgmental, interested more in justice than in sympathetic understanding.[13] According to Glasgow, he "accepted literally the most barbaric texts in the Scriptures, and was equally sound on doctrine, from the fall of Adam to infant damnation." [14] Yet, his very independence and sense of justice were also the source of his authority, at once repellent and attractive to Glasgow, which called into question the desirability of her mother's saintly sensitivity. Glasgow's autobiography describes her search for identity and reveals the tension she felt as she was pulled toward both parents; her struggles against what she at times thought of as the excessive selflessness represented by her mother are evident in her attempts to find an identity separated from others. As she did so, however, she seems to have understood that to define herself through separation and individuation, a staple of ego definition since Freud, alienated her from some ineffable sense of feminine self. The language she uses to describe her quest for self-knowledge replicates the tension inherent in using a male model of development as a means to female self-identity: "Always I have *had* to learn for myself, from within. Always I have persevered in the face of an immense disadvantage—in the face of illness, of partial deafness, which came later, of the *necessity* to blaze my own trail through the wilderness that was ignorance. To teach one's self is to be *forced* to learn twice" (*WW* 41; emphasis added). The words associated with imposition underscore Glasgow's discomfort with a means of self-education that demands enforced isolation. She felt the "necessity" of separation from a contextual female world, and that emphasis on individuation implicitly aligned her with a male tradition represented by her father. Just as in a woman writer's professional decision to either reject or accept (male) literary authority, the more personal attempt at self-definition required Glasgow, in her view, to accept a female tradition of relationship or a male one of individuation. If, as Glasgow asserts in her autobiography, her mother "had never known a selfish thought" (62), she could also be too passive, too accepting of her role as victim. And if her father acted out of a sense of impartial justice rather than taking into account the feelings of his family, he could also be powerful and authoritative. (It is revealing that, like Emily Dickinson, Glasgow frequently identifies her father with God the Father.) Often it seemed to Glasgow that to choose a woman's tradition was to choose victimization; to reject it was to embrace her father's "rock-ribbed" (16) masculinity.

Her story rings true for other women writers.[15] Glasgow felt torn between the authority and power represented by her father and the gentleness and sensitivity of her mother, and it was only much later that she learned to combine the best of what she had thought to be opposing traits. In the models of identity Glasgow formulated based on her parents, one could be either self-immolating or oppressive, could either serve others to the point of self-denial or serve oneself at the expense of others. Glasgow spent much of her early career, both professional and personal, seeking an identity that hovered somewhere between the life of caregiving that a woman's tradition had handed down to her (and that she along with others often interpreted as dependence, passivity, and isolation) and the patriarchal world of authority, public experience, and power. In the published fiction of roughly the first third of her career, from 1895 to 1911, Glasgow explores the traditions offered to her and searches for the way to write her own outline for a successful woman's story, to revise her mother's story in such a way that it allows for the salvation of self in a tradition of self-less giving. Beginning about 1911 with the realization that history and herstory differ, her story changes dramatically.

Early Friends, Early Fiction

An irony of Glasgow's early thinking about past and present women's lives is that in her anger about the limitations of the sphere of domesticity, she failed to recognize that the close-knit woman's world she lamented as unavailable was the world of her own childhood. Perhaps her lack of awareness is testimony to the completeness with which a tradition of female affiliation described by Cott and Smith-Rosenberg had at one time been erased from history. Whatever the reasons for her own unconsciousness about women's ties to one another, Glasgow, surrounded early by nurturing female caregivers and then by close female friends throughout her life, obviously drew more sustenance from her relationships with women than either she or her critics have recognized. Though female companionships rarely fully usurp the narrative center in her plots (a fact that reinforces the strength of masculine paradigms for fiction), they nevertheless tease us with a hinted awareness of alternatives to the traditional marriage plot. Glasgow's fiction from her first published short story in 1895 through her 1911 novel *The Miller of Old Church* shows her persistently exploring women's roles and searching for female identity for herself and her characters. The ambivalence in her own quest sometimes led her to accept the cultural values that mandated a peripheral role as wife and mother, sometimes to reject those standards in favor of a life centered more on a female self and her personal and historical relationships with other women. The fiction of these years fluctuates in the degree of hopefulness about the possibilities of heterosexual relationships. But always in the shadows lurks the suggestion that women's relationships might provide an "Eden of Friendship"—a term Glasgow will use later in *They Stooped to Folly* (1929)—separate from a postlapsarian world of heterosexuality.[16] Glasgow's works chart what was for her a difficult course as she made an important discovery: a woman's relational tradition of close female alliances, which she was tempted to reject as too self-less, was necessary to her identity as a woman. Some of the tension in Glasgow's fiction—in the simultaneous need to center on heterosexual pairings and to reject them, for example—results from her early efforts to reject traditions she found comfortable and, finally, necessary.

Whatever intellectual ambivalence Glasgow felt about a woman's tradition of connection to others, however, the conflict surfaced more in her writing than in her everyday life, which she lived surrounded by sustaining women friends and relatives. In fact, Glasgow put far more emotional energy into relationships with other women than she did into her much-discussed search for her ideal male mate (as did her contemporary, Edith Wharton, according to Susan Goodman). Drawn to a nurturing female world, throughout her life Glasgow gained personal strength from and came to self-definition in the context of close relationships with other women. In addition to her mother, in her immediate environment Glasgow enjoyed the nurturance of three older women: her black caregiver, Lizzie Jones, her mother's friend Virginia Rawlings, and her great aunt Rebecca ("Aunt Bec"). These women, who satisfied Glasgow's early physical and emotional needs, also were bound to Glasgow by a common thread: they fostered her early love for fiction and for fictionalizing. Their importance thus extends into Glasgow's later life as she makes a professional decision to become a writer, and their early and lasting influence on Glasgow emphasizes the significance of the personal and private to the supposedly impersonal and public, a significance feminist critics have sympathized with and argued for.[17]

Lizzie Jones, who joined the household when Glasgow was one month old, filled much of the space left vacant by Anne Glasgow, busy with her large family and distracted by her own nervous instability. Glasgow recalls as her "happiest years" those when she was "between the ages of three and seven," when quotidian life revolved around Jones. Together, Glasgow says, they lived "a life of wandering adventures" whose source was "not only in the tales we spun at night" but also in their daily travels, "when we roamed, hand-in-hand, in search of the fresh and the strange, through the streets and back alleys, and up and down the hills of old Richmond." She describes her "beloved" Lizzie as "an extraordinary character, endowed with an unusual intelligence, a high temper, and a sprightly sense of humor" (*WW* 18). With Jones, Glasgow created her imaginary childhood friend, Little Willie, and developed the ability to project herself into others' personalities by dressing as a gypsy and telling imaginary fortunes. Glasgow recalls Lizzie's bedtime tale–spinning as "more thrilling" even than their literal adventures during the day. Underscoring the mutuality of the relationship between the older woman and the little girl, Glasgow makes the stories theirs rather than either's: "Mammy and I would take up and spin out . . . the story we had left off the evening before." She cannot even remember whether her personal "hero" Little Willie, "the closest and dearest of companions," was first created by her or by Lizzie Jones (23–24). Jones was also responsible for extending Glasgow's circle of friendship past the imaginary Willie to the actual Lizzie Patterson, whose family employed Jones when Glasgow was seven (29). Patterson (later Crutchfield) would remain a close friend all of Glasgow's life. All descriptions of Glasgow's relationship to Lizzie Jones reinforce patterns of female connection: Jones introduces Glasgow to other friends, nurtures her ability to connect with others through fictionalizing, metaphorically represents Glasgow's mother through her caregiving, and even extends across generations of caregivers past, present, and future when Glasgow describes Jones's arrival as the replacement for Glasgow's mother's Mammy Rhoda (19).[18]

Two other older women whose significance has been overlooked are Virginia Rawlings, a close friend of Glasgow's mother, and Aunt Bec, Glasgow's father's sister. Both helped to provide an environment where nurturing was both literal and literary. According to Glasgow, Rawlings (no relation to Marjorie Kinnan Rawlings) had originally joined the family as Anne Glasgow's companion and the elder children's governess. She "stayed on permanently," Glasgow says in her autobiography, "as one of the family." Remembered for her storytelling talent and so, like Jones, a model for Glasgow's own creative penchant, Rawlings was a "large, happy, genial spinster" who had "the first short curly bob I had ever seen on a woman" (*WW* 38). Aunt Bec, like both Jones and Rawlings, was the "perfect story-teller," who recounted for the young Glasgows the plots of the Waverly novels in such a "magnetic" voice[19] that Glasgow began to teach herself to read

Scott's romances. Both of these older women—strong, independent, and unmarried—lived lives that posed an alternative to Glasgow's mother's life of childbearing and dependence. The positive message they sent, however, simultaneously suggested an opposition that Glasgow explored many times, particularly in her early fiction: marriage and attention to others are not easily compatible with creative endeavor. Had she acknowledged it, adding the servitude of a Lizzie Jones to the equation surely would have signaled disturbing hints of some similarities between caregiving and a more literal bondage.

In fact, Glasgow's earliest published fiction reveals the tension that the lives of Aunt Bec and Virginia Rawlings (and, differently configured, Lizzie Jones) represented. When she was twenty-two and twenty-three, respectively, Glasgow published her first short story and her first novel. "A Woman of To-Morrow" (1895) and *The Descendant* (1897) both oppose women's careers to heterosexual love. The conflict that reveals Glasgow's ambivalence is clear in these two works: a woman must either reject artistic integrity and authority or reject the standard of female affiliation; the two are incompatible. She decided early that if a female sense of self develops through affiliation and connection and an artistic self develops through independence and even rebellion, then for the woman writer, a personal identity is female whereas a public identity is male. No wonder we find the common tension in women's fiction (particularly that of the nineteenth century, when Glasgow began her public career) between art and life: *life* seldom meant anything beyond marriage and motherhood. The message suggested by Aunt Bec and Virginia Rawlings and explored in Glasgow's fiction is that one must choose between feminine and masculine paths to identity: the first is tied to love, marriage, children, and domesticity, and the second to art, power, and public success.

The conflict that arises from the necessity to choose between professional and personal development—between clearly demarcated masculine and feminine worlds—begins early in Glasgow's career and indicates the seriousness with which she considered the decision. At age twenty-one, Glasgow already saw the dangers to an incipient female self inherent in the choice to inhabit any male world, already sensed a woman's dual existence, spent straddling others' expectations and her own desires.[20] Glasgow's first female protagonist, Patricia Yorke of "A Woman of To-Morrow," tries to fit her role as woman and potential wife to her legal career. Just out of Yale, she envisions the marker that will announce her movement from the private world culturally assigned to her to the public world of business: "Patricia Yorke, Attorney-at-Law."[21] Signing herself into the public realm women have been excluded from, she seems to command her own destiny as a new woman; the narrator describes her as the "embodiment of freedom and the twentieth century" (WT 4). When we are told that Patricia wants "truth—truth only" (5), the wiser third-person narrator is quick to point out Patricia's flawed expectations. Patricia's naive faith that her ability to make free choices is a simple matter of independence is consistently undercut by the narrator, who frequently remarks Patricia's youthful ignorance and foretells her eventual capitulation to cynicism: Patricia has not *"yet"* experienced forces that will *"defy"* her, has not yet learned to *"prefer lies"* to truth (4–5; my emphasis).

One belief that Patricia naively accepts as a "truth" is her ability to successfully combine her public life as a professional and her private life as a wife. But Glasgow, in reversing the typical masculine and feminine roles in the story, exposes Patricia's sanguine expectation as one of the lies she will have to learn to prefer and identifies the confusion that results when women are perceived as overstepping their bounds. Patricia's lover, whose namelessness reinforces the insignificance of a typically feminine role, takes on the sense of "duty" ordinarily assigned to women.[22] He refuses Patricia's bold request that he leave his frail mother, who lives in an illusory world of wealth and Southern gentility, the world of lies she has learned to prefer to the truth of her poverty. "Don't you see?" he asks Patricia. "It is a question of duty. My post is here. I cannot desert it. I owe it to my family—to my mother" (WT 8).

As Patricia argues that his devotion to domestic responsibility is an "absurd" "remnant of that old chivalry—so called—of which the world is well rid" (WT 8), the conflict between them becomes Patricia's internal one and the larger cultural one: it pits women's professional ambition against domestic happiness and provides no way to reconcile the two. Patricia decides that to stay and "become a woman for his sake," to "suffer" and "be patient as other women were patient," would mean a loss of self: it would necessitate that she "merge her identity into his" (WT 9). Her locution acknowledges the cultural construction of femininity: in accepting passive, suffering domesticity she would "*become* a woman" (my emphasis). Moreover, she recognizes the loss of self, the merging, such an acceptance would bring. She renounces love and familial connection for professional and personal development, but ten years later, as the story concludes, she "burst[s] into tears" even as she reaffirms her earlier decision (14). Her ambivalence testifies to the complexity of the issues Glasgow explores from her earliest fiction: how to forge a female identity that requires affiliation without losing that identity by merging with others; how to accept an authoritative professional self without sacrificing feminine identity, without rejecting a woman's traditions. Even a tentatively satisfactory answer for Glasgow, however, is a long time coming.

Just two years later, in *The Descendant* (1897), Glasgow continues to see professional commitment—here in the form of artistic creativity—and traditional womanhood as mutually exclusive. But she also at least begins to imagine a more positive solution to this dilemma by placing her protagonist, the painter Rachel Gavin, in a tradition of female heroism. Though problematic, this tentative solution reveals Glasgow's incipient urges toward replacing masculine cultural constructions of femininity with her own female-centered tradition of authoritative and powerful women.

In *The Descendant,* sexuality assumes more prominence, further complicating a decision that is already less than simple. For Glasgow at age twenty-three, choosing authorship rather than marriage exposed her inclination to reject the traditional role of her mother. Glasgow's account of the publishing history of *The Descendant* highlights its place in her career as liminal: on one side lay sexuality, the traditional woman's (private) life of love, marriage, and motherhood; on the other lay professionalism, the innovative (public) life of a career as a writer. In addition to the patronizing advice offered by one publisher to produce fine babies rather than fine books (quoted above in chapter one), a literary agent offered more than advice. An attempt during the winter of 1892–93 to find a publisher for *Sharp Realities,* the novel Glasgow says she subsequently burned, resulted in sexual assault. According to Glasgow's autobiography, the agent, after asking whether her "figure" was "as lovely in the altogether" as it appeared when fully clothed, then proceeded to fondle her, demanding to be kissed, before she finally "struggled free." Glasgow, who, as she reports, "even as a child, had hated to be pawed over—especially to be pawed over by elderly uncles" was left "forever afterwards" with a "loathing for red and juicy lips," a sentiment that recurs in her fiction. She left "bruised," "disgusted," and "trembling with anger" (96–97). Glasgow's first two professional encounters served to reinforce her perception that sexuality and career could not easily mix (or, that they mixed all too easily, since these professional men assumed that her own professionalism made her sexually available to them).

As with Glasgow's experiences as a professional woman, identity becomes a question of sexuality as well as professionalism in *The Descendant,* which responds ambivalently to both issues. On the one hand, the novel suggests the redemptive power of heterosexual love. On the other, heterosexuality is the destroyer of artistic creativity, particularly for women but for men as well. Both Rachel Gavin and Michael Akershem, an angry young editor bent on reforming society, adamantly oppose heterosexuality for themselves. Michael "shunned" women and Rachel "left romance fastidiously alone."[23] Rachel is the first of many women characters repelled by heterosexual physicality; she surmises that, in contrast to her own feelings, "When one is in love, it doesn't nauseate one to be kissed" (*D* 73).[24] Love is too "exhausting" (73) until she meets Michael, who distracts her from her "great portrait of Magdalen." As in "A Woman of To-Morrow," the narrator laments that Rachel foolishly feels "emancipated" (83), even as she begins to reject art for love.

Rachel's unfinished portrait of Magdalen, the archetypal ruined woman, and a painting in the Metropolitan Museum of *Joan of Arc,* Rachel's virginal "shrine" (*D* 100), delineate the boundaries of womanhood that are possible without a man: sexual promiscuity or virginity. When Rachel succumbs both physically and emotionally to her love for Michael, she becomes beautiful through love's "transforming power," which "evolves . . . a Madonna from a Magdalen" (131). Figuratively eliminating any prospect of successfully interweaving professionalism and sexuality, Rachel abandons her Magdalen and embraces her role as a Madonna. Michael's love has made her, presumably, purer; her life has been completed by a man's love. Only now does she show him her Joan of Arc (painted, appropriately, by someone else), spiritual sister to the Madonna that Rachel has become. "It is my gospel," she tells him; "I would like to keep an altar-lamp burning before it, and to say prayers morning and night" (100). Rachel can paint her Magdalen only when no male defines her; only then does *she* control her image.

Just as Rachel has learned to see herself as purified by a man's love, Michael has learned to see as sullied a woman who succumbs to a man's physical advances. Michael's response still opposes Rachel's: Whereas she has come to see her sexual relationship as purifying her, transforming her from a Madonna into a Magdalen, he begins to view Rachel's passionate love for him as a sign of her "unworthiness" (*D* 189). She abandons her Magdalen to become Madonna, while Michael begins to see her as Magdalen. Though she eventually frees herself from Michael's judgment and exhibits her "Mary of Magdala" to critical acclaim, the ending of the novel applauds their reconciliation after an eight-year separation.

But this conclusion also contains a vision of Michael's death, and Rachel's identification with the Madonna and Joan of Arc suggests another interpretation: Rachel asserts the self-contained spirituality associated with her two virginal models most emphatically when threatened by earthy sexuality and by the assaults upon her autonomy and her creativity that accompany acceptance of Michael's love. Despite the ostensible focus on the power of romantic love, then, we are left with a successful, single, strong, creative woman who has triumphed professionally at the expense of the weak and dying man in her care. In this respect it is but a short step to Glasgow's mature work, *Barren Ground*. Though Linda Wagner argues that only when Rachel's suffering has paralleled Magdalen's can she "excel in her art,"[25] it seems more accurate to say that only when Rachel rejects Michael—and with him the requirement that she forgo art and publicity for exclusive privacy—and completes her painting can she finally excel.

Glasgow's use of Joan, Magdalen, and Mary introduces an important subject: women's traditions as they provide one kind of community. Along with these three female figures, Rachel accepts a diverse female tradition whose models are both virginal and sexual. Early in the novel when the lovers first meet, the narrator comments: "All the latent capacity for hero-worship, that had lain dormant since childhood, awoke with intensity" in Rachel (*D* 81). Rachel learns that her "hero-worship" for Michael and for the marginality he would require of her is misplaced. Her "hero-worship" turns instead toward Magdalen, Joan of Arc, the Virgin Mary—toward a *female* heroic tradition. Glasgow, connecting Rachel with three heroic female figures and separating her from Michael and his expectations, places her in a female tradition that includes her, protects her, and provides her with diverse models for female behavior.[26]

However, while these independent forebears in many ways give Rachel alternatives to conventional femininity, at the same time they exact their own high price: isolation and self-containment. They thus symbolize Glasgow's ambivalence. All three are saintly, exalted by definition above ordinary humans (the sanctity of Joan was legendary, even though she was not officially canonized until 1920). All must remain aloof (two are even certified virgins) in order to carry out the missions that make them special to begin with. All three women, in other words, are exceptional, a designation that Heilbrun and others have protested contributes to the further exclusion of women.[27] No less today than for Glasgow, their lives reify a problem inherent in the question of a separate women's tradition. Does independence from female traditions require exceptionality? Does it, paradoxically, demand an isolation from others at odds with women's experience? Does independence therefore undermine the very traditions that women might find satisfying? These three female heroes also prove to be disturbingly dependent upon male figures for their heroics. Both Marys depend upon the superiority of Christ, whose greater goodness justifies their patient attendance upon him (and Magdalen, as the reformed harlot, further requires male partners to reject as she is transformed from sexuality into transcendent spirituality). Joan depended upon male clothes and the indulgence of the dauphin for her heroic behavior. Under the surface of these heroines' apparent self-definitive acts and their self-willed behavior is a complex truth of conflicting impulses: isolation from the alternative women's tradition they would seem to define and dependence upon the male world they would appear to surmount.

Glasgow's complex response to heterosexuality, particularly to marriage, partially informs two short stories probably written around the time of *The Descendant*'s publication and published in 1899. In them, the issue of separation from a traditionally feminine world of caring assumes a criminal aspect. Associating with women and the relational world they represent has the capacity to save the criminals—both male—in "Between Two Shores" and "A Point in Morals." Glasgow's ambivalence about marriage is evident in both stories: though she still places male-female relationships at the plots' center, marriage benefits only the men, and she associates heterosexual love, especially marriage, with criminality and deception, and with the women's unhappiness. In "Between Two Shores," coincidence forces Lucy Smith into feigning marriage, and her submission to a deceptive and even cruel man concludes the story. The male protagonist of the interpolated tale in "A Point in Morals" is a murderer, and the frame narrative is the story of his suicide. His is a history not only of murder but also of his mistreatment of women, yet at the story's conclusion it is a woman who voices the strongest support on his behalf. As Richard K. Meeker, editor of *The Collected Stories*, suggests, Glasgow clearly used these stories as a forum for airing her views of marriage and of women's usual place in marriage,[28] and both stories offer little in favor of an institution in which, as Glasgow portrays it, women are exploited and victimized—and in which they even participate in their own victimization.

Marriage was still the only game in town, however, and a white, middle-class woman's traditional life left little room for more than courtship, marriage, and motherhood. But Glasgow was beginning to imagine for herself an alternative to the marriage plot, as the tension between marriage and artistic creativity in *The Descendant* clearly shows. She wrote later in *The Woman Within* that at the age of about seventeen, even though she still "was looking forward to the normal life of a Southern girl in [her] circle," she had "put aside, indifferently, the offer of the usual 'coming-out party' and the 'formal presentation to Richmond society.'" The conjunction that begins her next sentence tells why: "*For* I was writing, or had already written, a long novel, of some four hundred pages [*Sharp Realities*]" (*WW* 79). Glasgow's ambivalence is clear, but so is her dedication to her art. The remaining problem lay in imagining the means to resolve the ambivalence.

Though not yet quite able to see her life as other than a traditional woman's life, Glasgow certainly moved steadily toward rejecting that traditional story for herself, partly by imaging unhappy heterosexual relationships in her fiction. In her second novel, *Phases of an Inferior Planet* (1898), as in *The Descendant*, a major stumbling block to marital happiness is a woman's artistic ambition. Like *The Descendant*'s Rachel Gavin, Mariana Musin of *Phases* is an artist, this time a singer. Mariana's family history, a past filled with instances illustrating the unhappiness associated with marriage and heterosexuality, foreshadows her personal history. Her patriarchal ancestor emigrated to New York in search of freedom but "only succeeded in weaving matrimonial fetters"; his wife, in the first of many such occurrences in Glasgow's work, dies in childbirth.[29] Mariana, doomed in a fated Darwinian universe to repeat the ancestral cycle, gives up her singing career, falls in love with and marries Anthony Algercife, and proceeds to make the worst of it. As in *The Descendant,* any promise of heterosexual happiness is overshadowed by the misery the central relationship brings.

Initially, it is Anthony's "effeminacy" (*PIP* 74) that attracts Mariana. His touch communicates "not so much as a suggestion of sexual difference" (48); his is "a beauty which contained no suggestion of physical supremacy" (72). Unlike Michael Akershem's dangerous earthy sexuality or the short stories' male characters, whose appeal rests in part on their brutality, Anthony's spirituality signifies his safety: he "seemed one in whom passion had been annihilated" (75). For Mariana, Anthony serves to mirror a familiar female self; in mirroring her, he even objects to corsets, which "distort" (53) women's bodies into an ideal serving only to please male eyes or reflect a male gaze. Mariana marries Anthony precisely because she believes him to be more spiritual than physical, more feminine than masculine.

Phases of an Inferior Planet's most powerful prose chronicles the demise of a marriage that not only demands too much self-sacrifice —as Mariana gives up her music, Anthony his writing, and both their material well-being—but also gradually insists on an aggressive heterosexuality that threatens Mariana. The relationship collapses as the previously "effeminate" Anthony gains in masculine force. Their child, the outward manifestation of a sexual union that, according to Glasgow, demands female submission to male prerogative, falls ill and dies; Mariana recoils from Anthony "with an avoidance which was almost instinctive" (*PIP* 160), and eventually leaves him to return to her singing career.

In the novel's second section, heterosexuality succeeds best when idealized and hence unfulfilled; marriage is destroyed because of it, but unconsummated relationships are strengthened by renouncing it. As Glasgow demonstrates in Anthony's case, men are more companionable if they are asexual. After Mariana leaves and Anthony enters the priesthood, Father Anthony Algercife, "safe" in his celibacy, attracts sexually inexperienced women who idealize and spiritualize sexuality. The young woman with the "virginal calm face" and the elder woman whose eyes reveal "chastity unsurprised" (*PIP* 191) are, according to one husband, "driven" by Anthony "into a religious mania!" (192). An "Apollo turned celibate," a "Lothario of religions" (204), Anthony's appeal is greatest when he is least sexually threatening.

Mariana's attraction to Anthony strengthens as he becomes once again safely nonmasculine. Because of an illness, Mariana has also become spiritualized; "the brilliancy of her flesh had waned," and "in her faded eyes" Anthony sees "the clearer light of her spirit" (*PIP* 301). Their relationship is most fulfilling when Mariana's body has almost given way to spirit and Anthony's celibacy is ensured by his priesthood. Mariana's death and Anthony's continued priestly spirituality hint disturbingly at an ideal of femininity killed into permanent ideality and masculinity safely contained within institutionalized aheterosexuality.

That the love between Mariana and Anthony flourishes or declines in proportion to its fluctuating emphasis on spirituality or physicality introduces Glasgow's most important innovation in *Phases:* an actual female friendship to contrast to heterosexual relationships. Recognizing in her own life the increasing difficulty of combining "the normal life of a Southern girl" with artistic ambition and of imaging in her fiction a new woman's story, she broadened her plots to encompass more than just the choice between marriage and profession, as in *The Descendant*. In *Phases of an Inferior Planet,* for the first time in her fiction Glasgow suggests a possible way out of the prescribed marriage plot by positing friendships between women as a contrast—perhaps even a hinted alternative—to heterosexual relationships. Though Glasgow structurally marginalizes the theme of female friendship in *Phases,* the unhappy conclusion of the central heterosexual relationship pushes that marginalized relationship closer to the novel's emotional center. She senses that female friendship provides affiliation rather than alienation. If friendship can be conceptualized diachronically, even historical women such as those in *The Descendant* could be seen as less exceptional, more like friends from another era than isolated saintly role models. Joan of Arc and Mary Magdalen could become more genuinely representative of a woman's possible life, less exalted and more down to earth. And, important for Glasgow's own life as well as the lives of her characters, friendships between women can provide alternatives to male-defined plots for women's stories, since they modify, or even preclude, the marriage plot.

In a move that looks ahead to twentieth-century *Künstlerromane* as Rachel Blau DuPlessis has described them, Glasgow's *Phases* not only criticizes "heterosexual ties and the marriage relation,"[30] but also introduces female friendship as an experience that encourages the artistic integrity assailed by heterosexuality. Though not explicitly connected to Mariana's artistic fulfillment, the figure of Mariana as artist flourishes only apart from the heterosexual entanglements represented by Anthony and in conjunction with female-to-female bonds. The adult friendship in *Phases* between Mariana and "Miss Ramsey" is not the maternal-filial paradigm that DuPlessis discusses as typical, but a model of symmetrical female relationship based on equality. As a schoolgirl, Mariana's "passionate friendship" with an older "scholar" (*PIP* 21) corresponds to her "longings for fame" (22) as a singer. The novel argues that Mariana must move through this maternal-filial relationship to the later one with Miss Ramsey. Although never alluded to again in the novel, this schoolgirl "flame"— Havelock Ellis's designation in *Sexual Inversion* (1897) for the sort of dangerous relationship that led to adult sexual "inversion"[31]— provides an important context for Mariana's later friendship with Miss Ramsey. Although neither friendship assumes prominence in the novel, each contrasts women's friendships with one another to failed heterosexuality. Whereas in *The Descendant* Glasgow provides a tradition of female heroism that, even though it encourages women's self-fulfillment, nevertheless remains distant in time and problematic as a realistic role model, in *Phases of an Inferior Planet,* she gives her readers actual female friendships that enable her women characters to create themselves within a tradition of female artistry.

When, with the end of her schoolgirl relationship, "Mariana's emotions became theological" (*PIP* 21), Glasgow continues a pattern that began in *The Descendant* with the choice of a biblical figure (Magdalen) to represent Rachel Gavin's victory over the male protagonist. The shift from intense female friendship to the religion that replaces it could be interpreted to mean that Glasgow simply turned away from actual physicality in female relationships, and moved toward spiritual fulfillment derived from them. But the pervasive juxtaposition of female friendship with spirituality throughout Glasgow's work—the presence of her three saintly heroines in *The Descendant* is only one example—suggests that for her the two were linked closely. That link, moreover, was more complicated than a mere attribution to some version of the nineteenth century's ideology of separate spheres, in which a woman was assumed to be "naturally" superior morally, can explain. This emphasis on the superiority of female friendship to heterosexual love recurs in Glasgow's novels in the context of female companionship; friendships between women signify enough that they replace religion. Women's spirituality, shared with other women such as Mariana's schoolmate, becomes "theological." Glasgow wrote in *The Woman Within* of dismissing her father's Calvinism. She rejected her father along with it, and the complexity of her emotional relationship with him makes it impossible to say which rejection came first. But it is clear that, for her, abandoning conventional religion was tantamount to abandoning men as well. Glasgow's search for something to fill the void left by both rejections may be what led her to Darwin and to the social philosophers; it also led her to intense female friendship. Rachel Gavin calls the Metropolitan's Joan of Arc her "shrine" and her "gospel" (*D* 100) and speaks of praying to it; Mariana's schoolmate—her "divinity" (*PIP* 21)—is replaced by religion; religious language and imagery will continue throughout Glasgow's writing in connection with love between women, demonstrating that Glasgow's perception of a spiritual quality in women replaces her lost sense of religion and offers at least one reason for preferring relationships with women rather than men.

As she focuses on the spirituality of female friendship in *Phases*, Glasgow guides her readers to at least two possible conclusions: that heterosexuality overemphasizes physical sexuality; and that female friendships are somehow superior because more spiritual. She also suggests that heterosexuality would be improved by approximating female friendship; the relationship between Mariana and Anthony is happiest early and late, when it is spiritualized. What's more, by moving heterosexuality and homosociality closer together—by using their shared potential for spirituality to move them from opposition toward consensus—Glasgow subtly suggests that the one might be a replacement for the other. She centralizes (at least diagrammatically) female friendship by metaphorically superimposing it on heterosexual relationships. When the relationship between Mariana and Anthony fares better as it is less physically sexual, Glasgow implies that heterosexuality gains in appeal only as it imitates the spirituality of relationships between women.

As if to validate Ellis's belief (itself built on earlier theories, especially those of Richard von Krafft-Ebing in the 1886 American edition of *Psychopathia Sexualis*) that the danger in youthful "flames" lies in their later translation into homosexual "inversion," there is a woman, Miss Ramsey, who in adulthood fills a void left by Mariana's earlier schoolgirl crush.[32] To suggest Miss Ramsey's implicit encouragement of Mariana's singing career, Glasgow introduces Miss Ramsey as she accompanies Mariana to the opera. Though others vaguely describe Miss Ramsey as a "friend who lives with her" and Mariana as one about whom unspecified "odd things" are told (*PIP* 256), Glasgow clearly, if obliquely, delineates the close relationship between Mariana and Miss Ramsey. In one scene, Mariana underscores her desire for a relationship based on mutuality when she rejects Miss Ramsey's offers to serve her:

> "Shall I braid [your hair]?" [Miss Ramsey] asked.
> Mariana shook her head.
> "I don't want you to wait on me," she replied, half pettishly.
> "Janet [the servant] can do that. I want you to love me."
> Miss Ramsey smiled.
> "How shall I begin?" she inquired.

Mariana then "laid her head in Miss Ramsey's lap, and [Miss Ramsey's] voice sounded faint and far off" (261). When Mariana asks Miss Ramsey if she is "better" than she used to be, Miss Ramsey replies, "You are very good to me," implicitly ascribing her present "better" condition to her "good" treatment by Mariana. Mariana then "rose and kissed her good-night," and "when she awoke in the morning it was to find Miss Ramsey standing beside her, holding her breakfast-tray" (262). This scene's power is due in part to the pauses after the verbal cues; Mariana never answers Miss Ramsey's question about how she should begin to "love" her, for example, and such linguistic omissions invite the reader to fill in the silences with tender gestures on the part of the two women. When Mariana the next day orders new dresses for herself and Miss Ramsey and speaks to another friend in "low, almost affectionate voices, conscious of one of those outreaches of sympathy to which women are subject" (266), the ideal of female friendship is underscored, this time as an adult possibility.

Bonnie Zimmerman's observation that the "schoolgirl crush is central to the lesbian novel of development" underscores the significance in Mariana's adult life of her girlhood "passionate friendship" for her schoolmate, and thus gives greater weight to her relationship with Miss Ramsey as the reader retrospectively compares the two female friendships. Though Glasgow in *Phases* does not write a "lesbian novel," her interest in female friendships admits similarities. After Ellis warned about "flames," such friendships increasingly were seen as pernicious as the twentieth century became more and more intrigued with homosexuality. Perhaps Glasgow, writing in 1898, could include such a girlish crush with impunity, something she could not— and did not—include later, after the turn of the psychologically more sophisticated new century.[33] The friendship between Mariana and her scholar may indicate the unquestioning ease with which Glasgow viewed it at this time in her life and fiction.

Female Friendships: The Center of The Wheel of Life

Glasgow's own life at about this time and the critical interpretations of it mirror the fiction: readers have almost exclusively focused on Glasgow's presumed relationship with the elusive, pseudonymous "Gerald B—" of her autobiography, and they have marginalized her close relationships with female friends. Though Glasgow reveals in her autobiography the love affair with the married Gerald that is supposed to have begun around 1899 and ended with Gerald's death in 1905, there is as yet no convincing evidence other than Glasgow's word. The section of her autobiography that introduces him, furthermore, is tantalizingly titled "Miracle—or Illusion?" as Will Brantley also notes.[34]

Whatever the actual status of the man and the relationship, Glasgow's correspondence with more than one female friend at about the same time demonstrates that her warm feelings for her friends did not lessen. Among them, Glasgow's childhood friend Elizabeth Patterson—Lizzie or Lizbeth, to Glasgow—remained a confidante and companion long after their early jaunts at the Glasgows' country home, Jerdone Castle, or at the Pattersons' nearby home, Reveille. Glasgow's surviving letters to Lizzie, dated 1902 to 1916, chart a warm friendship, especially before Lizzie's marriage in 1915 to E. M. Crutchfield. They tell of Glasgow's cherished memories of their past, her longing to be with Lizzie, her jealousy of others who threaten to separate them emotionally, and her wistful sense of time passing, perhaps forcing them apart.

Reflecting the structural marginalization of women's friendships in *Phases* and other, later novels, critics have centered their attention on Glasgow's love affair and pushed aside her warm relationship with Lizzie, which, like that of Mariana and her schoolgirl "flame," began when Glasgow was about age ten. The earliest extant letter, and one of only two that have been published, dates from 2 January 1902, when Glasgow was twenty-nine. Addressed to her "Dear Girl," Glasgow's letter evinces closeness, nostalgia for a fading childhood happiness, and longing for Lizzie: "We so seldom see each now [*sic*] that I begin to fancy we are drifting in opposite ways until there comes, now and then, some realization that the past is quite as strong as the present and much more sacred. You are bound up, my dear, with some of the happiest memories of my life, and the older I grow the more earnestly I feel that the few intense joys of childhood are the best that life has to give."[35] With its emphasis on their "sacred" childhood friendship, the letter both lends resonance to and gains resonance from the schoolgirl romance in *Phases*. In March of the same year, Glasgow evokes for "My dearest Lizbeth" an almost literal "Eden of friendship" that connects the enjoyment of nature with a shared past threatened with extinction: "Did you know I wonder that my thoughts have turned so often of late to those dear lost springs in the big woods? Do you remember, too, those queer bell-like flowers we used to find . . . ? I have never seen them since."[36]

The sense of a special friendship subsequently unmatched—"I have never seen them since"—persists in Glasgow's letters to Patterson. In 1909, Glasgow, vacationing in Colorado Springs, writes: "Nobody can take your place. I am missing you all the time, & the further I get from England [where they had traveled together earlier that year], the more I realize what beautiful patience and sympathy you showed me every minute. I don't believe anybody else in the world would have been—or could have been—as understanding as you were there" (17 August 1909). On the same trip Glasgow writes: "Other friends are good & dear in their way, but . . . I love you more & more whenever I look back on it" (2 September [1909]). A little over a year later, Glasgow writes on Christmas Eve that she values the gift from her "precious dear" just as she "value[s] the past ones you gave me as precious possessions" (1910). On New Year's Day 1914, Glasgow assures her friend that her feelings haven't changed: "I love you all the time just as I've always done," and a year later, in the first surviving letter addressed to the new Mrs. E. M. Crutchfield, Glasgow writes that the Christmas gift "took me straight back to some of those happy days of my childhood & yours" (postmarked 27 December 1915).

A hint of jealousy on Glasgow's part and her sense that Lizzie might also be jealous creeps into at least one letter in 1909. After chastising herself for not visiting sooner, Glasgow explains that she'd heard Lizzie wasn't receiving visitors when she first arrived at home. But, "I heard the other day that you had a visit from Robert Munford so I suppose you would survive one from me." It's certainly not lack of interest in seeing her friend that has kept Glasgow away: "I've felt a perfect longing to see you for several days. You seem so near to me that I miss you all the time." Glasgow wishes they were going on a trip together, and is careful to explain that another friend's presence for a journey to New York can't make up for Lizzie's absence: "How I wish we starting [*sic*] to some warm country today! Louise [Collier Willcox] is going to New York for ten days with me (not as my guest) about the 20th—but I'd a thousand times rather be with my Lizzie" (29 December 1909).

Translating the closeness of girlhood friends that continues into a sustaining friendship between two adult women, Glasgow in 1906 published her sixth novel, *The Wheel of Life*. In it, the friendship between poet Laura Wilde and Gerty Bridewell assumes a greater structural and thematic importance than those in *Phases*. When Glasgow in 1938 wrote to another woman friend that her 1906 novel *The Wheel of Life* was the "only one . . . taken directly from experience,"[37] she might have been thinking partly of its origins in her actual friendship with Lizzie. The opening chapter, "In Which the Romantic Hero Is

Conspicuous by His Absence," focuses attention on the absent traditional male hero and prepares for the reader's necessary shift to a world that instead revolves around women. This initial chapter introduces the novel's major concerns: heterosexual love brings unhappiness because men and women are too different to comprehend one another, and the most genuinely satisfying relationships are between women. The first paragraph shows Gerty Bridewell (surely the irony of her last name cannot be accidental; we soon discover that she is anything but a "well" bride), reflecting on the fact that "the object" of her present "unhappiness" is her husband.[38] By contrast, Gerty's recollection of "her best friend, Laura Wilde," the "woman to whom she clung," brings the "peace which she had missed in the thought of her husband" (*WL* 5). Mirroring Glasgow's own exploration of the relative merits of heterosexuality and homosociality, *Wheel* demonstrates the truth of Gerty's initial feelings: marriage brings "unhappiness"; love between women brings "peace."

The three complexly intertwined heterosexual relationships in the novel—Gerty and Perry Bridewell, Roger and Connie Adams, protagonist Laura Wilde and Arnold Kemper—share features that call into question the common bases for heterosexual love. Both Gerty and Connie, for example, falsely accept the notion that if they maintain petty control over their husbands, they will be happy. In Gerty's metaphor for her marriage, she is the owner of a carriage driven by a male footman. Yet, her control has left her "wretched" rather than "produc[ing] in her the contentment of which she had often dreamed" (*WL* 4). Connie, wife of publisher Roger Adams, maintains control by seeing other men, amassing extravagant bills, and taking drugs. Roger's male friends pointedly note Roger's failed manhood when they wonder "why in the deuce he didn't keep a hand upon his wife" (49). As Roger admits, their marriage is "a pitiable failure" (123).

The novel seriously questions the probability of happiness in traditional romance plots by making mere physical attraction for the opposite sex a basis for love in all three pairings. Perry Bridewell is physically "magnificent" and "imposing," with characteristically "masculine" gestures. Gerty married him after a "restless infatuation" induced by physical attraction (*WL* 3–5). Even Roger Adams, whom Gerty calls "the brainiest man" among the Bridewells' circle of friends (11), fell under the spell of physical passion in marrying his wife, Connie. Though he now seems an unlikely candidate for such an attraction—he is a "scholarly looking man of forty years" and, according to Gerty, a cross between "a bookworm and a butterfly" (16)—in the past "his own senses had led him, he recognised now, to disastrous issues; his love for Connie had been the prompting of mere physical impulse" (54).

Laura Wilde seems an equally unlikely victim of physical passion. According to one man, she is not "worth much at love-making—the purpose for which woman was created by God and cultivated by man," because she "writes books" (*WL* 10). Reminiscent of Rachel Gavin's saintly heroines and Mariana Musin's spiritual friendships, Laura's poetry is "chastened and restrained," guided by a "cloistral vision" and a "conventual purity" (52–53). Describing herself as "not like other women," Laura opposes ideality ("dreams") and hetero-sexuality; as she explains, "I don't see how any one who has ever dreamed dreams" can "fall in love and marry—it is so different—so different" (37). But after Laura reads Arnold Kemper's "slim volume" (41), the "little novel" (19) published fifteen years ago, she succumbs to physicality and forceful masculinity. In Arnold's book, Laura believes she has "encountered the shock of a tremendous masculine force," the "life of the flesh, of vivid sensation." The reader, if not Laura, recognizes in the book's "slim" and "little" qualities its triviality.

As in *The Descendant* and *Phases*, here Glasgow suggests that female friendships encourage women's artistic fulfillment by revealing Laura's artistic self-doubt after she decides that Arnold's literary accomplishment is superior to her own. She begins to doubt the truth of her own work, suspecting that she has missed something by dwelling in too ethereal a realm. In a move that harkens back to Rachel Gavin's Magdalen, Laura's self-doubt draws her mistakenly toward Arnold in search of what she believes is the full expression of the "tumultuous, passionate instinct for life within her" (*WL* 41). Glasgow gives us a heterosexual relationship within a literary one, both of which serve to question, and therefore to damage, a woman's sense of her own worth.

If her critical eye fails her where Arnold is concerned, Laura correctly perceives in him the "life of the flesh." As Perry's "distant cousin," he shares Perry's forceful masculinity. Like Perry, Arnold has "a certain evident possession of virile power—a quality which women are accustomed to describe as masculine" (*WL* 12). The lengthy initial description of Arnold Kemper, often cast in Darwinian terms, emphasizes his primitive animalism and virility:

> He was not tall, and yet he gave an impression of bigness. . . . The development of his closely knit figure, the splendid breadth of his chest and shoulders, the slight projection of his heavy brows and the almost brutal strength of his jaw and chin, all combined to emphasise that appearance of ardent vitality which has appealed so strongly to the imagination of women. Seen in repose there was a faint suggestion of cruelty in the lines of his mouth under his short brown moustache, but this instead of detracting from the charm he exercised only threw into greater relief the genial brightness of his smile. (12–13)

Gerty remembers that "there was always a woman in the wind when it blew rumours of Kemper, though he was generally considered to regard the sex with the blithe indifference of a man to whom feminine favour has come easily" (13). Though Laura is at least temporarily won over by Arnold's traditionally masculine qualities, the narrator's negative judgment on the desirability of such "virile power" clearly forces the reader to question Laura's attraction to Arnold. Power is "masculine" because "women are *accustomed to describe*" it as such (12; emphasis added); power's dark underside is discernible in the "cruelty" lurking beneath Arnold's masculine exterior (13).

Where Laura sees in Arnold her low self-worth, Arnold sees in Laura his best self. Arnold's "mere dominant virility" (*WL* 94) makes Laura question her ethereality, the very quality that causes Arnold to want her so that she can uplift him. Gerty is correct in perceiving that some of what attracts Arnold to Laura is the "fresh sensation" of liking a woman for qualities other than sexual ones (85), but even more important is the fact that Laura confers upon Arnold a greater sense of self-worth than he has without her. When he realizes his interest in Laura is not physical, "a clean and perfectly sane satisfaction was the immediate result; he felt that he had grown larger in his own eyes—that the old Adam who had ruled over him so long had become suddenly dwarfed and insignificant. 'To like a woman and yet not to make love to her,' he repeated in his thoughts. 'By Jove, it will be something decent, something really worth while'" (88). Arnold as a mirror reflects Laura's inadequate self, whereas Laura as a mirror reflects Arnold's elevated, "larger" one. His attitude neatly encapsulates a male perspective in the ideology of separate spheres, where woman as spiritual mother leads man to his higher and best self. Raper argues that this kind of personality projection in Glasgow's fiction demonstrates her moving toward a sophisticated psychological realism that uses "phantasies," revealed through their projection onto other characters, as "an essential test of the reality within which her protagonists find themselves."[39] Such projection also has a gendered intepretation. For female characters like Laura, such projection reveals a woman's culturally constructed tendency to see herself as lacking and to look to a male for self-definition. For male characters like Arnold, such a view sees women as responsible for uplifting men spiritually. In any such occurrence, an obvious flaw in male-female relations is the inevitable tendency of one lover to view the other through the colored lenses of encultured expectation. With such clouded perspectives, Glasgow argues again and again, a stormy relationship is unavoidable, and the possibilities for men and women to understand one another, she implies, are limited at best. As Dorothy Chandler in Glasgow's short story "The Difference" (1923) says to her self-sacrificing friend Margaret Fleming, "When a man and a woman talk of love they speak two different languages."[40]

Laura's relationships with other women most pointedly illustrate the serious problems in her relationship with Arnold (and in heterosexual relationships generally). They also demonstrate an attitude toward female friendship that Glasgow will refine over the first half of her writing career: other women reflect a "second self," in Jean E. Kennard's term—a female image in which a woman can view a reflected female self instead of a reflected image of otherness.[41] Men, in this formulation, instead project a desired self, a male-defined female self that is foreign, other. Glasgow increasingly will come to believe that for a woman to see herself in a man's eyes is to experience a death of self. Consequently, when Laura becomes engaged to Arnold despite everyone's misgivings, she—like Rachel Gavin and Mariana Musin before her—simultaneously begins her estrangement from the things that matter most to her. She now has no use for her poetry, feels alienated from her true self, and, significantly, finds that her relationship with Arnold necessarily places her in unwanted competition with other women. Feeling obligated to work up enthusiasm for competing with one of Arnold's former lovers, Laura implicitly criticizes such conflict as an attack upon the female self, forced by competition for male attention. As Arnold demands nothing short of a battle between the women, Laura wonders: "Is it possible that I can ever enter into this warfare which I have always despised? . . . into this conflict of self against self, of vanity against vanity? . . . Shall I even come in the end to feel terror and suspicion in my love for Gerty?" (*WL* 404). As Diane Price Herndl observes of another of Glasgow's novels, female competition for a man is "sickening," and any perceived triumph is instead a "guarantee of eventual defeat." [42]

It is with this last possibility, "so terrible" to Laura that she "lacked the courage with which to face it" (*WL* 404), that the novel most seriously qualifies the heterosexual romance plot and offers female companionship as an alternative to it. Though at times pushed aside, Laura's relationship with Gerty occupies the emotional center of *The Wheel of Life*. When Gerty, in the novel's opening pages, contrasts the unhappiness of her marriage with the satisfaction she finds in her friendship with Laura, she recalls their first meeting twenty years ago, a recollection that parallels one of Glasgow's own in *The Woman Within* (44–45), when she had "first seen Laura Wilde as a child of ten" (*WL* 6). Gerty, at the time a "weak, bedraggled little girl" frightened by the other children, remembers being protected by the young Laura, who "folded her in her arms," kissed her, and promised to "love [her] best of all" (6). Laura's youthful "passionate friendship" with Gerty resembles Mariana Musin's schoolgirl crush in *Phases*. Unlike Mariana's friendship, however (except as it is manifest in the later relationship with Miss Ramsey), but like Glasgow's actual relationship with Lizzie Patterson, this friendship flourishes into adulthood. Gerty and Laura are so completely in sympathy that Laura can "feel" Gerty coming to visit (18), and both women readily spring to each other's defense.

Both Laura and Gerty are quick to uphold the ideal of female companionship against assaults from uncomprehending men. When St. George Trent, an aspiring young dramatist devoted to Laura, observes that Gerty's loyalty to Laura "seems a bit odd," Gerty is angered by Trent's assumption that friendships between women somehow lack the significance of those between men and women. Gerty lets St. George know that she would cross Brooklyn Bridge "on my knees for

Laura." If she "adored her" as a schoolmate, Gerty tells him, "I adore her even more to-day" (*WL* 76).

No less passionately, Laura defends her feelings for Gerty against male misrepresentation and skepticism. When Arnold asks Laura if she is "very fond of Gerty," she responds rapturously with a "smile [that] was a miracle of light. 'I love her more than anyone in the whole world.'" St. George Trent, "perplexed," protests: "I thought all women hated one another." Laura's "indignant" answer (which Glasgow will make more explicit in 1911 in *The Miller of Old Church*) is: "'That's because men have ruled the world in two ways,'": "'they have made the laws and they have made the jokes'" (*WL* 184). In fact, St. George Trent earlier *did* make a "joke" that displayed his prurient interest in female affection. When St. George's mother asked him if Laura Wilde's verse was "improper," he teasingly asked her: "have you been reading 'Sappho' at your age?" (58). The joke, though lost on the proper Mrs. Trent, does not escape the reader. Sappho had been associated popularly with what we now term lesbianism at least since Pierre Bayle's Critical Dictionary in the early eighteenth century,[43] and Glasgow's reference at once demonstrates her knowledge of Sappho, shades the relationship between Laura (like Sappho, a poet) and Gerty, and condemns St. George Trent by allowing him to make a tasteless joke at the expense of an ideal of female friendship.

Gerty's "adoration" and Laura's "miraculous" smile suggest the religious quality of their love, borne out by other such suggestions in this novel as it is elsewhere in Glasgow's fiction in the context of women's friendships. During her visit to Gerty when Laura is first introduced to Arnold, Laura's fascination is with her woman friend, not with her future male lover. Arnold eagerly takes up Laura's hint that she and Gerty have discussed him: "'So Gerty has told you that I'm a strenuous creature?'" But it is clear that Laura's interest is in Gerty: "'Perhaps. I don't remember.' She turned to Gerty, looking down upon her with a tenderness that suffused her face with colour'" (*WL* 89). Indifferent to Arnold, Laura kisses Gerty's cheek and, "folding Gerty in her arms," announces: "'I stopped for a moment to look at you. . . . It was a choice between looking at you and at the Rembrandt in the Metropolitan, and I chose you'" (90–91). Rachel Gavin's worshipful attitude toward the painting of Joan of Arc, her "shrine in the Metropolitan," is transformed here into adoration of an actual female friend. Arnold, unsuccessful at capturing Laura's attention, displaces his fears of female friendship, of Sapphic devotion, by reflecting on the almost religious nature of the women's relationship.

Where Kemper notes the religious quality of this friendship in order to safely contain it, Gerty uses the same quality to highlight the very seriousness of the relationship that Kemper finds threatening. Gerty even evokes the most sensuous of the sacraments in her thoughts about Laura; Gerty

> had come at last to feel, almost without explaining it to herself, that the truth was in Laura as in some obscure, mystic sense the sacrament was in the bread and wine upon the altar. . . . It made no difference that she should number among the profane multitude who found their way back to the fleshpots, but her heart demanded that her friend should remain constant to the prophetic vision and the promised land. Laura was not only the woman whom she loved, she had become to her at last almost a vicarious worship. (*WL* 349)

The unquestionably religious language consecrates Laura's and Gerty's friendship. As they do for Mariana Musin of *Phases,* other women characters in later novels, and other actual friendships in Glasgow's life, female friendships provide a spiritual fulfillment deeply satisfying enough to be interchangeable with religion.

The Wheel of Life's concluding chapters quietly demonstrate the healing nature of Gerty's and Laura's friendship. Laura, acknowledging her distrust of Arnold Kemper and realizing the impossibility of their marriage, flees. Taking refuge in the home of strangers, she stays past the wedding date and is sought by Gerty and Roger Adams. In an unlikely plot development, probably intended to make the ending more credible, Laura finally summons Adams, who in turn summons Gerty, "breathlessly" awaiting news of her friend. Gerty promptly abandons a dinner party with her husband, willfully abdicating her social and marital obligations. In trading the rest of the world for Laura, Gerty becomes a different, and presumably better, person; she "shone" with a new "beauty" and "her soul bloom[ed] in her face like a closed flower that expands in sunlight" (*WL* 459). Adams's announcement that "it's a woman that she wants" is borne out by the moving scene of almost wordless comfort that ensues: "For a moment, groping blindly for light, she hesitated; then her arms opened, and she caught Laura into them in spite of her feeble effort at resistance. 'Dearest! dearest! dearest!' she repeated, for she had found the word at last." This penultimate chapter concludes with an intimate scene befitting its title, "Between Laura and Gerty": "Neither philosophy nor religion mattered now, for presently she felt that her bosom was warm with tears, and when Laura lifted her head, the two women kissed in that intimate knowledge which is uttered without speech" (461–62). The actual experience of women's friendship replaces "religion," abstract "philosophy," and the relationship between a man and a woman. When Adams, incapable of helping despite his newly professed love for Laura, relinquishes his place to Gerty's superior sensibility, he—and the novel—acknowledges that in some instances, only a woman will do.

The concluding chapter, hopefully titled "Renewal," revises what has become a novel of female friendship with a traditional romantic ending. Even within the chapter, however, support for the rather abrupt Roger-Laura alliance is lacking. Laura first returns to Gerty's house, then goes "South" with Gerty at the beginning of the new year, comes and goes "at Gerty's bidding," and travels with Gerty in June to the Adirondacks (*WL* 464–67). Laura's "renewal" comes about in a transcendental moment of union with the natural world. Once she ceases to define "love" as narrowly focusing on an individual and begins to understand that it should instead touch "the boundaries of the world," Laura can begin to live fully (469). When Roger, in answer to Laura's explanation that she has finally found the "happiness of freedom," argues that he has "known [Laura's] heart" (471) better than she has, he is unpersuasive, as is Glasgow's attempt to leave us with a vision of their future love. We define love too narrowly when we view it as possible only between men and women, the novel implies, and its conclusion subverts the suggestion of an exclusive relationship between Laura and Roger by hinting at other kinds of love, such as that which exists "Between Laura and Gerty."

Laura's and Gerty's trip to the Adirondacks and the shared love of nature that it implies has its parallel in not only Glasgow's friendship with Lizzie Patterson but also her adult friendship with another Richmond writer, Mary Johnston, which flourished about the time of *The Wheel of Life*. Particularly between 1904 and 1908 (though they remained friends for many years), Glasgow and Johnston enjoyed a close friendship, marked by letters in which nature and natural beauty provide a basis for their friendship and their metaphors for communicating that friendship. In what is no doubt one of the earliest letters from Glasgow to Johnston, in 1904, Glasgow evokes the "gray skies," the "naked poplars," and the "eternal summer of which your letter was overflowing." [44] Johnston's *Sir Mortimer* "keeps wonderfully that peculiar golden light, as if of warmer sunshine." Glasgow especially likes Damaris, the "most attractive" of Johnston's "heroines," in the "love scene in the garden" (22 March 1904). A letter from Glasgow to Johnston in 1905 announces: "I can't tell you how often my thoughts will be with you this summer, & I shall think of you particularly when ever I see anything beautiful that you might enjoy with me." [45]

As in *The Wheel of Life,* a trip to the Adirondacks inspires Glasgow to appreciate the beauty of nature as a means to spiritual healing. During a vacation there in 1906, Glasgow writes Johnston: "Have you watched Venus, I wonder, this summer as closely as I have. I get a wonderful peace and the most exquisite pleasure from my friendship with the stars." [46] Also from the Adirondacks, an undated letter envisions a future including Glasgow and Johnston in a shared setting of natural beauty: "Someday, if all goes well, I may have a very simple cottage in the midst of fields of Timothy and harebells and black-eyed daisies and then you must certainly come up and spend a long quiet summer with me." [47] In another undated letter, Glasgow's letters to Johnston "would have fluttered like doves" had they been as frequent as Glasgow's thoughts of her. [48] In a philosophical mood, Glasgow writes to "Molly," as she often calls Johnston by 1908: "Voltaire said the last word for the philosophy of contentment when he remarked, 'Let us cultivate our garden.' There's my motto. Happy or unhappy, what does it matter when one can cultivate ones [sic] garden?" [49]

A shared belief in the possibilities of spiritual "renewal," as in the title of *The Wheel of Life*'s final chapter, forms the basis for a transcendent moment Glasgow describes to Johnston in a letter of 15 September 1906. Rejoicing that Johnston's letter brims over with "renewed vitality and a high heart for life," Glasgow describes her own spiritual vision that, like Laura's and Johnston's, was an "awakening" of self. During 1904–5, Glasgow says, "I was so dead that I couldn't feel even when I was hurt because of some curious emotional anaesthesia." Like Johnston, Glasgow "had to fight—fight" for her "very soul." Then, "at Brennerbad last summer I came out triumphant, and for three whole months it was as if I walked on light, not air. I was like one who had come out of a dark prison into the presence of God and saw and knew him, and cared for nothing in the way of pain that had gone before the vision." After affirming that such "rapture," though not sustainable forever, becomes part of the "eternal forces of one's spirit," Glasgow then brings Johnston back into her experience, re-emphasizing their shared awakenings: "We suffered in different ways, but we both suffered to the death—each of us saw at the end of her road the mouth of hell—and each of us turned and struggled back to life—you along your steep path and I along mine. It is something to be thankful for that now at last our roads may run a little while into one." [50]

Critics have assumed this spiritual experience revolves around the autobiography's "Gerald B—," and for evidence they have even mistranscribed "Mürren" for the actual place-name, "Brennerbad," mentioned in the letter. Following Glasgow's description in *The Woman Within* of a happy moment with Gerald in the Alps (*WW* 164), Rouse first identified the place as "Mürren," a place Glasgow associates with Gerald.[51] Though the word *is* difficult to read, not even a far stretch of the imagination would construe it as "Mürren." A surviving postcard from Glasgow's sister and traveling companion, Rebe, to their niece Josephine Clark, confirms the correct place: "Brennerbad, Tirol [Austria]."[52] Godbold, intent on tying Glasgow's earlier dark mood and the subsequent transcendent experience in the Alps to her relationship with Gerald, also transcribes the place as Mürren. Raper sees that Glasgow's version of this experience in her autobiography places the scene of transcendence *before* rather than after Gerald is supposed to have died in 1905, as Godbold would have it. Raper also recognizes that Mürren is probably a mistranslation and suggests "Blumen-tal" as a possible substitute, but leaves Mürren anyway because it "has associations with Miss Glasgow's earlier life," presumably with Gerald.[53] It is impossible to sort out the truth, especially with Glasgow's embellished account complicating it so thoroughly. The persistent critical misreading of this letter, however, goes beyond literal mistranscription to suggest an important truth of another kind: the episode in the Alps has been firmly, even stubbornly, connected to the ostensible sexual fulfillment that presumably brought Glasgow a rare moment of happiness. That reading centralizes heterosexual relationship, marginalizes female friendship, and distorts Glasgow's own words and quite possibly her meaning. The close resemblance of the spiritual fulfillment Glasgow describes to *The Wheel of Life,* with its focus on female friendship, makes the critical emphasis on heterosexual fulfillment even more problematic.

The final implication in *Wheel*—that confining love exclusively to heterosexual relationships restricts emotional possibility—also finds its way into a slightly earlier letter from Glasgow to Johnston, when Glasgow, still traveling in the Adirondacks, learns of her friend's recuperation from an illness: "I want to draw you, dear brave heart, not only back to work and play but back to us. . . . life to me means love just as it does to a child—love of many kinds and degrees, but each and all helping us on our way and bringing the journey's end a little nearer the knowledge of God. So love me, Mary, much or little as you can, and I shall love you back in my own measure." [54] In life as in fiction, there are many kinds and degrees of love, that between Laura and Gerty as well as that between Ellen and Mary.

Unpublished and previously undiscussed letters of 1905–6 to the older writer Louise Chandler Moulton (1835–1908) suggest the depth of Glasgow's emotional ties to women. A Connecticut author best known for her poetry, Moulton had also written children's stories, novels, sketches, and travel literature. More properly associated with the nineteenth century, and thus with a female literary tradition that preceded Glasgow's generation, Moulton was identified with the New York literary circle surrounding Richard Henry Stoddard from the mid to the late nineteenth century. Glasgow met Moulton in Paris in 1905, while touring Europe during the late summer and early fall. Forwarding a letter to Moulton from their mutual friend Amélie Rives Troubetzkoy, Glasgow writes in an undated letter of "Thursday night" that she would like to meet Moulton ("to know you"), but understands Moulton's fragile health may make that difficult. Open to the possibility of friendship with Moulton but concerned about her health, Glasgow's initial letter to Moulton hastens to assure her: "Don't let me be a burden, dear Mrs. Moulton, but if you do really feel that you would care to have me come to you for a little talk, send me word and

I will run to meet you." Though busy with preparations to embark, Glasgow would gladly "drop trifles light as ours for the sake of something really worth"—and here the letter stops, the remainder lost.[55]

Glasgow's letter following what was evidently her first meeting with Moulton is warm and enthusiastic about her new friend. Indeed, her effusiveness, characteristic of many letters to women friends, marks a rather dramatic divergence from a critical view of Glasgow, advocated by Godbold, as outgoing and socially adept but emotionally distant and reserved, or at least excessively self-protective.[56] Glasgow's letter to Moulton of 5 October 1905, written when their friendship can have been no more than a few days old, is emotionally unrestrained. Glasgow sends her "little message of love and farewell" to solidify her new friendship. The overwhelming "joy" of meeting Moulton, already Glasgow's "dear, dear friend," has rendered Glasgow's words inadequate: "There was so much—oh, so much I wanted to say to you today," Glasgow tells Moulton, but she was "a little shy." The "first thrill of joy" at knowing Moulton remains.[57]

Following Glasgow's effusive greeting to her new friend, the letter establishes a definite sense of a community of three inhabited by Glasgow, her friend Amélie, and now their mutual friend Moulton. She tells Moulton: "I feel, oh, my dear friend, with a sense that is above and beyond knowledge that we have come together—as Amelie and I have come—for some wonderful and lovely end." Most of Glasgow's letters to Moulton at least mention Amélie Rives Troubetzkoy. The community among women that in 1913 Glasgow will lament is missing clearly exists in some measure in the companionship shared in 1905 by these three friends. Glasgow writes in this same letter: "It is the liberation and the reconciliation of the spirit that I would make the joy that we hold and feel together, Amelie and you and I."

Glasgow's sense of "liberation" and "reconciliation" points to another characteristic of Glasgow's letters to Moulton: an emphasis on spirituality, which is evident also in the fiction and the letters to Mary Johnston of about this time. It was "beautiful," Glasgow continues in her letter to Moulton of 5 October 1905, "the way we came together not as strangers but as dear friends who meet again after a long absence and the sweet familiar recognition was the loveliest thing I have felt for a long time. You brought the spirit very close to me." Believing that the "soul" she "saw and loved" in Moulton is something she "must have known and loved before" leads Glasgow to observe in the same letter that "when one believes this the whole universe becomes not a wilderness but a home." It is difficult to say whether Glasgow's heightened interest in mysticism about this time results from some growing recognition on her part that spiritualized relationships with women were easier than with men, but certainly her willingness to portray such spirituality in her female friendships and to contrast it with her heterosexual relationships suggests that such an interpretation is possible, even likely. Elsewhere in this same letter, Glasgow asks Moulton not to think her "too great a mystic" when she feels that "where one meets constantly with wonderful ways of the spirit what else can one be but a believer in and a lover of the [wiser?]." Telling Moulton that "My love was with you before we met" and "will be with you always," Glasgow then incorporates their individual love within "that love which is both light and knowledge, the love in which we live and move and have our being." Meeting Moulton has connected the two women and has reconnected them both to a larger "spirit of love" that was "with us when we met." In closing, Glasgow addresses Moulton as her "dear newly *found* but not new friend."

The emotions expressed in Glasgow's eight letters to Moulton in 1905 and 1906 help to clarify Glasgow's hypothetical relationship from about 1899 to 1905 with the elusive "Gerald." Glasgow herself started others searching for Gerald by "confessing" to their love affair in her posthumously published autobiography. Her revelation is itself problematic, since her motives for revealing him are unknown. Critics have assiduously followed her lead, however. Godbold, noncommittal about identifying Gerald, nevertheless makes his significance to Glasgow and her fiction of central importance. Gerald becomes responsible for nothing less than "establish[ing] Ellen Glasgow as the first realist in Southern letters" by forcing her to "look to the future rather than sigh for the past." Raper reasons at length that Gerald is most probably Pearce Bailey, a friend and New York neurologist.[58] Even when acknowledging the problems associated with the search for "Gerald," as both Godbold and Raper do, the critical interest in that relationship helps to create the assumption that Glasgow's love affairs, especially those beginning with Gerald, are centrally important in her life and art, and that all else—including her close friendships with women—

is peripheral. The previously unexamined Moulton correspondence (October 1905 to December 1906), which spans the year Glasgow's relationship with Gerald presumably ended, serves as a reminder that the critical overemphasis on Gerald as Glasgow's great love has obscured other events and other relationships in her life. Regardless of the relative fictionality or actuality of Gerald and of Glasgow's affair with him, her life at the time was richer and fuller than has been emphasized. Had Glasgow foreseen the critical sleuthing aimed at discovering Gerald's identity, she might have echoed the impatient question posed by one of her female characters: "Why do you seem to think that the beginning and middle and end of my existence is a man?" (*MOC* 133).

In addition to the lack of evidence to corroborate Glasgow's account, there are several problems with the Gerald plot as it has been reconstructed. Though Godbold says that Glasgow's sister "confirmed" Glasgow's relationship with a man in New York, Rebe is adamant about Glasgow's "men" in a letter to Rawlings dated 14 November 1953: "It was I, not Carrie [Coleman Duke], who took all the trips with her to Europe and for months in Spring & Fall in New York and elsewhere and I can declare in *positive* terms that Ellen did *not* have a love affair of any kind in her youth." She continues later in the same letter: "I can assure you that during all the years I was [particularly?] with her men only entered into her life in a most casual manner." [59] Many people (including, at times, Glasgow herself) have seemed intent upon emphasizing Glasgow's love affairs with men, and many— including Rawlings, who thinks Gerald B— was Holbrook Curtis, an aurist (we would now refer to this specialist as an otolaryngologist) whom Glasgow consulted about her hearing loss—have speculated on the identity of Gerald. I think it at least possible that there was no Gerald; if he existed, certainly his importance has been overemphasized. The transcendent Alpine episode associated with Gerald by others recurs in the experience of Laura and Gerty in *The Wheel of Life,* in the letters to Johnston and Moulton about the same time, and much later in *Vein of Iron* (1935), connecting that episode as much with fiction and with Glasgow's female relationships as with Gerald. When, in *The Ancient Law* (1908), the male protagonist realizes that his male friend has "swayed his destiny" through the "simple power of the human touch," his vision affirms the possibility that friendship can liberate and expand the possibilities of love: "it was made plain to him at last, that the love of Emily, the love of Alice, and the love of Banks, were but different revelations of the same immortality."[60] The meeting with Moulton and the letters that followed would have corresponded with the period Godbold and others have described when Glasgow learned the devastating news of Gerald's death in August 1905, while Glasgow was in Europe, and her resulting depression. It is difficult not to perceive that they maintain a certain blindness to the emotionally satisfying female friendships evident at this time in favor of their bias toward a mysterious and romantic male object of Glasgow's affections. Even Glasgow's saying that he and her love for him existed does not make it so, particularly considering the probable strength of the pressure to *have* had such a man in her life. Her "truthful" autobiography would have been the perfect place in which to invent him.

Gleanings *from* The Miller of Old Church

By the time she published her ninth novel, *The Miller of Old Church,* in 1911, Glasgow felt keenly the pull in two directions: one toward a tradition of womanhood signified by isolation and passive femininity, the other toward a tradition of cooperative strength she also identified in her 1913 interview (see note 1 above). In her revised Virginia Edition Preface to *The Miller,* included in *A Certain Measure* (1943) as "The Miller of Old Church," Glasgow describes the tension she felt while writing the "curious blend of romance and realism" that characterizes this novel. Even though she "had broken with tradition," she says, she had "not yet escaped entirely from the influence of its emotional patterns." She was "still feeling the backward pull of inherited tendencies," both drawn to and repelled by the past glories of a "code of beautiful behaviour."[61] Though apparently she refers to the willful blindness she elsewhere calls "evasive idealism" as it translates into stylistic practice, Glasgow's statement also sums up her struggle with tradition as it defines gendered behavior. Although she can almost envision a countertradition of self-determination to offset the tradition of passivity and selflessness she has associated with one powerful woman's tradition, she still feels the pull of simpler times. She begins to find, in *The Miller of Old Church,* a middle ground between completely rejecting and completely accepting a woman's tradition of self-sacrifice. As her protagonist, Molly Merryweather, rewrites her mother's story and changes its ending, Glasgow rewrites *her* mother's story and in so doing suggests it is possible for all women to find and redefine a usable woman's past. Again, in the theme of women's friendship, Glasgow discovers an important connection between women's need for one another and their need to tell their own stories. She comes to the insight that female friendship in fiction effectively silences the men, who usually do the telling for women. Representing close female companionships, therefore, is tantamount to letting women themselves tell their unheard stories.

Early in the novel, the "sex hatred" (*MOC* 120) that typifies male-female relationships suggests that any satisfactory outcome from the conventional marriage plot is impossible. Betsey Bottom, spokeswoman for independent womanhood and indisputable ruler of Bottom's Ordinary, the inn that bears her name, introduces the idea that for women to find the voice for their own experience, men must be silenced. Since marrying William Ming ten years earlier, she has "successfully extinguished his identity without materially impairing her own" (4). Betsey, who "saw through men early" (83), announces that if women did their learning after marriage, as one male frequenter of the inn asserts, "thar's precious few of 'em that would ever set foot into the estate!" (124).

The younger Molly Merryweather seems to agree. "Savagely pure" (*MOC* 32) and fiercely virginal, Molly refuses even to shake hands with young Jonathan Gay, nephew of the aristocrat who exploited and betrayed her mother. At one point later in the novel Molly lashes out at Abel Revercomb, her would-be suitor and the miller of the title: "Why do you seem to think that the beginning and middle and end of my existence is a man? There are times when I find even a turkey more interesting" (133). Molly has "seen enough of marriage," she tells Betsey, to realize that she "shouldn't like it" (92).

Molly revises her mother's story by refusing to be a passive victim of male pursuit, and in doing so she establishes a countertradition to the conventional marriage plot. Current relationships are foregrounded by the betrayal of Molly's mother by old Mr. Jonathan, constantly present in Molly's continuing revision of the outcome of her mother's experience. The tradition of bad relationships suffuses the atmosphere of Old Church. Sarah Revercomb, the miller Abel's mother, had been "disappointed" in marriage (*MOC* 40); Abel's sister, Blossom Revercomb, secretly marries young Jonathan only to find that the love that she had expected to "fill her life" now looks "as if it might be poured into a teacup" (228); Judy Hatch, married to Abel after he is rejected by Molly, foolishly pines away for the Reverend Orlando Mullen, who preaches that "If the womanly woman possessed a talent, she did not use it, for this would unsex her" (100). Against this backdrop we are asked to believe that Molly, "savagely pure" though she is, comes to want Abel Revercomb enough to beg, literally on her knees, for his forgiveness and love.

In trying to define a female self against a male tradition of possessiveness, assumed superiority, and attempts to dominate, Glasgow implies that women are too easily convinced of their inferiority and their need for male support, and too quick to assent to the diminished view of themselves reflected back from a male gaze. Molly knows that if she succumbs to Abel, she might well lose her self: "The sense of bondage would follow; on his part, the man's effort to dominate; on hers, the woman's struggle for the integrity of personality" (*MOC* 199). Molly's assiduous efforts to avoid the tradition of almost literal female selflessness required by conventional romance are central means by which she defines herself. Though descriptions of Molly as a caged bird longing for freedom abound in the pages between her "struggle" and her relinquishment of it, somehow by the novel's conclusion, where romance with Abel triumphs, Molly has completely forgotten her earlier reservations. Glasgow's own ambivalence about traditions of male and female behavior may well explain the forced shift toward a conventional romance plot's conclusion. Certainly her admission in her Preface that she had not entirely succeeded in breaking with "tradition" would in large measure explain the novel's ambiguities.

Perhaps in partial response to her own ambivalence toward the women's traditions that at once ask for connection with and caring for others yet demand—in the context of male definitions and expectations—extreme selflessness, Glasgow introduces in *The Miller* an intense attraction between Molly and Blossom. Though Wagner calls this "emphasis on friendships among women" an "innovation" for Glasgow,[62] in fact it builds on many earlier fictional (and actual) friendships, and looks ahead to many more. With more depth than male-female relationships in *The Miller,* this understanding between women offers an alternative pairing based on connection without loss of self, fulfillment without demand, relationship without tension. The placement of the scene with Molly and Blossom just prior to the reconciliation between Abel and Molly undercuts the novel's conclusion. Molly, haunted by a troubled look on Blossom's face, offers aid to Blossom in words that emphasize the need for women to tell their stories to other women: "You're in trouble, darling—tell me, tell Molly about it." Excluding Jonathan—who relives his patriarchal history by betraying Blossom—from the circle of sympathy occupied by the two women highlights male failure to comprehend genuine love that does not ask for selflessness. As Molly and Blossom embrace "in a passion of despair and pity," Jonathan perceives his diminished position as outsider and observer. Traditional heterosexuality "was dwarfed suddenly by an understanding of the relation of woman to woman" that was "Deeper than the dependence of sex, simpler, more natural, closer to earth, as if it still drew its strength from the soil." Silenced, Jonathan "realized that the need of woman for woman was not written in the songs and the histories of men, but in the neglected and frustrated lives which the songs and the histories of men had ignored" (*MOC* 320–21). As in her letters to Lizzie Patterson, Glasgow argues here that "the relation of woman to woman" is "more natural" than that of "woman to man" (321). Echoing a masculine assumption that women *are* nature ("closer to the earth"), which Sherry Ortner has found pervasive across many cultures,[63] Gay's response simultaneously reveals awe and fear of women's relationships and acknowledges their threat to the status quo. And friendships between women, Glasgow implies here, only seem more uncommon than heterosexual ones because they are unsung, a theme to which she will return later.[64] This brief yet intense scene severely qualifies the heterosexual reunion of Abel and Molly with which the novel closes just fifteen pages later. The structure of the novel—and, more importantly, of culture, Glasgow suggests—may only appear to centralize the relationships between the Mollys and the Abels of the world (and thus easily deceives formalist critics who share the very patriarchal assumptions Glasgow here subtly condemns).

When Glasgow, through Jonathan Gay, articulates a realization that although plenty of stories have been told, they have been told not *by* women but *about* women, she recognizes what has been a stumbling block in her own thinking about her identity as a woman and her place in a woman's tradition: the simple fact (with complex implications) that the storytellers have been men. Her confusion about women's heritage has been exemplified in her simultaneous attraction to and revulsion from the tradition of feminine nurturing, her conflicting desire to embrace a culture of female companionship and simultaneously to inhabit the world of canonized literature, and her search for a means to self-definition that includes both nurture and power. Even if these conflicting needs are not resolved, they are at least in great measure explained in Glasgow's realization of women's historically obscured lives. *The Miller of Old Church* changes the way Glasgow, at thirty-eight, looks at women's traditions, by helping her recognize the implications of *his*tory. From that point on—if not in a neat, uncomplicated, linear fashion, at least with determination— Glasgow can allow herself to fit into a woman's tradition she had been resisting all of her adult life. Moreover, by combining in this novel an intense female friendship with the recognition that women need to tell their own stories, Glasgow implies a connection between self-knowledge and its expression and women's relationships with other women. Depicting female friendship in her fiction becomes a way to self-definition and, simultaneously, to redefinition of both literary and cultural history. As Janet Todd has said of women's literary friendships, they allow a woman to "mirror herself, not a man, [as in] the traditional female role,"[65] a role that has been defined both fictionally and experientially. And that self-mirroring becomes a tool for discovering a female self unmediated by (male) cultural definitions, untransformed, insofar as that is ever possible for anyone, by patriarchally imposed expectations.

Glasgow's relation to a woman's heritage of a female world as defined by Carroll Smith-Rosenberg is marked by ambivalence, fluctuation, and complexity. Early in her career, her definition of a woman's tradition still revolved around the marriage plot. She was not yet fully aware of the extent to which, for her at least, that story was a male-defined one, and was still not fully aware of the extent to which her own friendships with women offered an alternative to the usual story. As Glasgow began avoiding the traditional marriage ending (both as a personal option and as a literary convention), she thus abandoned what she still thought of as a woman's tradition. As she offered female affiliation as an alternative to heterosexual love relationships, however—realizing that in her own life female companionship brought greater satisfaction—she thought she was rejecting a female tradition. As she began to realize and vocalize more emphatically what she had come to see as the errors of male-imposed views of traditional womanhood, she also came to understand that self-definition, for her, depended more on the connection with women that she herself had experienced. Her unmistakable anger toward men and male attitudes in many of these texts reveals an increasing awareness that stereotyped expectations of her (and of her female characters) expose the dangers of self-denial and the loss of identity associated with rejecting a woman's tradition and accepting a mediated self offered by male standards. She realized, that is, that the female traditions she tried to deny—passivity, selflessness, dependence on men—are really male traditions of womanhood, since they had been defined by men. Further, the tradition she obviously wanted to embrace—that of female friendship, a sense of connection to other women—belongs truly to a *woman's* tradition, and is even threatening to accepted male standards of experience.

The story of Glasgow's attraction to a nurturing, connected female world passed on from literal and literary female precursors and of her recognition that the passivity and victimization often associated with that tradition was in fact a male tradition recounts a familiar narrative. Indeed, in many ways her story as I have reconstructed it is itself a part of a woman's tradition of assessing her place in a tale of woman's strengths turned against her: caring for and identifying with others becomes, from an altered viewpoint, evidence of obsessive selflessness and weakness.[66] In "What I Believe" (1933), Glasgow said of another subject that it is "wiser" to "profit by the past than to ignore or deny it."[67] She might have been speaking of her own complex and evolving relationship with one woman's tradition. Along with many other actual and literary women, Glasgow, in the very act of confronting the realities of gendered difference and interpreting its meaning in an individual life, narrates another traditional woman's story. The problem she wrestled with—how to embrace a tradition and yet transform it, separating it from its negative and externally imposed interpretations—remains vitally important in both the theory and the practice of women's experience.

THREE

Traditions Old and New:
Fall and Redemption

The ruined woman is an invention of man.

Glasgow, "Notes for They Stooped to Folly"

Queen or slave or bond or free, we battled,
Bartered not our faith for love or gold;
Man we served, but in the hour of anguish
Woman called to woman as of old.

Glasgow, "The Call" (1912)

IN AN ESSAY titled "Feminism," published in 1913 in the *New York Times Book Review,* Glasgow begins with the specter of Clarissa Harlowe, one of her favorite examples of what she elsewhere calls "literary woman myths":

> When the most popular of men's heroines, after being blighted by love, went to the undertaker's to select her coffin, ordered that a broken lily should be engraved on the lid, and had it sent home to be used as a writing table during her decline, an admiring eighteenth century public exclaimed that this touching episode had immortalized the womanly woman. No other heroine in fiction has been so passionately eulogized or so widely mourned, and even to-day she remains the most convincing of the feminine prigs with which the imagination of man has enriched the pages of literature. For Clarissa belongs not only to the evolving novel, but to the evolving masculine ideal of woman.[1]

According to Glasgow, Clarissa may be a "womanly woman," but she certainly is not a woman's woman. This "most popular of men's heroines" not only failed to imagine herself into being, she failed to imagine even that she *could* imagine herself. Priggish in her devotion to a male ideal, Clarissa at last dies, giving literal reality to the death of self she already has experienced, Glasgow suggests, by adhering to men's valuation of her worth. Glasgow goes on to admit that strength of personality on the part of a woman and acumen on the part of male novelists would be unexpected, since both men *and* women have participated in creating the mythic version of the ideal woman. But women, long conditioned to view themselves *other*wise, Glasgow argues, must learn to see themselves rather than a reflected image: "Ages of false thinking about her on the part of others have bred in woman the dangerous habit of false thinking about herself, and she has denied her own humanity so long and so earnestly that she has come at last almost to believe in the truth of her denial" (F 27). The real meaning of the women's movement, Glasgow believes—its "profound significance" (31)—lies in its fight for the right of woman to search, unhampered by the ideals created by man, for her self. Feminism is, finally, "a revolt from pretense of being," a "struggle for the liberation of personality" (31–32).

Not surprisingly, these words were published in 1913, the same year that produced *Virginia,* the most successful of Glasgow's earlier novels to realize that women's traditions and men's versions of women's traditions were two very different things, and that a woman's search for her own identity must take that difference into account. In *The Romance of a Plain Man* (1909) and *The Miller of Old Church* (1911), Glasgow, shifting her focus toward gendered tradition itself, recognized that men have written women's stories and distorted them in the process. She concludes that women must, with the help of other women (whether diachronically through generations or synchronically in conjunction with female friends), rewrite those stories and change those traditions that dictate women's roles. With heightened emphasis beginning in *Virginia,* Glasgow fully explores women's roles as men have defined them and examines the relationship between the male-defined "woman myths" of Glasgow's 1928 essay and the truth of women's experiences as they know them. Glasgow settles on women's relationships with other women, which she had begun to explore in her earlier novels, as the surest way to self-definition, and increasingly comes to believe in a world of close-knit women as a way of defying externally imposed definitions of a woman's place. She affirms a tradition of female connection that has provided a context for her own experience. By 1922, with *One Man in His Time,* she has rejected a male tradition of the "womanly woman" and has more consciously adopted a tradition of female friendship to replace it.[2]

The stereotypes of gender (especially those of women's roles) explored in *The Romance of a Plain Man* (1909) and evoked in *Virginia* (1913), *Life and Gabriella* (1916), *The Builders* (1919), and *One Man in His Time* (1922), are symbolic of what has become for Glasgow the problem of women's traditions: they represent not so much the women's traditions themselves as male-defined and male-imposed views of womanhood. After the pivotal *Virginia,* Glasgow moves to a newly re-visioned woman's tradition of connection and female companionship, one purged of the selflessness and victimization she had earlier seen as unhealthy symptoms of it. Certainly by the time she begins *Barren Ground,* published in 1925, Glasgow has come to an awareness that connection to others does not have to mean self-denial. What has been called "mature dependence"—a firm and independent sense of self that simultaneously accepts an "ethic of responsibility" toward others—becomes, in Glasgow's newly reconstructed female tradition, a real possibility.[3] Perhaps more radically, in maintaining her power *to* reconstruct traditions of womanhood, Glasgow both acknowledges a truth of socially constructed gender roles and the possibility of changing them, at least for herself. Glasgow's renegotiated woman's tradition can thus rebuild a model for her own self-definition. It can embrace what might be called a relational metaphysics: affiliation without loss of self, connection that aids rather than hinders self-definition.

From History to Herstory:
The Romance of a Plain Man

Working toward a synthesis of female friendship and traditions of womanhood, Glasgow, in *The Romance of a Plain Man,* emphasizes women's responsibility, especially across generations, to educate other women in gendered traditions.[4] This novel marks a noticeable change in attitude toward men, women, and the traditions that bind them to certain gendered behaviors. There is more generalizing about the sexes, and more overt hostility between them (characteristics that are also true of the novel that follows, *The Miller of Old Church*). Male characters typically patronize women, and the women in turn suffer—often not silently—for the limitations imposed on them by men. Moreover, a new emphasis on a tradition of "sex hatred" (*MOC* 120) on the passing down of gender-based antagonisms, marks Glasgow's own deeper questioning of gendered inheritance. Acknowledging legacies of gendered hostility, Glasgow glimpses in women's cooperation positive possibilities that span boundaries of time, possibilities she had hinted at in novels such as *The Descendant,* with Rachel Gavin's "hero-worship" (*D* 81) of historico-mythical women figures such as Joan of Arc and Mary Magdalen. Now, however, it is actual, living women who provide the impetus for others. Women of one generation, Glasgow suggests in *The Romance,* can help younger women rewrite their mothers' stories, transforming old plots into revised, more successful ones. Using tradition positively—as an instrument of change for the better—rather than negatively, as a reminder of the burdens of isolation in a separate sphere, women can, with the help of other women, transform history into herstory.

It is against the stagnant views of General Bolingbroke, keeper of *his*tory and representative patriarch, that the women in *The Romance* must work in order to re-vision themselves and their lives. Transmission of the General's rigid scheme of separate spheres for men and women seems assured, particularly through his teenaged nephew and namesake, who "hate[s] women," and through the General's protégé, young Ben Starr.[5] The insufferable General, whose authority rests on his money and his misogyny, asserts his right to define the proper traditions of womanhood when he announces that any true "Virginia lady" is "content to be what the Lord and the men intended her" (*RPM* 171). Impelled by the power of past ideals and the devotion of like-minded men to maintain a masculine status quo, the General teaches that "principles do not apply to ladies" (76). He advises Ben Starr not to "fall for a woman with ideas" since "a strong-minded woman" has "unsexed herself" (143).

Though traditions of separate gendered spheres clearly will not be transformed by *his*tory as espoused by the world's General Bolingbrokes, Glasgow acknowledges that women will not automatically do the transforming, either. In the character of the unworldly Mrs. Chitling, Glasgow shows us both the powerful appeal for some women of their idealization in an ideology of true womanhood and the danger of countering with another idealization: unswerving sisterhood.[6] Despite the novel's emphasis on women's responsibility to act as educators and models for other (especially younger) women, Glasgow recognizes that many women decline to participate in such subversions of the social and cultural status quo and instead remain loyal to a patriarchal standard that confers upon them status, if not autonomy. Mrs. Chitling articulates a womanly woman's tradition of submissive attendance on men's needs, further arguing that such attendance grants her honor and even power: " 'My kitchen is my kingdom,' " she says "with dignity" (*RPM* 63), and such a kingdom should be wide enough for any woman: " 'the woman who wants pleasure outside her do' ain't the woman that she ought to be, that's all. What can she have, I ax, any mo' than she's got? Ain't she got everything already that the men don't want? Ain't sweetness an' virtue, an' patience an' long-suffering an' childbearing enough for her without impudently standin' up in the face of men an' axin' for mo'? Had she rather have a vote than the respect of men, an' ain't the respect of men enough to fill any honest woman's life?' " (64). Even if Mrs. Chitling's inferior social status and consequent powerlessness undercut her opinions, she nonetheless gives voice to an additional woman's tradition: indifference to challenging patriarchy.[7]

That position starkly contrasts with the tradition of female rebelliousness represented by Matoaca Bland. She is the "slave of an ancestry of men who oppressed women and women who loved oppression" (*RPM* 165). However, Matoaca literally gives her life to the cause of women's equality: she dies after marching in a suffrage parade. Matoaca's role as foremother to her niece Sally Mickleborough consists mainly of her position as spokeswoman for a tradition not of rigidly separate private (female) and public (male) spheres but of equal access to both. Her frequent conflict with General Bolingbroke is a representation of a powerful and (to him) threatening new tradition of womanhood set against the old patriarchy. Matoaca bears the brunt of the General's barbed condescension; he taunts her for advocating women's rights and at the same time salves the pride wounded years ago when Matoaca broke her engagement with him on the eve of their marriage because she objected to the "masculine morals" that permitted him his "airy wanderings" (103). As he now badgers her to "confess" (75) that she reads the political headlines in the papers she surreptitiously buys—there is no man in the house and so no newspaper is regularly delivered!—her "shoulders straighten" and her face "glow[s]." Steadily she pronounces her basic principle: "'I consider that taxation without representation is tyranny.'" He retorts: "'But what would you do with a vote. . . . Put it into a pie?'" (76–77). Later, his opinions echo Mrs. Chitling's: "'Talk about taxes without representation exactly as if she were a man and had rights! What rights does a woman want, anyway, I'd like to know, except the right to a husband?'" (103). He advises Ben to marry "a good sensible woman" with no "opinions of her own" if he wants "peace." A woman infested with the "maggot" of "heathenish ideas" ceases to believe in "gentleness and self-sacrifice," the General reasons, and hence she "ceases to be a woman." Without irony he concludes: "Every man knows there's got to be a lot of sacrifice in marriage, and he likes to feel that he's marrying a woman who is fully capable of making it" (143).

Missing his own unintentional irony—"sacrifice" in marriage doesn't mean by *men*, of course—he seems merely foolish. But the General has good reason to take seriously his responsibility as the bearer of male tradition: older women in the novel work assiduously on younger ones to undercut traditional male authority. Sally's grandmother objects to "nothing" more than "a boy" (*RPM* 43). Though Matoaca at times verges on martyrdom, she provides Sally with a model of independent thought and action. Even Ben thinks that Matoaca "had suffered from a greater mental activity than was usually allotted to the women of their generation." He momentarily marvels: "what battles of conviction against tradition must have waged!" (138). While Sally's "great-grandmamma" felt obliged to turn to her husband when asked whether her tooth ached ("'Does it ache, Bolivar?'"), Matoaca speaks for herself and offers a model of resistance to traditional gender values.

Matoaca's role surpasses that of simple example. Several times Sally almost *becomes* Matoaca, an act of identification that looks ahead to Sally's reluctant and ambivalent acceptance of her traditional feminine role at the end of the novel. General Bolingbroke perceives that Sally has "plenty of that outlandish spirit of her aunt's" (*RPM* 143). Sally, in writing to Ben that she will defy even her Aunt Matoaca's unwillingness to assent to their marriage, ironically resembles her aunt. Using Matoaca's methods, her spirit, the counter-tradition of defiance that she provides, Sally writes: "I'm not suffering half so much from love as I am from indignation. If it keeps up, some day I'll burst out like Aunt Matoaca, for I've got it in me" (168). The General warns Ben that Sally threatens to "begin talking politics presently like her Aunt Matoaca" (175). When Matoaca marches in a suffrage parade, Ben, in "bewilderment," looks at Matoaca and "sees Sally" (181). As Sally merges with her aunt, Glasgow creates Sally as the inheritor of Matoaca's independent thinking.

The issues of tradition and the strength of inherited beliefs regarding gender recur later in the novel, after Ben and Sally have married. Though Ben ostensibly sees his "future triumphs" in "the overthrow of the things for which [General Bolingbroke] and his generation had stood" (*RPM* 87), his actions and words suggest that the pull of patriarchal tradition is strong. Early in the novel he tells Sally he "shouldn't like" his wife to "go to the polls." Sally perceives his traditionally masculine possessiveness and inevitable focus on women primarily as marriageable objects: "It's funny—isn't it?—that when you ask a man anything about women, he always begins to talk about his wife, even when he hasn't got one?" (128). Ben fails to live up to his earlier vision of the nature of his "triumphs" and, in an ironic mirroring of Sally's increasing resemblance to her defiant Aunt Matoaca, he becomes instead more and more like the General. Ben gives lip service to rejecting the "moth-eaten tradition" of the General and others, but his actions toward his wife belie any genuine dedication to progressive ideas about women's rights. He quite literally takes her inheritance and loses it in foolish speculation, ignores her when his business subsequently flourishes, and attempts to circumscribe her social activity. Only when Sally turns to another man's friendship does Ben finally realize that what he has "lost" is "Sally herself—not the outward woman, but the inner spirit" (344–46), shaped and guided by a sense of herself as a woman within a tradition that expects passive acceptance of male authority.

Ben's realization of his loss supposedly prepares us for a "happy" ending, but both his earlier attitudes toward Sally and the language as he presumably rediscovers his more understanding self mitigates against any such unequivocal conclusion. Ben's attempts to renew his marriage and rewin Sally, if successful, presumably would justify an ideal of women's fulfillment in marriage and the motherhood she anticipates. But Sally's illness, which Ben had failed to perceive, renders further childbearing impossible (their first and only child died in infancy, a typical occurrence in Glasgow's fiction). Their attempted reunion thus begins inauspiciously by precluding the motherhood intended to contribute to Sally's fulfillment. Moreover, Sally, according to Ben, subtly rejects him: "something within her," he observes, "turned from me, seeking always a clearer and a diviner air" (*RPM* 360). (The spirituality in the "Eden" of women's friendships possibly resonates in that "clearer," "diviner air.") Ben turns down the coveted railroad presidency because Sally needs "daily and hourly care" in a milder climate (362); he plans to become the caring husband he has not been. But the language describing Sally's response does not allow us to rejoice. Instead, it reinforces Sally's inevitable second-class status as the submerged partner in a traditional marriage, particularly when she will be bereft of maternity, one of the few sources of authority open to the True Woman. At Ben's assertion that *she* is his "career," Sally kissed his hand "gently," then "let it fall with a gesture that expressed an acquiescence in life rather than a surrender to love" (363). I find it hard to accept C. Hugh Holman's characterization of this novel as a "gentle and appealing love story,"[8] particularly in light of *The Miller,* which gives misandric women a voice to counterbalance expressions of misogyny like those of the General. The "tragedy" lies more in the failure of a woman's alternative tradition of self-determination— which Matoaca tries to pass down to Sally—to receive its full expression. Though Sally at one point realizes that her Aunt Matoaca was "right in believing that women must have larger lives" (313), she cannot completely expand her own. She recognizes the necessity of a "larger" life, only to become, like her aunt, a woman who "suffered from a greater mental activity than was usually allotted" to women. Glasgow observes in the Preface to *The Romance* that while "men novelists, from Defoe onward, have never hesitated to write of women in the first person singular" (x), she struggled against assuming the voice of Ben Starr in her only novel to use first-person narration. Glasgow's uneasiness with her own subjectivity, especially as it assumed (and presumed upon) a false gender identity, itself demonstrates the difficulty both in changing a (literary) tradition and in finding an authentic voice in the midst of countervailing pressures.

Women, the Tyranny of Tradition, and Virginia

Glasgow's relationships with women in her own life—beginning in the period during which she wrote *The Romance of a Plain Man*, *The Miller of Old Church*, and especially *Virginia*, which charts the demise of true womanhood—helped Glasgow to clarify, or to re-vision, her attitudes toward certain women's traditions, especially that of friendship with other women. Rejecting female self-definition according to a male ideal—eschewing the Clarissa Harlowe syndrome—Glasgow in this period searches for the way to reconstruct a self according to some unknown female-identified standard that, for her, had not yet been described. Both *The Miller* and *Virginia* (1913) are dedicated to Glasgow's sister Cary (the first was published in 1911, the year of Cary's death, and the latter composed during Cary's long illness), and in many ways the sisters' relationship provides the measure for Glasgow's shifting attitudes toward the place of other women in her life and for her growing realization that, despite her sometime attraction to them, the traditions of female connection she had worked to reject because they signaled self-denial were more accurately men's traditions of womanhood and woman's place. Her dedication in *The Miller*, "the last thing Cary read before she became unconscious" according to Glasgow (*WW* 191), reads: "To My Sister Cary Glasgow McCormack in loving acknowledgement of help and sympathy through many years." The verb tense of *Virginia*'s dedication, "To the Radiant Spirit Who Was My Sister Cary Glasgow McCormack," marks Cary's death in 1911, just three months after the publication of *The Miller*; its tone reflects the increased closeness Glasgow felt with her sister. *Virginia*'s dedication also suggests Glasgow's understanding that Cary's death, like that of her protagonist Virginia, symbolized the passing of a certain kind of womanhood for which, Glasgow had come to understand, she had been unfairly blaming women rather than men. Her first dedication thanks Cary for her quite literal help in writing, seeking out publishers, and providing books and intellectual guidance for Glasgow. Her second dedication pays tribute to the kind of selfless woman Cary had been—as their mother had been also—and reveals Glasgow's increased devotion to her sister in particular, to her mother, and to women in general, and her sense that with their help she could discover a self that yet remained vaguely defined.

Cary's life in many ways illustrates the traditional women's roles about which Glasgow felt such ambivalence and the place those roles were to occupy in Glasgow's experience. Though Cary was "brilliant" according to Glasgow, it was Cary's husband, Walter McCormack, to whom Glasgow most often turned for intellectual tutelage. Perhaps through Cary's courtship with Walter, Glasgow vicariously experienced the traditional story for a young woman's life. Ten years Glasgow's senior, Cary was wooed and courted by the handsome and intelligent Walter. Glasgow was nineteen when Cary and Walter married in 1892. The marriage of two attractive people based on intellectual companionship and mutual respect for one another must have seemed to Glasgow close to idyllic; surely it provided a positive model for a young woman ambivalent about marriage and traditional womanhood and seeking her own identity as a woman.

But the relationship between Cary and Walter, and then Glasgow's with the two of them, shows subtle signs of being less than idyllic. For one thing, the "brilliance" Glasgow perceived in Cary was subsumed, according to the standards for many typical Victorian marriages, under the presumably stronger male intellect of Cary's husband. With Walter's guidance, Glasgow read Darwin and social philosophy, not only shifting her intellectual allegiance from Cary to Walter, but also shifting away from a literary tradition associated with Cary and toward what was seen as a more masculine scientific one. Cary, who had once aspired to be an author herself, was supplanted by Walter and Darwin and Spencer.[9]

Glasgow's perception of Walter and Cary's relationship was colored by the slow decline of Glasgow's mother's emotional and physical health, in Glasgow's view largely brought on by her father's insensivity (*WW* 161–64). Mrs. Glasgow's death in 1893, the year following Cary's marriage, seemed to Glasgow (at least according to her autobiography) a logical result of her traditional role as dutiful wife and mother. Cary's marriage now took on increased importance for Glasgow as the test case for what happens to women in that traditional role. The horrible story has its climax in Walter's suicide in a New York boardinghouse, reported only after a silence of several days because he had registered under an assumed name. Cary spent the insurance money on an elaborate tombstone and haunted the site of Walter's grave. Moreover, as if admitting her intellectual inferiority to her husband, Cary began reading Walter's favorite books as intellectual preparation for meeting Walter in an afterlife. Cary's actions after Walter's suicide suggested her acceptance of the idea that her inferior life had little meaning apart from her husband and her marriage; money, intellectual energy, and spiritual meaning became important only insofar as they served her diminished role as wife. Glasgow, watching her sister turn into the ghost of the brilliant and happy self Cary had been, said she felt as if she were "living in a tomb."[10]

The message of the literal death of her mother and the figurative one of her sister seemed to be that marriage kills women, that the traditional wifely role drives them to mental instability and bequeaths to them a shadowlike existence when they are left alone. When Cary died in 1911, probably of uterine cancer (as if in grotesque reminder that the source of her death must be her very femaleness), the message must have seemed even clearer. By the time of *Virginia*, Glasgow had made an important shift in her thinking: rather than blame women for their passivity, perhaps she should hold men responsible for their imposition of it. Even her favorite brother Frank's suicide in 1909 must have seemed a grim confirmation that traditional masculinity kills: Glasgow's father had tried to toughen the sensitive—Mr. Glasgow would have said effeminate—Frank, and Frank's suicide at his father's workplace seems a pointed condemnation of Mr. Glasgow and his world. Frank's death also must have been an eerie reminder of Walter; both men were, at least as Glasgow portrayed them, sensitive, compassionate, and ill at ease in a world of patriarchal values. The conclusion seemed harsh: women must be sacrificed to masculine definitions, and men who attempt to refrain from such defining are no safer.

One bright spot in this period when death seemed inextricably bound to traditional female roles (and to male ones as well for men such as Walter and Frank, who were uncomfortable with them) was the arrival of Anne Virginia Bennett in 1910. Hired to care for Cary during her illness, Bennett's efficient manner served as a reminder that other stories were possible for women. Though traditionally feminine in her role as professional caregiver and nurturer of the ill, Bennett was also independent and authoritative. From her arrival in the midst of a spirit of gloom that proceeded partly from a sense that women's lives haven't much of a chance to develop as long as they remain true to ideals of true womanhood, Bennett represented a female tradition based on something like Gilligan's "ethic of care" or "morality of responsibility" but without the loss of self Glasgow associated with her mother and sister.[11] Bennett, unmarried and apparently happy in her independence, also served as a reminder of the possibilities for women's companionship without male intervention.

Though her significance to Glasgow has been at best understated, Bennett undeniably became the most important person in Glasgow's life, a fact Glasgow acknowledged most publicly by bequeathing her estate to Bennett. The critics' de-emphasis results from familiar causes, primarily an assumption that the marriage plot provided the only real possibility for fulfillment in Glasgow's own life, but also from an uneasiness with the potential implications of Glasgow's and Bennett's long residence together. The critical myopia delineated earlier sees Bennett's role in Glasgow's life through similarly distorting lenses. If a woman's fulfillment depends upon marriage or at least a conventional romance, then the thirty-year companionship between Glasgow and Bennett presents a problem for critics.

With the notable exception of Monique Parent, scholars have undermined the importance of Anne Virginia Bennett in Glasgow's life and art, dismissing Bennett's significance by ignoring her or treating her cursorily,[12] or by interpreting the relationship as essentially pathological. The latter method, evident in Godbold's biography, undercuts his often-helpful use of crucial information, notably that gleaned from notes made by Marjorie Kinnan Rawlings as she prepared to write the biography of Glasgow that she did not live to complete. Godbold's characterization of Bennett's and Glasgow's friendship as a "bizarre" one in which Bennett "became intensely jealous of anyone who tried to wait on" Glasgow, and in which Glasgow treated Bennett "as her personal possession" plays too freely with questionable information, and leaves little room for a sympathetic understanding of an intense personal relationship.[13] That Wagner's study omits Bennett entirely may be a testimony to the influence of Godbold's earlier assessment. The effects of both approaches are similar: they undermine the most important relationship in Glasgow's life; distort the significance of Glasgow's embracing the friendship of women as an alternative to the traditional marriage story; falsify other relationships, notably those with men, by casting them into deceptively high relief; and, perhaps most important, deny Glasgow the right to tell her own story of friend-ship rather than marriage.

It is within the context of her relationships with her sister and Anne Virginia Bennett that Glasgow in her 1913 *Virginia* most openly and completely confronts questions about women's legacies that she had been contemplating. *Virginia* most clearly marks Glasgow's changing attitudes toward some women's traditions, which the novel itself helps her sort out. The title reveals the layers of meaning asso-ciated with many women's lives and with Glasgow's in particular. The novel is at once the personal story of the prototypical virginal woman and the political story of her native state, whose name echoes that of the virginal monarch and whose ideological base rests upon solid patriarchal principles of sexual and racial oppression. The title represents as well more personal connections to Glasgow's life and actual women in it: her mother's friend Virginia Rawlings and her own now-essential friend Anne Virginia. The body of the woman—"Virginia"—becomes the body politic, the state of Virginia, to be ex-ploited as it tries to construct (or to Reconstruct) itself in the turbulent years following the Civil War. The racial and sexual oppression that victimizes on a personal scale repeats that victimization politically.

Glasgow herself admitted *Virginia*'s important place in her canon, calling it her first really "mature work" (*WW* 188). Its maturity can be traced to a shift in Glasgow's tone, occurring during the writing of the book, toward the main character, Virginia Pendleton. Anne Good-wyn Jones has observed that Glasgow began by intending to "em-balm" the southern lady and ended by "enshrining" her, and Elizabeth Ammons accurately perceives *Virginia* as a turning point in Glas-gow's "self-confrontation." But Jones's perception of enshrinement and Ammons's argument that Glasgow's change in attitude sentimen-talizes the tradition of true womanhood and so "collud[es] in the very ethic that she ostensibly regrets" depend upon a reading that misses the irony of the novel's conclusion.[14] Rather, the ending, because of (not in spite of) Glasgow's sympathy for her protagonist, condemns even more forcefully the socialization that has made Virginia's life so impoverished.

Glasgow's later Preface (1938) to the Virginia Edition of her novel addresses the shift in her feelings toward her main character. Mid-novel, Glasgow says, she began to see Virginia not "ironically," as she had initially envisioned her character and the "Victorian tradition" that surrounds her, but sympathetically. "I discovered," she says, "that my irony grew fainter as it yielded at last to sympathetic compassion." As she neared the novel's conclusion, "the simple goodness of Virginia's nature had turned a comedy of manners into a tragedy of human fate." [15] Originally intending to damn a woman's tradition that relegated Virginia to selfless inaction and to denounce the women who freely accepted this role, Glasgow, in creating her character, came to see the practical impossibility of Virginia's ever being otherwise than she had been defined by the patriarchal world, here that of the Reconstruction-era South. Virginia was, Glasgow came to realize, "more than a woman; she was the embodiment of a forsaken ideal" (*V* xii). Moreover, like other women before and after her in Glasgow's fiction and in her experience, Virginia's participation in her own loss of self results from the subtle but strong internalizing of social standards. "If Virginia is absorbed into the Victorian tradition," Glasgow asserts, "even more compellingly she has absorbed that tradition into her own consciousness" (*V* xvi). With this novel Glasgow seems to fully realize that for a woman, constructing a self is often falsely based not on interior truth but on exterior "tradition" (*V* x) that has merely seeped "into her own consciousness" (*V* xvi). As with Clarissa Harlowe, the "ages of false thinking" (F 27) are the real culprit.

Virginia is, primarily, a novel about establishing an identity: "Reconstruction" describes the main character's project of self-definition (and even the reader's and the author's) as much as it designates the historical time period of the novel. The book's opening chapter makes clear at the outset the difficulties any female character will be up against as she tries to construct a self in Dinwiddie; the narrowness of vision is metaphorically apparent in the images of literal confinement with which the book opens. Miss Priscilla Batte's school, the Dinwiddie Academy for Young Ladies, is founded on the principle that "the less a girl knew about life, the better prepared she would be to contend with it." [16] Miss Priscilla's garden does not tempt exploration or the search for knowledge, but instead demands respect for a falsified and dead past; it looks backward rather than forward. Like the plants in her old-fashioned garden, Miss Priscilla "stood firmly rooted in all that was static, in all that was obsolete and outgrown" (*V* 12–13; 10).

Miss Priscilla's life, confined to her small space like her bird in its cage, represents to Virginia and her friend Susan the life that they can expect for themselves as the matronly inheritors of Dinwiddie. Only once, fleetingly, does Priscilla Batte allow herself to question the traditions of womanhood she has always believed to be essential components of a young woman's education. Watching Virginia as she leaves, she *becomes* Virginia and (like Matoaca and Sally in *The Romance of a Plain Man*) thereby emphasizes the generational transmission of women's traditions. Fleetingly, Miss Priscilla admits the discrepancy between expectation and reality:

> She saw herself . . . standing flushed and expectant before the untrodden road of the future. She heard again the wings of happiness rustling unseen about her, and she felt again the ardent challenge that youth flings to destiny. Life rose before her, not as she had found it, but as she had once believed it to be. . . . for she, also, . . . had had her dream of a love that would change and glorify the reality. The heritage of woman was hers as well as Virginia's. And for the first time, standing there, she grew dimly conscious of the portion of suffering which Nature had allotted to them both from the beginning. (*V* 25; 20) [17]

This momentary disillusion at the close of the first chapter establishes as a major theme the difficulties of self-determination in a world where the only acceptable woman's story is the traditional heroine's text, which seems in its solidity to be allotted by Nature rather than constructed by culture. Compounding those difficulties is the fact that the purveyors of the tradition are sometimes the women of the previous generation, who, in occasional flashes of self-awareness, themselves recognize the dishonesty and the narrowness of the vision of "happiness" they inculcate in the younger women. Miss Priscilla, echoing Glasgow's adjective for her sister in the novel's dedication, wonders: "Would life yield nothing more to that radiant girl than it had yielded to her or to the other women whom she had known?" (*V* 25; 20). The image of "*wings* of happiness" recalls the canary who "spent his involuntarily celibate life" (*V* 4; 4) in a cage listening to Miss Priscilla's "earnest exhortations" about the "joys of cage life for both bird and lady" (*V* 5; 5).[18] The irony is not lost on Miss Priscilla for the moment as she watches Virginia walk away from her porch and the reader shares her gaze into Virginia's future. Together with Miss Priscilla, the reader implicitly questions the value of a woman's tradition that requires passing along the attitudes that elicit Miss Priscilla's final observation: "Strange how the terrible innocence of youth had moved her placid middle-age as if it were sadness!" (*V* 25).[19]

Of course it is Virginia's mother, Lucy Pendleton, who has the primary responsibility for preparing her daughter for a woman's role.[20] As firmly rooted in the past as Miss Priscilla, Lucy also fleetingly questions her own advice as she contemplates Virginia's approaching marriage. Though she concedes that her daughter's determination to call her husband by his first name is probably acceptable in a new-fashioned world, she knows that Virginia's grandmother would have been "horrified" and admits that it "does seem lacking in respect" (*V* 199; 152). Unself-consciousness about her own abstract notions of female passivity, however, Lucy exhorts Virginia to remember that "gentleness" is her "strength," that her "first duty" is to her husband: "His will must be yours now, and whenever your ideas cross, it is your duty to give up, darling. It is the woman's part to sacrifice herself" (*V* 199; 152). Even as she speaks, however, Mrs. Pendleton, if only briefly, doubts her own words:

> In Mrs. Pendleton's soft, anxious eyes the shadow darkened, as if for the first time she had grown suspicious of the traditional wisdom which she was imparting. But this suspicion was so new and young that it could not struggle for existence against the archaic roots of her inherited belief in the Pauline measure of her sex. It was characteristic of her—and indeed of most women of her generation—that she would have endured martydom in support of the consecrated doctrine of her inferiority to man. (*V* 200; 153)[21]

Glasgow's irony is inescapable as she moves from Mrs. Pendleton's belief in the "Pauline measure of her sex" (*V* 200; 153) to Virginia's daily reading of the marriage service and the reflections that accompany her reading: nothing could be "more beautiful or more sacred than to be 'given' to Oliver—to belong to him as utterly as she had belonged to her father" (203; 155). With equally unmistakeable irony, this chapter, titled "Virginia Prepares for the Future," winds down as Virginia contemplates with happy anticipation the "daily excitement of marketing," the "perpetual romance of mending his clothes," the "glorified monotony of pouring his coffee." She "ecstatically" pictures herself in the "immemorial attitude of women": "waiting—waiting happily—but always waiting" (204; 156).[22]

As Virginia learns to live the tradition of Miss Priscilla, the "other women" of her thoughts, and her mother, however, Glasgow begins to view the tradition as more suited to tragedy than to irony. Particularly as the momentary self-doubts of Miss Priscilla and Lucy Pendleton hint at awareness that male standards have prevailed in defining female lives, the novel begins to shift the responsibility for what *was* too easily seen as Virginia's and other women's ready acceptance of their place. Two early chapters are juxtaposed to highlight one of the novel's most damning pronouncements on male hegemony: the conflation of sexual and racial oppression by men. In "White Magic," as Virginia hopes for Oliver's dance request, she first envisions her experience as one she shares with other women: "Suspense! Was that a woman's life, after all? Never to be able to go out and fight for what one wanted! Always to sit at home and wait, without moving a foot or lifting a hand toward happiness!" And worse even than the passivity, Virginia recognizes, is the loss of self that accompanies it: "Never to be one's self—never to let one's soul or body relax from the attitude of expectancy into the attitude of achievement." The others' "faces" as they dance fuse "into one, and this was the face of all womanhood" (*V* 152; 116–17).[23] As Helen Fiddyment Levy also notes, Virginia's fleeting realization of a woman's life's "tragic vision" echoes the thoughts of the older women; it thus connects her life to theirs in acknowledgement of a tradition of passivity.[24] Like them, she recognizes that only "expectancy," never "achievement," can be hers. The image of the other women "whirling" rather than moving purposefully reinforces a sense of shared tragedy. "All womanhood" from Miss Priscilla and Lucy to Virginia and her peers joins in the tradition comprised of "Love, sorrow, hope, regret, wonder, all the sharp longing and the slow waiting of the centuries— above all, the slow waiting" (*V* 153; 117).

But Virginia's blossoming awareness that stronger ties to other women might counterbalance the eternal passivity dictated by tradition is interrupted by a goal also dictated by that tradition: male attention. Oliver gazes so closely into Virginia's eyes that she becomes "dizzy" and fears she might "lose her balance and fall" (*V* 154; 117). Metaphorically, of course, she does "fall" into an imposed ideal of womanhood and away from the impulse to join with other women. As she accepts Oliver and the terms he represents, she eschews female community, noting that "the distance between her and the whirling figures in white muslin seemed greater than the distance between star and star" (154; 118). Oliver pulls her even farther from the others as she "follows" him to the summerhouse. She is "separated" from those with whom she had briefly shared a "tragic vision" of womanhood, and senses instead her connection to the damaging tradition of self-denying womanhood: "The longing of all the dead women of her race flowed through her," and she accepts the "inherited ideals of self-surrender, of service, pity, loyalty, and sacrifice" (159; 121). Virginia's acquiescence in following Oliver and separating herself from other women diagrammatically illustrates the problem Glasgow now discerns in a woman's quest for identity: a man always seems to determine the boundaries and the direction of female self-exploration.

With Oliver and Virginia isolated together, cut off from a complicating world outside the summerhouse, male definitions of woman's experience can seem the whole truth. Here he literally circumscribes her world's parameters, in metaphoric reminder that men *do* define women and announce the place that they will occupy. Glasgow emphasizes Virginia's silent acquiescence—she "did not speak"; "Her tongue was paralyzed"; her "irresistible appeal" lies partly in "the poverty of her speech"; Oliver finds "her monosyllabic responses" "adorable"; she waits with "mute patience"; she accepts the "voiceless entreaty for happiness" that her subconscious recognizes (*V* 155–59; 119–21). Virginia's loss of voice underscores how powerless she and, implicitly, other women are to define themselves, to articulate their own submerged wishes.[25] It is surely no accident that both Miss Priscilla and Lucy earlier only *think* their doubts. This very silence on Virginia's part is precisely what appeals to Oliver; her mute acceptance of his standards represents her passivity and his own power over her. After Virginia responds to him with silence, Oliver "read the effect of his words" in "every line of her figure, in every quiver of her lashes, in every breath that she drew" (157; 120). She literally embodies passive acceptance; the "effect" of Oliver's "words" is his recognition that *he* holds all the power: "Never before had he realized the power that was in him!" (158; 120).

In the familiar terms of Victorian gender ideology, and as with other Glasgow men in and out of Glasgow's fiction, Oliver casts Virginia in the role of his spiritual savior; her purity, defined by him, will save him and confer worth on him. Virginia becomes merely a vehicle, a mirror of his own importance, and his definition of her passive nature is a requisite part of that mirroring: "To have her always gentle, always passive, never reaching out her hand, never descending to his level, but sitting for ever aloof and colourless, waiting eternally, patient, beautiful and unwearied, to crown the victory—this was what the conquering male in him demanded" (*V* 158; 121). When Virginia denies that confessing his "troubles" indicates Oliver's selfishness—of course she denies it!—by affirming that "a man's work means so much to him," her "words seemed to him to embody all the sympathetic understanding with which his imagination endowed her" (159; 121–22). Virginia's capacity for language is limited to "words" that reinforce Oliver's imposed definitions; tragically, they have no power to define her.

Although the succeeding chapter, "The Great Man Moves," seems to redirect attention away from the romance plot, in fact, its central issue is the patriarchal Cyrus Treadwell's ability to control women (or, as he might say it, to put them in their place), the same "power" that the younger Oliver is discovering in himself. The chapter demands a comparison between Oliver and Cyrus. Though much is made of the conflict between them, both are Treadwells (Oliver has the unmistakeable "Treadwell nose" [*V* 15–16; 13]), in all that this designation implies, and nephew and uncle become increasingly indistinguishable as the novel progresses. This chapter, juxtaposed with the awakening of Oliver's and Virginia's relationship, suggests the similarity in the Treadwell males' attitudes toward women. Further, it broadens the implications of those sexist attitudes to include racism as well.

Glasgow's ironic reference to Cyrus as "the great man" points in two directions: one toward Cyrus himself, who turns out to be anything but "great" in his relationships with others, and the second toward the social standards that equate greatness with patriarchal or entrepreneurial aggressiveness. Earlier Cyrus had been described as a typical late-nineteenth-century robber baron, whose "rebuilding of the tobacco industry" and immediate "elevation" to a railroad presidency had assured his status as a "great" man in the eyes of Dinwiddians (*V* 74; 57–58). Like "most men who have suffered in their youth under oppression," Cyrus's "ambition" serves "not so much to relieve the oppressed as to become in his turn the oppressor" (75; 58). Miserable in a marriage to a wife he treats more miserably, his "dogged male determination to override all obstacles" (89; 69) finds its outlet in oppressing his wife, Belinda, his daughter, Susan, and his black former mistress, Mandy. That Mandy in the past bore Cyrus a son, Jubal, whom Cyrus now willfully ignores, highlights Cyrus's generally oppressive sexual and racial attitudes, and emphasizes the connection between Belinda and Mandy as mothers, and Susan and Jubal as children.

Cyrus's petty but consequential tyranny is pervasive. Sitting on his porch, he asserts power by spitting on the flowers that dare to bloom "valiantly" in their untended "bleak strip of earth." Cyrus feels the "vacuous contentment" that "men of small parts and of sterile imagination" call "happiness" (*V* 163; 124). (The surely intentional pun on "small parts," which contrasts with Cyrus's alleged greatness, is appropriately reinforced by the "sterility" of Cyrus's imaginative capability.)[26] The "dried husks of his nature" (170; 129) make him not even an "animal" but a "machine" (164; 124), and extend the metaphor of Cyrus's "parts": he is merely an impotent mechanical automaton.

With people as with flowers, Cyrus controls through denigration. Male prerogative combined with an "inherent contempt for women" (*V* 166; 126) enables him to set the standards for womanhood, a power Oliver is discovering. Thus, Cyrus can oppress even strong women like his daughter, Susan. Her announcement that she wants to go to college is "a direct challenge to the male in Cyrus" (164; 125). " 'Tut-tut," he tells her: "If you want something to occupy you, you'd better start about helping your mother with her preserving' " (164; 125). Cyrus at once trivializes her intellectual impulse and pointedly reminds her of her domestic duty. Even money is less important than his inflexible will to power over women, as Susan discovers. At stake is a woman's proper place, which he will designate. In one blow humiliating his daughter, asserting his authority, and denying further discussion, Cyrus notes that since Susan's "schooling at Miss Priscilla's" is "still owing," he will "take it out in help about the housekeeping' " (165; 125–26). As Susan departs with only "shreds of dignity," Cyrus, "with a contented chuckle," spits "benevolently" on the flowers at his feet (165; 126).

Mandy's appearance following Susan's defeat points to the close relationship between Cyrus's patriarchal attitudes and both misogyny and racism. Initially, Mandy is deferential as she attempts to fulfill Cyrus's expectations of her as a black woman. Cyrus fails to recognize in his condescension the irony that his original attraction was to Mandy's appearance, to her apparent sexuality; he patronizingly interprets her habits of dress as "primitive attempts at Sunday adornment" and describes her once "graceful" "figure" as "heavy" (V 172; 130). Accustomed to Cyrus's devaluation of her, Mandy now wears the "trustful," "humble, inquiring look" of a "tamed" "wild animal" (172; 131). Mandy, "deprecating" and "uncertain," hesitatingly greets the "superior" Cyrus (172–73; 131).

But Mandy is unwilling to collude entirely in Cyrus's deprecation of her. Knowing that her only source of power over Cyrus lies in his past sexual vulnerability, she uses it to triumph momentarily over him. As Cyrus remembers that Mandy "couldn't have been over fifteen" when she arrived at the Treadwells', "a look of cunning" crosses Mandy's face, and she recalls her dismissal by Cyrus's wife, Belinda: " 'En Miss Lindy sent me off befo' de year was up, Marster. My boy Jubal was born de mont' atter she done tu'n me out.' She hesitated a minute, and then added, with a kind of savage coquetry, 'I 'uz a moughty likely gal, Marster. You ain't done furgit dat, is you?' " (V 173; 132). Mandy's words, instantly effective, "touched Cyrus like the flick of a whip on a sore" (173; 132). Unlike Virginia, and even the more independent Susan, who both respond to male definition with silence, Mandy tries out the "cunning" use of language as a weapon for rebellion. Even as she momentarily wins, however, she realizes the necessity to submit, and her "humble and deprecating look" as she retreats announces the failure she doesn't literally articulate: " 'I don't understand, but I submit without understanding, because you are stronger than I' " (174; 133).

The ultimate powerlessness of Mandy's speech-making is most poignantly revealed as she realizes its uselessness in saving her own child. Though she positions herself as an obstacle in the walkway and enjoins Cyrus to help get her—their—son out of jail, it is not her privilege but Cyrus's to wield language, and he uses it, as with Susan, to remind Mandy of her place: "Your race has got to learn that when you break the law you must pay for it" (V 366–67; 283). Using the "law" and "justice" that codify and uphold his superiority, Cyrus maintains his authority when Mandy tries to revive her earlier tactic.

But this time her pleading rather than commanding tone foreshadows her failure, and, hypocritical yet powerful, Cyrus remains in control. Mandy "had gone too far" (367; 283) by alluding to his paternity and, worse, to evidence of her past power over him. He repudiates her and their son with a fifty-dollar bill and a dismissal. Cyrus's treatment of Mandy—of all women—demonstrates a truth recognized by Sethe in Toni Morrison's *Beloved*: "definitions belong to the definers, not the defined."[27]

And there is no question that the men in *Virginia* are the definers. Structurally framing the novel's middle section, "The Reality," with a wedding and a threatened lynching, Glasgow conflates the misogyny and racism that characterize male (here Southern white male) hegemony. This structuring, which emphasizes a male prerogative to set boundaries within which female self-definition must take place, turns that prerogative against the patriarchate. In the section's final chapter, "The Problem of the South," a lynch mob threatens an innocent young black man. Glasgow adroitly turns back on the definers the familiar phrase that provides the chapter's title: the "problem" lies not in the black community but in its oppression by the white one. The suggestive framework circumscribes the patriarchal world of the novel, reinforcing the connection between marriage and slavery: both, Glasgow suggests, are products of a white male world that defines the acceptable limits of others' experience. Sexual oppression equals racial oppression. It is Glasgow's full realization of this truth and its implications that accounts for her shift in tone as she writes the novel. Glasgow comes to recognize that Virginia's passivity and self-effacement result not from willful blindness on Virginia's part but from internalized standards of male-defined womanhood that Virginia shares with all women. It is in this new awareness that Virginia becomes tragic rather than ironic. "Created" by "man," Glasgow says in her 1938 Preface, "out of his own desire," Virginia was "the perfect wife as man had invented her" (*V* xvi).

At one poignant moment in the novel, Glasgow attributes much of Virginia's tragedy to a corollary truth: men have tired of the women who most adhere to their invented ideal. Though Virginia's appearance has suffered by the neglect born of her selfless attention to her family, including Oliver, he criticizes her indifference, especially noting her formerly "pretty" hands (*V* 305; 235). Comparing her to the unmarried and funloving Abby Goode, he admits, with maddening contradiction, that though Abby remains physically attractive, "somehow she doesn't seem womanly" (306; 236). Despite his criticism of Virginia, she remains Oliver's "ideal." Blindly accepting as "divine fact" that "woman" is "dependent upon man for the very integrity of her being," Oliver cannot "see her at all" beyond this formulation. This attitude's prevalence almost seems to prove its divinity. As the narrator comments, "Oliver, his Uncle Cyrus, the rector, and honest John Henry, however they may have differed in their views of the universe or of each other, were one at least in accepting the historical dogma of the supplementary being of woman" (307; 236).

If Oliver and other men share a belief in women's inferiority, Virginia and other women (even throughout time) share a tragic awareness of this fact. Just after Oliver criticizes Virginia's worn hands, she envisions herself and other women in a long tradition of service to men and children: "In a flash of memory, she saw the reddened and knotted hands of her mother, and then a procession of hands belonging to all the mothers of her race that had gone before her. Were her own but a single pair in that chain of pathetic hands that had worked in the exacting service of Love?" (*V* 305; 235). The central image—a "chain" of hands—points to a complex response to a woman's tradition of female connection that makes *Virginia* such an important text in the evolution of Glasgow's thought about women's available traditions.[28] In a play on words reminiscent of Sarah Grimké's "bonds of womanhood" that Nancy Cott has borrowed for the title of her book, that "chain" is, on the one hand, a symbol of enslavement, of bondage to the kind of service to others that demands loss of self. It is this "chain" that both Miss Priscilla and Lucy Pendleton earlier divined at moments when they felt responsible for transmitting an ideology of selflessness to Virginia. On the other hand, this "chain" also connotes positive attachment, relationships among women that provide sustenance outside the demands of patriarchal definitions of womanhood. It is the first "chain" that prompts the realization of the need for the second, and it is the second that will provide Glasgow with her most satisfying response to questions about her own place in a woman's traditions.

The consistent presence of female friendships, the "chain" of connection, provides a hinted alternative to patriarchal definitions of woman. Indeed, the novel's most significant if not most evident relationship between women, that of Belinda Treadwell and the unmarried dressmaker Miss Willy Whitlow, exists in direct defiance of the novel's representative patriarch, Cyrus Treadwell. Their friendship, a constant reminder of the threat of women's emotional closeness, contrasts sharply with the Treadwells' dismal marriage of "five and thirty penitential years" (*V* 88; 69). Cyrus "resented" Miss Willy, who spends most of her time at the Treadwells' house and provides "the only companionship his wife really enjoyed" (91–92; 71). He surmises correctly that his wife confesses her innermost feelings to Miss Willy—or, as he puts it, that she has "whimpered out her heart to the whirring accompaniment of Miss Willy's machine" (92; 71). Though Belinda's helplessness and ineptitude usually represent the worst of a woman's tradition of passivity, she resolutely stands behind her right to Miss Willy's friendship. When Cyrus attempts to "rise in his authority" and banish Miss Willy, Belinda stands firm: " 'If I can't see her here, I'll go to her house' " (92; 72).

Similarly, the friendship between Susan and Virginia sustains them; it is Susan who ultimately perceives Virginia's marital trouble. Even the comparatively superficial relationship between Virginia and Abby Goode, to whom Oliver unfavorably compares his wife, is a reminder of the difference between women's personal relationships and those same relationships as soon as they are mediated by male definitions. Virginia likes Abby and even defends her against rumors of a flirtation with Oliver. But as soon as Oliver forces competition and Virginia believes Oliver to be "happier with Abby" than with her, she decides to fight for her husband's attention: "As [her father] the rector had gone to war, so she was going now to battle with Abby" (*V* 321; 247–48). Flattered that he is the prize to be won, Oliver becomes interested enough in his wife to put down the newspaper, the customary physical barrier that symbolizes the profounder spiritual barrier between them. Sadly, Virginia's "one thought" as she prepares for the war between women that she does not wish to fight only reinforces the idea of men's power to define women: "she must be, at all costs, the kind of woman that Oliver wanted" (324; 249). Virginia's triumph during the ensuing foxhunt is an empty victory. It leads her only to recognize the pointlessness of her war in the first place, and the bathos of unseating Abby: " 'What is the use?' " After winning the

battle, represented by the fox, Virginia realizes she has "risked" everything "for the sake of wresting a bit of dead fur out of Abby's grasp"
(328; 252–53). Rather than recapture her husband and give new life
to their marriage, she only gains "a bit of dead fur." Virginia's brief
recognition that she has no wish to compete demonstrates the truth of
the narrative comment that a woman is relentlessly asked to "adjust
her personality to the changing ideals of the man she loves" (323–24;
249).[29] The "chain" of connection among women is easily threatened
by male prerogative.

The "chain" of enslavement to patriarchal culture is the tradition
that triumphs in this novel, a victory made painfully clear by the conclusion. Virginia's bondage to this tradition is most tragically exemplified in her growing resemblance to her mother. Using vision metaphorically, Glasgow demonstrates the narrowness of Lucy Pendleton's
life and the tragedy of Virginia's fate as she reenacts her mother's incapacity to imagine any existence other than the selfless one expected of
women. After her wedding, Virginia "looked back" on her departure
from her parents (209; 160), and in so doing foretold her repetition
of her mother's connubial role. Much later, again in the Dinwiddie
of her own upbringing, "the tapping of a blind beggar's stick on the
pavement" provides a "plaintive accompaniment to the lullaby she
was singing" (270; 207). Virginia's shortsighted conception of being
a wife and mother, like her mother's, is no less "blind" than the beggar below; her blindness, the reader shortly discovers, keeps her from
seeing that she has lost her husband already. Her "personal life" had
"restricted her vision of the universe to that solitary window of the
soul through which she looked" (283; 217). She had, like her mother
and her mother's mother, the "narrow outlook of women who lead
intense personal lives" (301; 232). As Miss Priscilla watches Virginia
through her own solitary window, she thinks "for a minute that 'Lucy
Pendleton had returned to life.' So one generation of gentle shades
after another had moved in the winter's dusk under the frosted lamps
of High Street" (452; 349). Virginia, her mother, Miss Priscilla—all
become unreal "shades" of the women they might have become.

The novel's conclusion leaves the reader with a final image of
Virginia's limited vision, her enduring acceptance of the traditions of
womanhood passed down by her mother. It reinforces the idea that a
woman's life is not her own to "see"; she sees rather a life reflected in

the defining gaze of others, mirrored in male eyes. The final chapter, ironically—or tragically—titled "The Future," shows Virginia embracing her mother's outdated past even as she attempts to cope with her modern impending divorce. The contrast between Virginia and her daughter Jenny, named for her yet distinguished by the different spelling, provides a painful reminder that not all daughters accept a maternal legacy of self-effacement. While Virginia's vision narrows to the restrictive past of her mother, Jenny's "vision" is "wide" (*V* 500; 386). Virginia wanders the streets of Dinwiddie "looking for something" (502; 388). In her search she goes "back" to the church and rectory of her childhood, moving "as softly as a ghost" (one of Miss Priscilla's "gentle shades"?) in the garden (502; 388). Looking in the window she "almost expected to see the face of her mother, with its look of pathetic cheerfulness" (503; 388). She shops at "the old market" because "her mother and her grandmother had used it before her," and where "one of the older generation might have mistaken her for her mother" (507–08; 392). Miss Priscilla thanks Virginia for a gift and remarks: "How like you that was, Jinny. You are your mother all over again. I declare I am reminded of her more and more every time that I see you" (510; 394). In being herself—"how like you"—Virginia is also her mother.

Hopeless about her marriage, Virginia stands at her house's literal threshold, the threshold between past and future. Incapable of her daughter's "wide" vision, and long accustomed to looking back or not seeing at all, she can only see a future of emptiness without others to give her definition: "Ahead of her stretched the staircase which she would go up and down for the rest of her life. On the right she could look into the open door of the dining-room, and opposite to it, she knew that the lamp was lit and the fire burning in Oliver's study." It is still an empty staircase, still "Oliver's" study. But she sees a letter on the table: " 'Dearest Mother, I am coming home to you, Harry' " (*V* 525–26; 406). Virginia's vision can only "see" rescue from her son, continuing the patriarchal transmission from father to husband to son that is her legacy. Her "instinctive reliance on masculine protection" (522; 403) now leads Virginia to depend upon her son to rescue her from a future void of "usefulness," as she earlier phrased it, primarily because she cannot envision a future any different from the traditional one handed to her, even though it failed to provide new answers. Not at all the "contrived 'happy ending'" that Wagner-Martin sees,[30] the conclusion, with Harry's return to his mother, is instead tragically deterministic. Glasgow has carefully prepared for the failure of vision and the continued dependence on male definition that marks the end of Virginia's story as we know it. Virginia's mother, who "had not thought of herself" for the "more than forty years" of her marriage (388; 299), could not do so once her husband died; the source of her very being had died with him. The "inherited habit" that "had made it possible for Mrs. Pendleton to efface her broken heart" (391; 302) allows Virginia, also faced with a destiny of dependence on men, to look to her son to take over where her now-absent father and husband left off.

The "tyranny of tradition" that Glasgow speaks of in her Virginia Edition Preface refers at once to the larger social fabric of Dinwiddie, with its refusal to move forward out of the outdated habits of its antebellum past, and to the related traditions of womanhood that shape the town's women. Tradition for them means the tyranny of an inherited inferiority, a destiny of self-effacement and dependence that refuses them self-determination. And Dinwiddie is merely representative; "human nature" there "differed from human nature in London or in the Desert of Sahara" (V 15; 12) only in habits of eating and styles of dress. Many women, Glasgow implies, share the same traditions. The change in Glasgow's attitude toward Virginia from irony to compassion marks the accompanying shift in her attitude toward the traditions of her own foremothers. As Glasgow speculates in her Preface, her transformed perspective on Virginia and Virginia's "tragedy" are tied to Glasgow's relationship to her own mother, after whom she patterned the young Virginia. Like Adrienne Rich in "Heroines," Glasgow, in *Virginia,* comes to understand the paradox of many a woman's traditions: they oppress, they close off options for a woman's search for selfhood; yet they also seduce, they even represent, as Glasgow says in her Preface, "the thwarted human longing for the beautiful and the good" (V xxi). The overarching question—as Glasgow came to understand it and as Rich articulates it in the fragmented pieces of a problematic history—asks how to "honor" the "legacy" of past women's "courage" and yet acknowledge that legacy's inadequacy.[31]

The sense of nurturance, connection, "mature dependence" that Glasgow provides as partial answer to Rich's question had been present, as I have argued, from the start of Glasgow's publishing career. The difference for her, beginning with *Virginia,* seems to lie in her recognition that accepting an ethic of care doesn't have to mean a loss of self if one can simultaneously reject a male-identified tradition of selflessness in the exclusive service of male hegemony. It is connection gone awry, nurture transformed into its ugly twin "self-immolation" (*V* 393; 303), that causes Virginia's tragedy. The relationships among women—Miss Priscilla and generations of women before her, Susan and Virginia, Belinda and Miss Willy, potentially even Virginia and Abby—provide an undercurrent of connection without self-destruction that can help *re*place a *mis*placed ethic of care for others. After *Virginia* and this positive alternative, I think, Glasgow's work and personal life are never quite the same.

Art and Life: The Builders

The years from about 1914 to 1920 were difficult ones, when Glasgow confronted most directly—perhaps because forced to—her personal relationships with both men and women. Partly to escape the memories associated with Cary's death, Glasgow traveled to Europe with her friend Louise Collier Wilcox in the spring of 1914 and, with her lifelong companion Carrie Coleman (later Duke), to Colorado in July 1914. Glasgow moved to an apartment overlooking Central Park in New York City in 1915,[32] but after the deaths of her older sister Emily late in 1915 and her father in January 1916, Glasgow returned permanently to Richmond.

She went back to a house that, in her words, "belonged to the dead" (*WW* 222). But her relationships with the living, specifically Anne Virginia Bennett and Henry Anderson, whom she met in the spring of 1916, caused more conflict in this period of Glasgow's life than did figures from her past. In *Life and Gabriella,* written during her stay in New York and published in 1916, Glasgow could fictionalize a "woman of courage" who confidently declared "I can manage my life" and expressed "disgust" for "the sordid and ugly sides of sex," the "emotion which drew men and women together," the "light in the eyes, the touch of the lips, the clinging of the hands,"[33] assertions that seriously qualify the novel's romantic ending. But in *The Builders*

(1919), women's relationships with both men and women demand a complex treatment that more accurately mirrors her own conflicted relationships with Bennett and Anderson.

Most critics agree that Glasgow's relationship with Henry Anderson, her collaborator on *The Builders,* informs that novel. But they have often overlooked Bennett's influence. Anderson's known collaboration certainly invites personal speculation, but the less frequently acknowledged relationship between Glasgow and Bennett also needs to be factored into the complex equation that resulted in *The Builders.* Once Glasgow's father died, the house was vacant except for Glasgow and Bennett, who had stayed on as Mr. Glasgow's nurse. Alone together, the two women would have been faced with the question of the future. Bennett volunteered for Red Cross duty overseas during World War I, left Richmond in 1918, and had returned to Glasgow's house at One West Main by 9 November 1920.[34] Whatever earlier uncertainty Glasgow and Bennett might have experienced never seems to have surfaced again, and Bennett remained in the house even after Glasgow's death, as Glasgow had expressly wanted it. It seems reasonable to assume that if Anderson is partially transformed into the character of the politician David Blackburn, Bennett provides a model for the nurse-protagonist Caroline Meade, conflicted about her personal allegiances and volunteering for service in France. The novel addresses very real concerns in Glasgow's life as she tries to balance confusing relationships with both Anderson and Bennett. Anderson's presence in particular created a tension that in some ways was never resolved, a tension that included Glasgow's uncertainty about the appropriateness of men in her life.

Gabriella's intriguing and seemingly offhand remark in *Life and Gabriella* that her friendship with her sister-in-law was "compensation for any lack" (*LG* 174) of happiness in marriage suggests the importance of women's complex friendships in *The Builders,* where they both promise fulfillment and invite conflict. In *The Builders,* Glasgow's interest in female friendship and the man who first facilitates it, but then intervenes, leads her to explore the relationship among two women and one man much like the one in her own life at the time. What becomes in *The Builders* the destructive potential of women's relationships is particularly devastating because those friendships begin with such promise. That promise and the destruction that instead results particularly damns men whose intervention causes that destructiveness.

Glasgow carefully distances her protagonist, Caroline Meade—the capable, rational, and orderly nurse in *The Builders*—from any tradition of submissive, dependent womanhood, in part by noting her traditionally masculine characteristics: her "wide white brow," "a shade too strong and thoughtful for a woman," seems "almost masculine."[35] Intellectually, she conforms to a masculine stereotype of strength and rationality; being "lucid," she "despised the melodramatic" (*B* 17), and believed that "thought, not emotion, is the only permanent basis of happiness" (26). The descriptions resemble many of Anne Virginia Bennett, and Caroline's hard life, which had "trained her mental processes into lucid and orderly habits" (25), may have its parallel in Bennett's life.[36]

By contrast, Angelica Blackburn, Caroline's new employer, lives up to the image of ethereal feminine beauty suggested by her "angelic" name, and the force of Caroline's attraction to Angelica testifies to the equally forceful appeal of her traditional womanhood. "Small," "delicate," and "golden," Angelica's skin and features seem "perfect," as if "chiselled in marble" (*B* 38). She is as suited to the outdated Victorian excess of her home's decor as Caroline is out of place in it, and the novel's emphasis on dying traditions suggests that her role as invalid and dependent female is another of the world's waning traditions.[37] The almost mythic force of traditional womanhood represented by Angelica is reinforced by the fact that Caroline is in love with the *idea* of Angelica before she even meets her. As she prepares for her new post as nurse to the Blackburns' daughter, Caroline feels "as if this stranger with the lovely name were the 'something different' she had waited for in the past" (18). Arriving at the house, appropriately named Briarlay (like Jane Eyre's Thornfield) for the emotional entanglements it will harbor, Caroline is awestruck at her first sight of Angelica: "For once the reality was fairer than the dream; the woman before her was lovelier than the veiled figure of Caroline's imagination." She senses "delight and expectancy, on the edge of a new emotion, of an undiscovered country." Caroline again notes the difference between other events and this one: "This was not only something beautiful and rare; it was different from anything that had ever happened to her before" (38). Caroline's immediate "vow of dedication" and acknowledged "bond" to Angelica take on "the nature and the obligation of a covenant" (40).

Despite the familiar religious language of vows and covenants, which testify to mutuality and spirituality in the women's depth of feeling, Angelica's reliance on men for self-definition causes her to betray Caroline's devotion by feigning jealousy and indignation at Caroline's supposed romantic entanglement with Angelica's husband, David. Because she so thoroughly conforms to Victorian gender roles, Angelica, like Virginia before her, can imagine no relationship with Caroline but a competitive one. Unlike Virginia, however, whose similar dependence on male definition was tragically unconscious, Angelica willingly manipulates others, including women. Just as she competes for her sister-in-law's fiancé's attentions, Angelica attempts to force Caroline into a tug-of-war for her husband, a battle both David and Caroline refuse to enter. As Caroline later must learn to recognize, Angelica is only too eager to "sacrifice" Caroline (*B* 303) to her own selfish need for the male attention that gives her self-definition.

Glasgow levels her criticism not so much at fictional individuals as at rigid gender traditions that force uneasy relationships. Angelica's betrayal of Caroline is caused by what Glasgow sees as a common problem in women's relationships with other women: men's definitions of women have insisted that competition for male attention replace a sense of connection and cooperation. Moreover, she targets a male tradition that defines a woman as either angel or demon, leaving no room for anything between idealized perfection and degradation.[38] Angelica Blackburn—even her name delimits the boundaries of her angelic or demonic possibilities—can be ethereal or subhuman according to a male myth of woman's role in either raising him above the material world or dragging him into the dirt; she cannot be merely human. And in either function she is not herself; she plays a role given to her. Appropriately, Angelica even escapes censure for negligent motherhood when she chooses to appear in a tableau rather than stay with her sick child—that is, when she obviously plays her part and assumes her role as the fixed object of a (masculine) gaze. Angelica's rakish brother describes her in the tableau as "a stunner . . . The Washington *Examiner* spoke of her as the most beautiful woman in Virginia" (*B* 181). As long as she fills a male-identified role as stunning beauty or dangerous manipulator, she acts within the confines of others' expectations of her.

Because potential close friendship with Caroline lies outside the realm of either extreme, there is no model against which to measure its worth. The "Sistine Madonna" that hangs in the stairwell because there is no place for it in the drawing-room serves as a reminder of women's choices between the imposed role of Virgin or of Whore. Such beauty as Angelica possesses may be "a power" (*B* 152), as Caroline once observes, but it is a power limited to the confines of the very patriarchal standard that defines it as a power in the first place. Angelica's willingness to play the roles asked of her demands in return that she forfeit her true self, so that she is, finally, as Caroline eventually realizes, a "vacancy" (152). For Caroline, the tragedy revolves around female support and cooperation, once possible but now betrayed: "I thought her so good and beautiful. I would have worked my fingers to the bone for her if she had only been kind to me. . . . It would have been so easy for her to have kept my love and admiration" (299).

If traces of Anderson and Bennett are evident in the individual characters David Blackburn and Caroline Meade, Glasgow and Anderson as a couple have their parallel in the relationship between Caroline and Roane Fitzhugh, Angelica's brother and Caroline's would-be suitor. Anderson's expectations about Glasgow's role in his life turn up in particular in the fictional couple and help explain Roane's fictional role, which wavers between providing a minor annoyance and facilitating a major cultural critique of gender stereotypes. Roane's attitude toward Caroline, who finds him repellent, asks that she raise him out of the dross of his materialistic existence, an attitude that the novel itself addresses generally. The extremity of Roane's degeneration is manifest in his drunkenness, his simpering, and, more seriously, his physical abusiveness. Roane calls Caroline "the angel in the house" and wishes she could "nurse" *him* rather than his niece (*B* 136). Roane's idealization of Caroline makes explicit his need for her help in resurrecting him. When Caroline defends David, Roane notices, her beauty is spiritual rather than fleshly, giving her "the rare and noble grace of a marble Diana." In comparing her to that legendary virgin, Roane acknowledges his belief that Caroline is "above [the rest of] them." Though merely a "dark, slender woman, with a gallant heart," she seemed to Roane "as remote and royal as a goddess." Transforming the high brow earlier associated with Caroline's masculinity, Roane observes the "light on her forehead" "gathered in benediction" (140). Later, Roane implores her to "make me the kind of man you like. You can if you try. You could do anything with me if you cared—you are so good" (200). "Honestly," he tries again, "you could make a man out of me. . . . I'll do anything you wish" (201).

Similarly, as Godbold and Wagner have also observed, a constant theme in Henry Anderson's letters to Glasgow is her spirituality compared to his materiality, her capacity to raise him to her higher spiritual level. Godbold interprets Anderson's expressions of inadequacy as the natural result of Glasgow's presumed continual assault on his worth, an assumption, perhaps unconscious but nonetheless striking, that rests on an inference that Glasgow was to blame for Anderson's feelings of insecurity. In fact, evidence suggests that Anderson's feelings of inadequacy were endemic, and that he did indeed see Glasgow's role as lifting his unworthy self to her "spiritual heights."[39] During the summer of 1916, in the first months of their relationship (they had met on Easter Sunday), Anderson's letters already make this theme apparent. Though Godbold speculates that "undoubtedly" Glasgow "preyed" on Anderson's insecurities,[40] one early letter thanks her for the "sweetest letter possible." Far from feeling berated by her, he worries about living up to her: "My dear I am entirely unworthy of such thoughts and it makes me feel very humble and small." He continues by saying that he will try to "at least see the spiritual heights on which you dwell" (7 September 1916). A week later he writes that her life is so full of "the great and good in spirit" that he wishes he were "better and bigger" to deserve her (13 September 1916).

Anderson's letter of 27 December 1916 defines Glasgow's role as Beatrice to his Dante:

> I can only express my thanks by striving in my own imperfect
> way to live nearer to the high ideal which you see. You are always
> an inspiration to that end and to idealistic effort . . . I feel very
> humble, my dear, before your estimate of me, very unworthy . . .
> and now more than ever before I have longed to be all that you in
> your vision see, to rise higher and higher in thought and achieve-

ment until my spirit may rise to your heights and stand side by side with you on the highest peaks of life . . . like Beatrice to Dante leading me from the depths of material things to the heights of idealism which we may well call Paradise. (box 9)[41]

In undated letters probably written between 1916 and 1920, Anderson "need[s]" her "help and sympathy," and though he probably doesn't "deserve" her understanding and forgiveness, asks it nonetheless ("Monday night").[42] In another, he feels "reverence" for Glasgow, but doesn't "admire" himself ("Tuesday"). Once, overcome by a letter from Glasgow, he is "humbled" by his "unworthiness." He implores her to "help me, and lead me along the ever rising path if I am ever to reach a level with you, or even the foot of the spiritual throne on which you dwell." He concludes: "my spirit is at your feet" ("Tuesday night").

Anderson frequently hints that at least one reason for his constant striving to rise to Glasgow's level of spirituality is their quarrel about his desire for a more physical relationship. Though it is difficult to imagine the genteel and reserved (even fastidious) Anderson as the embodiment of threatening physicality, the letters in fact suggest that at least on occasion Glasgow may have seen him as such. Just as Roane Fitzhugh of *The Builders* regards Caroline as either his angelic guide to spirituality or the object of his physical desires, Anderson's letters suggest a similar view of Glasgow. In an undated letter of "Sunday night, Midnight," Anderson writes of one of their Sunday evenings together:

> I deserve your judgement . . . I cannot understand my own weakness, for never have I reverenced you so much as today. . . . Yet I have sinned and must pay the price. I cannot think of those quiet evenings as ended, yet I know what you say as to the impossibility of some things is true for I know you. *It is a very humiliating thought that you cannot see me alone* but if that is your judgement I must accept it, until I win again the privilege by showing myself more worthy. (emphasis added)

Another letter on "Sunday morning" promises that Anderson will be on his good behavior, presumably that evening: "There will be no repetition today of anything to which you object. If the penalty is loss of your friendship I can do some very hard things . . . Until a modus vivendi is reached you need have no fear of the unpleasant incidents—if they are to you—I can of course see your point of view and, respect it—." A cryptic "Wednesday" letter shows a confused Anderson: "The unfortunate part is I am 'doomed either way' since I offend if I am reserved and am liable to do so if I am not." In one brief undated note Anderson tries a humorous reference to their relationship: "We had a very delightful evening—thanks of course to my angelic disposition!!!" And on 31 August 1916, perhaps half in jest, Anderson invites Glasgow to come to see him before he leaves for New York, and to bring "a chaperone too, if you need one."

I don't want to portray Anderson as the villain. The relationship was complicated, marked by confusing signals on both sides. Glasgow seemed to want Anderson and not want him simultaneously, and he wanted someone to read his speeches, support his political aspirations, and bolster his ego. But the view of Glasgow as excessively demanding bespeaks an attitude that Glasgow's critics have shared with Anderson: women exist to support men's more important endeavors, often reminding them of their potential spiritual heights, and they exist to gratify men's sexual desires at the same time. Angel/demon, virgin/whore—in terms of expectations, it is but a short distance between Roane and Henry Anderson.

Anderson articulated many of his ideas to Marjorie Kinnan Rawlings when she was collecting notes in the early 1950s for her planned biography of Glasgow. In a letter of 6 January 1953, Anderson offered Rawlings his views on men and women:

> I do not agree with your view that it is necessary to stand up for the woman as against the man in controversial cases in actual life. . . . At present the women have all the rights of women and are claiming all the rights of men; they can not have both. There must be an adjustment somewhere. My own belief is that women are happier where the dominance of the man in the relationship is recognized, at least to the extent of his obligations. After all, happiness is the ultimate objective of life. I do not like weak men, nor do I like women who are too aggressive.[43]

Implicitly questioning Rawlings's choice of biographical subject, at one point Anderson told her, according to Rawlings's notes, that " 'A woman writer (Ellen) lives such a secluded life—really not much to write about her. A man lives a life of action." A few months later, Anderson evades Rawlings's questions about an actual engagement to Glasgow. Rawlings describes his explanation: "Ellen and I were very close friends. We were very different. She was very emotional. You know, there are two elements, one, the emotional, which is the feminine and the affirmative, the other, the mind or the intellectual, which always says 'Be careful. Be careful.' This is the negative and the male. She represented the emotional and I the intellectual." During the same conversation, Rawlings says that "2 or 3 times" Anderson characterized Glasgow as a "personal person." Anderson's behavior during Rawlings's inquiry consistently reveals a man threatened by women, afraid of unpleasantries (admitting this, he calls himself an "escapist" who "likes to avoid disagreeable things"),[44] and still uneasy about his relationship with Glasgow more than thirty years earlier. He shows his preferences for submissive women (which Glasgow was not) and domineering men (which he was not), preferences that make it remarkable that the two got along at all. Glasgow's brother Arthur, upon hearing that his sister's memoirs contained a chapter about "Henry," is reported to have said, "astonished, 'Henry *Anderson?*'" Indeed, the astonishment is, not that there was never a marriage (a subject Anderson repeatedly refuses to discuss with Rawlings), but that there was ever anything even approaching an engagement.[45]

The conflicted allegiances in *The Builders,* in which Caroline transfers her emotional focus from Angelica to David (though to both uneasily), as well as the novel's open-endedness, accurately reflects Glasgow's personal life at the time: her own "story" had no foregone conclusion. Feeling the pull of her relationship with Anderson and at the same time sensing that marriage was not for her, and simultaneously envisioning a life of independence and female companionship with Bennett for domestic and professional support, Glasgow's own text's conclusion was equally uncertain. Moreover, and importantly, the two possibilities seemed irreconcilable. Near the end of *The Builders* David Blackburn says goodbye to Caroline. Her feelings enlighten Glasgow's reluctance to privilege heterosexual love over companionship: "It was friendship, not love, she knew" and "friendship was all that she asked—friendship satisfied her heart, and filled the universe with a miraculous beauty" (*B* 332). The novel concludes with Caroline on her way to France and David and Angelica in the midst of an unpromising reconciliation. As Caroline sees Angelica she thinks: "never, not even in the days of her summer splendour, had Caroline felt so strongly the invincible power of her charm and her pathos" (378). The final comment—"it seemed to her that, beyond the meadows and the river, light was shining on the far horizon" (378–79)— holds out a vague promise of happiness, but the inconclusiveness of the relationships in the novel make it difficult to predict what that happiness should consist of. The pull of friendship certainly seems at least as strong as that of romantic love between men and women.

One Man in His Time *and*
Redemptive Female Friendships

One Man in His Time (1922) clearly recognizes women's friendships as alternatives to heterosexual relationship, and views those friendships as enabling a reconciliation between a woman's problematic heritage and her possible future. The novel imagines a new tradition blended of the best of the old and the new, a merging figured in the relationship between Patty Vetch and Corinna Page. Corinna vividly illustrates Glasgow's attraction to the old-fashioned woman of her mother's generation. Genteel, calmly beautiful, discerning, appreciative of the fine things in her antique shop, Corinna's appeal seems as ageless as Campion's famous lute player of the same name, who evokes old-fashioned feminine appeal.[46] At forty-eight—Glasgow's age at the time—Corinna resembles "an October morning": fresh, but also reminiscent of time passing, beautiful but outdated as a standard of beauty.[47] But, as Adrienne Rich's "Snapshots of a Daughter-in-Law" implies, that standard of beauty was not Corinna's in the first place. Like Richardson's Clarissa, Rich's Corinna is but the reflection of male desire:

> When to her lute Corinna sings
> neither words nor music are her own.

Even her hair falling "over her cheek" and the "silk against her knees" are "adjusted in reflections of an eye."[48] Just as Rich revises Campion, Glasgow revises male-defined traditions of womanhood, insisting that Corinna learn to reconstruct old and new into a re-visioned tradition. Corinna, however appealing, must temper her tradition of womanly beauty by incorporating into it newer traditions of womanhood represented by Patty Vetch. These two women form a friendship based on complementarity. With one as traditional and the other as re-visioned womanhood, together they propose a solution to the problem of reconciling past female traditions with those of present and future.

Corinna's material environment defines her incomplete appeal: she is a work of art, at home among the fine objects in her shop, but the independence of her artistry from interaction with others has limited its effectiveness. She is so at ease in her setting that she is "Corinna *of*"—rather than *in*—"the Old Print Shop" She looks "as if she stepped out of a portrait by Romney" (*OMHT* 37) (a comparison Glasgow also makes in describing her sister Cary [*WW* 102]), and seems to "belong in one of the English mezzotints on the wall" (*OMHT* 48). The women she resembles in the paintings harken to an aristocratic, old-world past whose definition of artistic and aesthetic worth (whether of women's beauty or of painting) is disappearing as fast as are the classist pretensions of the Virginia that serves as the novel's background. Corinna resembles a duchess in "an engraving" and the "bewitching face of Lady Hamilton," who was in fact painted by George Romney. Corinna's "place" seems to be "among those vanished beauties of a richer age." (48–49).

But these images of Corinna fixed in frames (like Rich's snapshots) in an old print shop where no one purchases the art are reminders of the limitations of her appeal, and of the objectification she has undergone. She exists, statically and alone, "amid the rare prints which she never expected to sell." Returning from residence in France and Britain and presumably exchanging the Old World for the New, Corinna had instead clung to the old by opening a "quaint" and "ridiculous old print shop." Not at all the bustling, quintessentially American entrepreneurial enterprise suggested by her shop's address in Franklin Street, Corinna's shop had "never sold an engraving" (*OMHT* 37). To her young cousin Stephen Culpeper, the shop was "another world" of dreams, warmth, "colour," and "magic." If outside was "real life," inside the shop was an "enchanted fairy-ring where children played at making believe" (40).

If Corinna is the color of mezzotints and old roses, the younger Patty Vetch is the vivid reds and greens of the tropical birds she evokes (*OMHT* 9, 16, 55). Lacking the cultural and artistic refinement that characterizes Corinna, Patty longs for Corinna's grace and charm. Patty, the daughter of the upstart new governor, was "born in a circus"

(93), and her New Womanly facade indicates vitality and adventurousness but does not give her confidence. Unlike Corinna, who seems to have stepped out of an idealized portrait of a lady, Patty looks "absurdly like a picture on the cover of some cheap magazine" (8). Patty goes to Corinna for instruction, asking "as many questions as Socrates" (55) about the objects in Corinna's shop; she shows particular interest in the portraits of the aristocratic women. Patty plans linguistic self-improvement, too; she studies a page of the dictionary every morning and practices the words during the day (101). Corinna correctly perceives that a "sense of inferiority" (101) lies close under the surface of Patty's daring appearance, as her incipient tears after a social snubbing reveal (14).

Whereas Corinna conforms to the standard of beauty and worth traditionally defined and celebrated by men—by Campion, by Romney, and by the novel's Stephen Culpeper—Patty defies that standard. As the representative of some new and as-yet-undefined component of a future standard of womanhood, Patty, appropriately, is not beautiful to men like Stephen, raised to admire Corinna and women like her. Patty, according to Stephen, is "not exactly a lady" (*OMHT* 9). Corinna exposes as typically male Stephen's inability to understand Patty: it is "simply" because he is "a man" that he fails to see Patty's intelligence and inquisitiveness (55). Corinna knows that Patty is likewise bound by gender restrictions. Corinna's broader understanding of male-female relationships allows her to see what Stephen cannot: much of Patty's behavior around him—of women's behavior around men—is an act. "Some girls," Corinna tells him, "are for ever acting" a "vulgar part" they "learned before they were born" (55).

But neither Patty's apparent crudeness nor Corinna's old-fashioned perfection is a workable solution to the problem of women's place in the world, a problem emblematized by the Woman Question Patty so vividly represents. If Corinna's cool aestheticism distances her too often from human involvement, Patty's bold adventurousness threatens to centralize her in a heightened human drama and to make her unable to remove herself even momentarily from its emotional tangles. The circus she was born into surrounds her with melodramas of betrayed love, romantic elopements, abandoned children, and the extremes of humanity represented by the "freaks" she so loved to hear about as a child (*OMHT* 94–96). Patty reveals her confusion about her place in the world and her relation to others when she wonders what Corinna, "who looked as if she had stepped down from one of those old prints, thought of her" (123). Sitting at her dressing table, the site of many women's attempts to make themselves over into an image men admire, Patty worries about her appearance: her powder is "too white," she decides, and her "prettiness was merely the bloom of youth, nothing more" (132). Like many women in fiction and out of it, she knows that glitzy youth is attractive to men, and that once it is gone her appeal may go with it: "In ten, fifteen, at the most in twenty years, I shall have lost it all." "Then," she thinks, "I shall get fat and common looking; and everything will be over for me" (132).

Patty's longing for the mother she never knew defines her relationship with Corinna and reinforces the necessity of uniting the worlds they represent in order to forge a new order. Patty inquires of her own reflected image, " 'I wonder if Mother could have helped me if she had lived?' " She imagines her mother as a circus performer/fairy godmother complete with tulle skirt and a "short silver wand, with a star on the end of it." But the shortcomings of such a romantic and idealized mother are poignantly revealed in the terse story she has been told of her mother's inglorious fate: a neighbor has told Patty that "her mother had lost her mind from a fall in the circus, that they had taken her away to an asylum, and that now she was dead" (*OMHT* 133). Rather than the "sanctified wives and mothers" Linda Wagner sees satirized in Glasgow's early fiction, here there simply is no mother; she must be replaced.[49] The mother Patty needs must be human, not a fairy godmother.

Corinna shows Patty the value of female relationship with characteristics of both the mother-daughter bond and the bond of a mature friendship, and their companionship demonstrates the nurturing possibilities in such a union for both women. Together, they learn the lessons that Glasgow implies many women must learn in order to situate themselves in the world of men and at the same time to fashion a new tradition for women that both maintains connection and encourages independence. Patty will provide Corinna, as Corinna herself predicts, with the "interest in life" (*OMHT* 101) that she lacks; Corinna will be for Patty the mother she has needed. Patty admits to herself that "ever since her first visit to the old print shop, she had tried to copy Corinna's voice, the carriage of her head, her smile, her gestures" (141). In the concluding section of the novel, Patty learns that her mother had been a drug addict and a murderer and that the man she calls her father had adopted her out of kindness. Corinna experiences her own kinship with impoverished women at the scene of Patty's enlightenment and feels that she had "faced life for the first time" (360). Patty, now able to distance herself from sentimental notions about motherhood, marriage, and love, resolves to help save her "father" from political scandal. This mutually enabling relationship has allowed Corinna to step down from her detached position as artistic object and Patty to step away from her emotional chaos to the clear resolve she exhibits at the end.

As in *The Wheel of Life* earlier in Glasgow's career, the chapter here called "Patty and Corinna" usurps the structural and thematic center of the novel away from the plots of love and marriage and political maneuverings. In this chapter Patty also usurps the place of Corinna's suitor, substituting what Corinna refers to as the watchlike, "monotonous regularity" (*OMHT* 142) of men for the friendship Patty affords. Having searched for that absent "something" in relationships with men, Corinna realizes that "perfection," or idealized romantic love, has left her unfulfilled. Announcing to Patty, "You shall have a friend—a real friend—from this day" (158), Corinna affirms the satisfactions of female relationship: affiliation without dependence, and an emphasis on the "daily miracles" (158) associated with women's experience rather than the romanticized love associated with men. Corinna, in her "golden middle age," will "accept the milder joys, the daily miracles, the fulfilled adventures" (158).

Patty's satisfaction seems even stronger; her "real" friendship with Corinna "was like first love without its troubled suspense, this new wonderful feeling! It was like a religious awakening without the sense of sin that she associated with her early conversion. Nothing, she felt, could ever be so beautiful again! Nothing could ever mean so much to her in the rest of life!" (*OMHT* 160). In the language of their mutual awakening, Corinna, rather than removing herself from life, goes to its "heart" (158); Patty, rather than descending into the tangled web of her chaotic emotions, experiences through Corinna a spiritual conversion that enables "her first clear perception of the difference between the things that mattered a little and the things that mattered profoundly" (160). Though *One Man in His Time* retreats from its brief focus on these two women as quickly as it placed them at the center, the novel's final message is intricately related to the knowledge represented by them: the necessity for human compassion and under-standing, together with independent judgment and calm evaluation. Not separately but together, in close friendship, Patty and Corinna embody a redefined tradition of womanhood that combines the best of a legacy of mutuality with a new independence.

The years surrounding the composition and publication of both *The Builders* and *One Man in His Time* were difficult ones for Glas-gow, and her search for an identity as a woman and a woman writer both complicates and is complicated by events in her life. The "con-flicting stories," to use Elizabeth Ammons's phrase, that waver be-tween traditional romantic love and deeply felt female friendships are both fictional and real. Glasgow's complicated relationship with Henry Anderson beginning in 1916 forced Glasgow to confront di-rectly her feelings about men and heterosexuality, feelings I think she had been able to repress fairly successfully until then. And it was not Anderson alone who presented a problem for Glasgow: it was Ander-son squared off against Anne Virginia Bennett, who by the time of Anderson's arrival had been living in the house for six years.

And they did square off. Though much of the conflict between Bennett and Anderson only came to light later, especially in Rawl-ings's interviews with Bennett, it is clear that these two saw them-selves as rivals for Glasgow's attention. When Anderson complains of Glasgow's need for a "chaperone" in his presence,[50] he probably refers partly to Bennett's constant companionship, confirmed by many sources (including casual references to Bennett in letters from and to Glasgow). In interview notes, Rawlings quotes Blythe Branch (Glas-gow's brother Arthur's brother-in-law) that Bennett responded to Anderson's invitation to live with him and Glasgow after their mar-riage by saying that "she wouldn't spend one [n]ight under his roof." Bennett wished Glasgow would marry him, Branch told Rawlings, and told Anderson: " 'then I'd want and expect her to divorce you after 24 hours.' " Carrie Coleman Duke, Glasgow's lifelong friend, said to Rawlings: " 'Anne Virginia hates men. She's awfully upset that I've rented the top apartment to three men.' "[51]

Though impossible now to reconstruct these years in all their complexity, certain facts are clearly established. Glasgow and Anderson became engaged the night of 19 July 1917, the eve of Anderson's departure for Red Cross service in Rumania. It is difficult to discern Glasgow's real feelings about this engagement. The autograph statement that Linda Wagner describes as "an ecstatic note" is, in fact, curiously devoid of emotion. "I became engaged to Henry this evening" is penned on a piece of monogrammed note card such as Glasgow used for brief correspondence. Though Godbold describes it as "written on a half sheet" of paper "with no other markings on it,"[52] in fact this brief statement with its date is cut out of a larger piece of paper, as if deliberately, and the tops of words that followed it are visible at the bottom. It looks more like a part of a letter now cut away. The surviving letters from Anderson, particularly frequent from 1917 to 1920, are warmest when either Anderson or Glasgow is at a distance. Those written when they are seeing each other frequently in Richmond show the strains of their relationships and often hint at arguments. Anderson returned from Rumania for about five months in 1918 (July to November), then permanently in the fall of 1919. Certainly by late 1920 (or earlier, if one accepts Glasgow's frequent comments in *The Woman Within* about the unsuitability of marriage for her), it seems they had given up on marriage or a lasting romance.

What Glasgow obviously had decided in favor of, however, was the permanence of Anne Virginia Bennett and a preference for her women friends, though the former decision in particular presented its problems, too. Like Anderson, Bennett also left for war duty; she went to France as a volunteer nurse, leaving in early 1918 (probably March, judging by a letter of March 26 from Glasgow to her brother Arthur), a few months before Anderson's temporary return that summer. Though the precise date of Bennett's return is uncertain, a letter of invitation in early November 1920 makes clear Bennett's solid position as cohost by that time: "The house and the welcome and Miss Bennett and I are waiting."[53] As if to formally mark the end of their engagement and, perhaps, to relinquish his place to Bennett, on Christmas Eve 1921, Anderson presented the two women with a Sealyham puppy, their beloved Jeremy, the "one perfect treasure" from Glasgow's years with Anderson. It is, perhaps, no coincidence that the dog's name, before Glasgow changed it, had been Llangollen, the place associated with the two eighteenth-century Welsh women famous for eloping and setting up house together (*WW* 246).[54]

Bennett and Glasgow lived together until Glasgow's death in 1945, upon which she left the bulk of her estate to Bennett and from which Bennett seems never to have fully recovered. Bennett's pain is fully apparent in Rawlings's interviews and correspondence from 1953.[55] Monique Parent confirms Bennett's devotion to Glasgow's memory.[56] But however settled the two women seemed from about 1922 on, the journey toward that permanent companionship was difficult for Glasgow, and her feelings about female friendship remained complex throughout her life. The conclusions of many of her novels, with their frequent uneasiness with the traditional romance or marriage plot, must be read against the backdrop of their fictional and actual alternative of women's friendships in Glasgow's life. Her mother, sisters, aunt, and mammy; then friends Carrie Coleman (later Duke), Lizzie Patterson (later Crutchfield), Mary Johnston, and many others in her childhood and youth and later, provided a nurturing circle of women in whose presence Glasgow obviously felt less tension and more encouragement to discover an identity as a woman. As she grew older she only enlarged that earlier circle of women friends.

When Glasgow remarked in her 1938 Preface to *Virginia* that her heroine's "tragedy" was not of her own making but had sprung from her status as a "forsaken ideal" (*V* xii), she articulated something she had begun to realize fully as she wrote that novel early in the second decade of the twentieth century: women have not been just themselves, but male-defined ideals. Men have written the songs and made the jokes, as she said in *The Wheel of Life*, and have put women in their circumscribed places in the bargain. When Glasgow in 1913 defined feminism as "a revolt from a pretense of being" and a "struggle for the liberation of personality,"[57] she grasped a common truth about feminine selfhood—that men had mediated the definition of self that women had for too long falsely accepted—that would make possible her redefined woman's tradition of connection, of community. What she had seen in her mother's generation—even in her sister Cary's—as the inheritance of selfless dependence and shared victimization could be transformed into a new tradition allowing an independent self simultaneously capable of independence and affiliation, what Chodorow calls "mature dependence." After the pivotal *Virginia* and certainly by the early twenties, Glasgow discovered, for herself, at least, that the self defined by gazing in the mirror of simi-larity—at a female friend—is the self unmediated by an other's expec-tations. A woman's tradition of connection and affiliation helps her discover a female self rather than to lose that self as it filters through male definition. By the early 1920s, Glasgow realized that for herself, a woman's community—even a community of only two—provided the solidarity and relation that made her revolt and struggle against patriarchal definition possible.

FOUR

Gothic Imaginings:
Five Stories

Shade after shade, they approached, looked at me,
without stopping, and vanished into complete darkness . . . The past was the present, and past and present
were equally haunted. . . . The house belonged to the
dead. I was living with ghosts.

Glasgow, *The Woman Within*

[The Angel in the House] died hard. Her fictitious
nature was of great assistance to her. It is far harder to
kill a phantom than a reality.

Virginia Woolf, "Professions for Women"

The Victorian ideals of femininity lay as an incubus
upon the earlier fiction of the period—for it is, after
all, an imperfect transcript of life that paints man as a
human being and woman as a piece of faintly colored
waxwork.

Glasgow, "Feminism"

To the extent that Glasgow's engagement with traditions of
womanhood led her to recognize that it was not life itself but an
"imperfect transcript of life"—largely one written, she felt, in a masculine hand—"that paints man as a human being and woman as a
piece of faintly colored waxwork," she succeeded at what contemporary feminists have described variously as re-visioning, writing beyond
the ending, and changing the story.[1] Reimagining women's traditions

as positive forces for change rather than as negative justifications for stasis represented a bold move for Glasgow, one that allowed her to acknowledge her preference for the company of women, to embrace her mother's generation's grounding in a community of women (if not her mother's passive acceptance of marginalization), and to redefine selfhood in context rather than in isolation.

I do not wish to oversimplify such new awarenesses, however, or to imply that, especially after *Virginia*, Glasgow's newly imagined traditions of women meant she saw the process of awareness as completed (she did not), or that she no longer grappled with the complexities of actually using them to instigate change (she did). Five Gothic short stories, written between 1916 and 1923, openly address the difficulties of reinventing stories for women. This time using not only personal women's traditions but also a literary tradition associated predominately with women writers and characters (and readers) in order to imagine tradition as it affects women, Glasgow at once acknowledges the old traditions, recognizes the need for new ones, and imagines the difficulties inherent in not only finding the new ones but in making them work. Glasgow writes of gendered identity in the fictional context of the past (tradition), and of both identity and the past within the larger context of the literary tradition that Ellen Moers in *Literary Women* first termed the female Gothic. In doing so, Glasgow makes use of an extratextual past as empowering for women, and at the same time she highlights intratextually the difficulties in making practical use of such empowerment to effect change.

In *The Woman Within,* Glasgow acknowledges her special feeling for the female Gothic literary tradition in describing a pilgrimage to the home of the Brontë sisters. During an 1899 trip to England, she and two of her sisters "walked in pale sunshine over the moors" of Yorkshire in search of the "bleak parsonage" where the Brontës had lived at Haworth. The trip was prompted, Glasgow says, by their "feeling for the Brontës, especially for Emily" (*WW* 149). Finding the cottage "unchanged, beside the forsaken churchyard, with its toppling headstones" (150), Glasgow remarks the "essence of solitude" (150–51) pervading the place and Emily Brontë's deep attachment to her home and its environs, so uninviting to the outsider.

Glasgow refers to the Brontës again in a 1934 essay, "One Way to Write Novels" (later revised as the Virginia Edition Preface to *The*

Sheltered Life), perhaps written near the time she wrote the autobiography's passages above. She uses the Brontës, especially Emily,
to illustrate her belief that, while novels should be written out of
"illuminated" experience, experience needn't be "eventful." "Several
of the most thrilling lives in all literature," Glasgow observes, "were
lived amid the unconquerable desolation of the Yorkshire moors." But
neither Byron nor Lawrence, she imagined, contained "such burning
realities as were hidden beneath the quiet fortitude of Emily Brontë."[2]
The "burning realities" beneath the calm exterior of Emily Brontë's
female life, not the male lives of Byron or Lawrence, were what intrigued Glasgow. And it was this hidden female interior, whatever
name we might give it, that called forth Glasgow's five stories in the
Gothic tradition of Brontë. No doubt Glasgow also identified with
Emily Brontë's seemingly perverse attachment to her desolate region:
Glasgow herself often questioned the intellectual aridity of her native
Richmond and the cultural isolation of the South that H. L. Mencken
in 1917 had famously termed "The Sahara of the Bozart." Glasgow
retrospectively identified her own physical and spiritual space in 1916,
following the death of her father, as desolate, as the first epigraph to
this chapter reveals. Her "haunted" existence allowed her to appreciate the Brontës and the experience of desolation she shared with them
(*WW* 221–22).

Of course, Glasgow's admiration for the Brontës does not necessarily explain her engagement, beginning in 1916, with the Gothic
tradition with which they are often closely associated. Glasgow herself probably wouldn't have called the five stories that I will discuss
Gothic, as others would not.[3] To Glasgow, Gothic connoted the un-
necessarily violent and even perverse fiction of, for example, Faulkner and Erskine Caldwell, and she made certain she dissociated herself from it. Nonetheless, five of Glasgow's stories—"The Shadowy
Third" (1916), "Dare's Gift" (1917), "The Past" (1920), and "Whispering Leaves" and "Jordan's End" (1923)—are modern updates of
the traditional Gothic plot as Claire Kahane describes it. In Kahane's
terms (though Kahane does not discuss Glasgow), each of Glasgow's
stories has its "imprisoning structure," a house; its female protagonist,
not always "young"; its sexually charged male, not always "powerful"
(and usually obstructing if not threatening); and its mysterious, secret
"center," not always a literal space. Though the existence of the pro-

tagonist's mother is usually left ambiguous, motherhood is often an anxious focal point in the stories (an anxiety Moers first discussed as a typical feature of female Gothic fiction). The "boundaries" between life and death are indeed "confused," often through a supernatural figure knowable by and known to the protagonist. For my purposes, an even more significant confusion of boundaries, which Eugenia DeLamotte has seen as the salient feature of Gothic fiction, occurs between self and other.[4]

It is in her concern with the relation between female self and other —that is, with gendered identity—that convincingly places Glasgow's stories in the tradition not just of Gothic but of female Gothic fiction.[5] Though Moers locates her definition of female Gothic rather vaguely in "the work that women writers have done in the literary mode" called the Gothic, her focus on the female Gothic as expressive of female self-loathing urged others toward more precise descriptions. A characteristic "horror of the self," or of "female physiology," Juliann Fleenor argues in *The Female Gothic,* "is closely tied to the patriarchal paradigm." That paradigm, I would add, posing as normality or reality in the world of the Gothic, forces silence and erasure for the Gothic heroine. The normative world that Gothic fiction hopes to restore at the end of a nightmare vision of confusion requires self-hatred in the female protagonist. This "tyranny of the normal," as Nina Auerbach calls it in another context, is precisely what female Gothic fiction works against, since "normal" for the heroine is likely to mean, among other commonplace horrors, female idealization and objectification, domestic imprisonment, and the inadequate self-worth that Moers and others have noted. Identifying whatever specific conflict the Gothic heroine typically internalizes, however, as Michelle Massé provocatively suggests, has led us away from the very subjectivity at the center of female Gothic concerns. Locating Gothic conflict or anxiety variously in "self, mother, father, heterosexuality, and homosexuality" often leads us to "a forced synthesis" that masks a "more ominous" characteristic: "the refusal of the heroine's existence as subject." Because the typical Gothic conclusion moves toward marriage, Massé argues, "the woman can exist only in relation to another— usually as a daughter in the beginning and as a bride at the end." When we insist on this movement as progress, we "rewrite the Gothic and assure its repetition."[6] It is precisely the resistance to this refusal to recognize female subjectivity that, for me, most clearly identifies the female Gothic. In fact, Glasgow's imaginative interest in one passage of Emily Brontë's *Wuthering Heights* suggests that questions of female subjectivity form one link between Brontë's and her own brand of female Gothic. In her copy of Maurice Maeterlinck's *Wisdom and Destiny* (1903), Glasgow marked heavily a discussion of Catherine Earnshaw's well-known and unsettling assertion, "I *am* Heathcliff!"[7] The female subjectivity that Catherine has just obliterated (or at least altered radically) by her statement is the focus of the concern that unifies Glasgow's five stories.

The setting for the protagonist's construction of gendered self-identity in Glasgow's stories is not the Gothic castle of earlier writers, but the more modern house, with its associations of domesticity and feminine space. DeLamotte cleverly characterizes Gothic novels as centrally concerned with "women who just can't seem to get out of the house."[8] Reading *house* as a metaphor for the myriad structures that limit or confine women, we can appreciate the rebelliousness that has transformed Gothic into female Gothic for writers such as Glasgow. Rather than featuring the isolated Gothic heroine, for example, Glasgow usually provides her female protagonist with another woman (or other women) to help her. The traditional unprotected and threatened heroine acting (or *not* acting) alone is thus exchanged for the protagonist acting within empowering female companionship. Unlike the male-centered Oedipal plot that Leslie Fiedler identifies as quintessentially Gothic,[9] in Glasgow's female Gothic stories men are eerily absent, except as something to be overcome. In a different configuration of what Massé terms "marital Gothic," marriage in these stories functions as a source of anxiety rather than of the romantic (although, as Massé argues, ultimately undercut) promise of reality. Glasgow's reliance on the past in her five stories (one of which is even called "The Past"), rather than accepting typical Gothic remoteness, instead highlights the past (or tradition) as something that threatens to be present, something to avoid repeating. This version of the past as an "incubus" constraining the present (as do the "ideals of femininity" in this chapter's third epigraph) views the past, in Massé's words, as the "nightmare from which the protagonist cannot awaken and whose inexorable logic must be followed."[10] Certain nightmares and their logic, I would argue, did seem almost inexorable to Glasgow at the time she was writing these stories, and it is her resistance to the seemingly inevitable relinquishment of her own agency that the stories partially record. The female Gothic as a literary heritage provided Glasgow the venue for exploring self and sexuality in the context of her engagement with women's traditions. In these five stories, Glasgow situates herself in a literary tradition associated with women's search for selfhood within a hostile cultural setting, and directly confronts the roles of men, marriage, and female friendship in her fiction and in her life.

The circumstances and timing of Glasgow's Gothic stories, beginning with "The Shadowy Third" and ending with "Whispering Leaves" and "Jordan's End" in 1923, are suggestive. It was Anne Virginia Bennett who proposed (probably early in 1916) that Glasgow write a short story for the income it would bring. Marjorie Kinnan Rawlings's notes of her interview with Bennett record the scene: "sitting in front of open fire—she [Glasgow] hated the darkness. A.V.: 'We need money for things—why don't you write a short story?' "[11] After an initial protest, Glasgow responded by writing and publishing "The Shadowy Third" (December 1916), her first Gothic story. That Bennett provided the initial impetus in such a cozy domestic scene exemplifies Glasgow's increasing reliance on companionship with women, particularly Bennett, about this time. Also, these stories, spanning as they do the time of her closest involvement with Henry Anderson, express anxiety about her relationships with men and about the domestic space that encloses women in marriage. Finally, and closely related to her anxiety about men, her father's death in January 1916 signaled to Glasgow a new freedom, but one complicated by a new limitation as well. Though its patriarch Glasgow had died and the daughter was now the head of the Richmond house of Glasgow, that house both literally and symbolically represented conflicted emotions about her mother and women, about her father and men, and about an ideology of separate spheres that demarcates acceptable space for women and men. Further, her father's infirmity had been the reason that Bennett stayed in the house after Glasgow's sisters had died, Cary in 1911 and Emily in 1915. Without them, Glasgow was in the position of needing to justify Bennett's presence.

It seems fitting, given the anxieties revolving around the house and its associations, that Glasgow's Gothic stories share an exploration of domestic space. As with much fiction in the female Gothic tradition, spatial constraints in the form of houses are symbolic of male domination, particularly in marriage; they are "an emblem of male oppression and control," according to Lloyd-Smith.[12] Houses are, for example, both literal places of residence and metaphoric descriptions of the family called by its patriarchal name, as in the House of Windsor or Hanover (or Usher or Glasgow). Historically, the patriarchal "house" stands for the obliteration of women, effectively imprisoned in domesticity. Houses represent a tradition of male hegemony, of primogeniture and the legal silencing of women associated with the passing down of property to which they had little legitimate access.

A physical house has been an important medium of exchange in the marriage marketplace, too: it was first the lure by which a man of property could catch a worthwhile mate and subsequently the place where she ostensibly ruled. From the late eighteenth century on, houses have also located a woman's proper sphere, the domestic setting that, with particular emphasis beginning in the nineteenth century, has designated the boundaries of a woman's power and influence, even of her existence. *Feme covert,* the term used to describe the submersion of a woman's legal identity into her husband's upon her marriage, can be seen to have referred to a woman's being legally "covered" by more than her husband's name and legal legitimacy; it more literally alluded to her invisibility within the house that had become her only domain.[13] The irony of a woman's supposed reign as the angel in the house whose very terms of ownership actually denied power to her was not lost on female Gothic writers. As Glasgow adopts the female Gothic tradition, she translates that irony into an awareness of the absurdity of women's being asked to search for female identity in a (domestic) setting that attempts to obliterate a female self even while it professes to elevate her. I will observe for Glasgow, as she might have, that angels, even in the house, are by definition dead. The Gothic convention of "live burial" that Eve Kosofsky Sedgwick discusses so provocatively easily describes the "life" of the angel in the house that Virginia Woolf recognized women had to kill if they were to write.[14] Spatial limitations in Glasgow's Gothic stories play out the anxiety and anger that follow upon her awareness of the limitations imposed on women's lives by the domestic ideal.

Spatial constraints also represent generic constraints that say

"Gothic" (i.e., popular) fiction lacks the respectability of serious "realistic" fiction, a literary debate argued with particular fervor in the United States during Glasgow's early years. And though Glasgow always avowed her connection to a realistic literary tradition, in her Gothic stories she demonstrates her willingness to question principles that underlie that very realism—that *realistic* necessarily means "superior" because not "popular." The little criticism of Glasgow's short stories that exists reinforces that bias. In his Introduction to Glasgow's *Collected Stories*, Richard K. Meeker is perplexed that Glasgow asks her readers to believe in ghosts. With Godbold, Meeker assumes that only money could have prompted Glasgow to write "ghost stories," since the genre lacked respectability. In his early scholarly study of Glasgow, Frederick P. W. McDowell finds the stories "negligible" because they take as their subject "the supernatural." Lacking in "subtlety," the stories are "thinly imagined," McDowell argues, unlike Glasgow's "best stories" of "real life." Even Raper, who treats the stories most fully and seriously, finds the "ghost stories" both "a little opaque" and "simpler" than the others.[15] But just as her life and often her fiction emphasized female-centered relationships to criticize the cultural dictates of a male-centered world, Glasgow chose a female-identified literary tradition to offer a generic alternative. She defied all kinds of "authority"—male, institutional, generic—by aligning herself with the female Gothic tradition and representing herself within its terms.

This self-representation was, of course, cultural representation as well. From the turn of the century through the early 1920s was a time of particular urgency about a woman's place; the ostensible new freedom signified most prominently by the ratification of the Nineteenth Amendment in 1920 invited women and men to reassess and redefine gender roles and responsibilities. It could be argued that Glasgow, in choosing the female Gothic form, placed herself within a tradition and thus in one sense accepted a status quo. At the same time, however, in a repetition of the same kind of tension she had experienced all along regarding tradition and innovation, the female Gothic tradition she chose was one that represented subversion of the status quo, as many commentators have observed.[16] She thus gave herself at once a comfortable place and a revolutionary position, and from that standpoint could continue her ongoing re-visioning of a newly defined woman's tradition. As with her personal experience, in her Gothic stories what she proposed against the patriarchal status quo was a community of women that usurped man's place by joining together, at times transhistorically—even, in these supernatural tales, metaphysically—to subvert male power.

Other than Henry Anderson's letters to Glasgow (discussed in the previous chapter) and Glasgow's autobiography, *The Woman Within,* little remains to document Glasgow's personal life during these years. Even a simplified account, however, suggests a kind of Gothic quality to Glasgow's actual life at the time. Her turn to Gothicism can be seen as a way of sorting through a confusing time in her life as well as a creative experiment. Certainly Glasgow felt little warmth toward her father; in her autobiography she says that he was "growing old, and old age was making him *more* irascible and dictatorial" (*WW* 183; my emphasis). Even so, his death in January 1916 at the age of eighty-six would have made the house—and dwelling—he had ruled for so long seem a bit empty, and it did leave Glasgow more on her own (including financially) than she had ever been. The large, elegant house at One West Main in Richmond had been home to Glasgow since 1887, when she was fourteen. As the eighth of ten children (though not all ten survived childhood), she was accustomed to the presence of family members. Upon her father's death, she lived in the large house with only Anne Virginia, and she felt deeply its relative emptiness even as she enjoyed the freedom that emptiness signaled. After the death of her mother and Walter McCormack's earlier suicide (1893 and 1894, respectively), the seven years from 1909 to 1916 had brought their share of death too: her brother Frank's suicide in 1909; Cary's death in 1911; the death of another sister, Emily, in 1915; her father's in early 1916. She even tried leaving One West Main in 1911 for One West 85th Street in New York, but managed only a few months there each year, and returned permanently to Richmond by 1916. Add to these family sorrows and Glasgow's attempt to escape them the tension of her new relationship with Anderson; his departure for the Balkans in 1917; his more painful return in 1918, when it was evident that the relationship was over; Bennett's departure in 1918 for Red Cross service in France; and the horrors of the war itself. Like many a Gothic heroine, she apparently felt trapped in a house full of painful memories and haunted, as she says, by the ghosts of the past. In *The Woman Within,* she even goes so far as to explain her "illogical" relationship with Anderson as a result of her "desperate need" to escape from her "inescapable past." She felt "an unconquerable isolation" "closing in," and a "loneliness" that was not that of "the spirit in freedom" but an "utter desolation" that was "peopled with phantoms" that "haunted" her. Her inability to escape the past affected the present: "The past was the present, and past and present were equally haunted. . . . The house belonged to the dead. I was living with ghosts" (*WW* 221–22).

Had I been Henry Anderson, I might have been uneasy about the implications of Glasgow's first two Gothic stories, published in 1916 and 1917. Both "The Shadowy Third" and "Dare's Gift," products of the early stages of Glasgow's and Anderson's relationship, contain male protagonists who are killed through the agency of a female character who shows no regret. I doubt that Glasgow felt literally murderous toward Anderson, but these first two stories in particular reveal a persistent underlying anxiety about men and marriage, subjects that Glasgow's relationship with Anderson made it impossible for her to ignore. Her ambivalence about marrying Anderson, compounded by her frank dislike for her father, informs these stories, which exude suspicion, even hostility, toward men and the things Glasgow often associated with them—war, domination of women, capitalistic exploitation. Moreover, in both tales it is not the isolated Gothic heroine who must take action; rather, it is the agency of a woman in conjunction with another woman (or other women) that overpowers a male character or characters.

Conflicting Loyalties in "The Shadowy Third"

Nowhere is anxiety about heterosexuality and marriage more evident than in "The Shadowy Third." Nurse Margaret Randolph, the naive first-person narrator, has recently completed her nurses' training in her native South. Like Virginia Pendleton, her general education seems to have been based on lack of knowledge; her sense of reality, particularly as it pertains to relations between men and women, is gleaned from sentimental novels. Summoned to private duty as nurse for the wife of the "great surgeon" Roland Maradick, she sees herself as playing heroine to his hero.[17] Already under his "spell," Margaret observes that he was "born to be a hero to women" (*CS* 57, 53).

What Maradick, accustomed to hero "worship" (CS 57), fails to anticipate is Margaret's even stronger attraction to his wife. Counting on Margaret's inexperience and infatuation to aid him in assuming control of his wife's fortune, Maradick is blinded by faith in his own sexual power. Margaret quickly comprehends the source of Mrs. Maradick's "malady": she sees the ghost of her young daughter, Dorothea, who died of pneumonia two months earlier, and Margaret sees the child as well (CS 57, 58). As Margaret lives in the house and shares Mrs. Maradick's ghostly vision, she discovers the exploitative side of Maradick's sexual power. Just as Margaret sees the child, she perceives the consequences of marriage: since marrying her husband, Mrs. Maradick's daughter has died, her property has been threatened, and she is literally imprisoned in her own room with the constant threat of more permanent exile to an asylum. What Margaret learns is to fear male sexuality and its links to male economic and professional status, and to cherish a female community that cannot sustain itself under the same roof with men. The message of the story manifestly asserts that men and women cannot live together; someone has to go, and the conflict in the story revolves around the question of who is powerful enough to decide who stays.

The house itself is the modern version of the "contested castle" that Kate Ferguson Ellis sees as central to Gothic fiction. In "The Shadowy Third" power resides with whoever controls the house, Mrs. Maradick's family home on Fifth Avenue, and the house itself is the source of the underlying tension between Roland Maradick and his wife. The house, Margaret eventually learns, was an issue in a disagreement between the Maradicks before their marriage. Though Maradick wanted to move "uptown" after marrying his wife, she had been "obstinate" and had "clung, against his wishes" to her ancestral home (CS 55). Mrs. Maradick dies in the asylum shortly after her husband succeeds in sending her there, and Margaret learns from the housekeeper that Roland Maradick has already made plans for the house's destruction. Committed to the upward mobility (even moving "uptown") that denotes capitalistic success, Maradick has sold the property to developers who will build an "apartment-house" (69).

Dr. Maradick's fixation on the house as a source of power has its basis in the matrilineage metaphorically represented by it and reproduced in the matrifocality of the story itself. Mrs. Maradick "had been born in the house" and "had never wanted to live anywhere else" (*CS* 55). When Dr. Maradick first met his future wife, she was a widow living in her house with her daughter. The butler, Gabriel, had come with Mrs. Maradick's mother; it is his subservient position and his connection with matrilineage that allows him, though male, to see Dorothea's ghost. The house also serves as a double reminder that a woman loses selfhood in marriage. For one thing, *Mrs.* Maradick's name is only that, except for the brief moment when we are given her "maiden name," Calloran, a name that functions more as a reminder of the traditional heroine's plot as she is transmitted from father to husband than it does as a marker of independent selfhood. Second, in marrying, Mrs. Maradick relinquished her monetary inheritance; she loses personhood as one who can rightfully inherit. The fact that the money passes matrilineally to her daughter makes it necessary for Roland Maradick to extinguish the daughter's personhood too. Dorothea "was so much like her [mother] that you would have known them anywhere for mother and daughter" (54). Mrs. Maradick has "clung" to the house, understandably, because it represents her identity apart from her husband, and because, in the familiar ideology of separate spheres, it is the only place in which she has a measure of control. And it is the only power she can pass on to her daughter as well.

Astutely and wickedly, Roland Maradick uses the very seat of his wife's ostensible power to highlight her actual powerlessness. By turning her domestic interior space into a prison, he reminds her that the much more powerful patriarchal world still does the defining. Like the doctor-husband of the narrator in Charlotte Perkins Gilman's *The Yellow Wallpaper* (1892), Dr. Maradick uses his professional power to justify his treatment of his wife's "malady" (*CS* 57). Also as in Gilman's story, and in a Brontëan Gothic plot device, here the wife is literally incarcerated in her room on the third story; she is "allowed" only the "fresh air" from "her windows" (65) and is "never left by herself for an instant" (53). Mrs. Maradick says she can't go outside because her husband " 'wouldn't like it' "; Roland "doesn't want me to go out,' " she tells Margaret (66). In emphatic contrast, Dr. Maradick "was always going somewhere"; as Margaret says, "I believe he didn't dine at home a single evening that winter" (63). Maradick's oppressive use of the domestic space that supposedly grounds his wife's authority to remind her of her lack of it also has another subtle parallel to Gilman's text. S. Weir Mitchell, the nerve specialist whose famous "rest cure" treatment Gilman's and Glasgow's female characters both endure, reveals in *Fat and Blood: And How to Make Them* (1877) his similarly vindictive motives:

> The rest I like for them is not at all their notion of rest. To lie abed half the day, and sew a little and read a little, and be interesting and excite sympathy, is all very well, but when they are bidden to stay in bed a month, and neither to read, write, nor sew, and to have one nurse,—who is not a relative,—then rest becomes for some women a rather bitter medicine, and they are glad enough to accept the order to rise and go about when the doctor issues a mandate which has become pleasantly welcome and eagerly looked for.

Mitchell's emphasis on the importance of the doctor's superior will, of his forceful character, of his ability to induce in women a "tractable" nature, further dichotomizes stereotypical masculine and feminine personalities.[18] Glasgow's story is a reminder that (male) doctors' use of professionally conferred authority—conferred in the public world that marked men's more significant separate sphere—was not a dead issue more than twenty years after the publication of Gilman's text.

Mrs. Maradick's attempt to hold on to a matrilineal heritage that confers, if not much actual power, at least a stronger female identity, reinforces and is reinforced by the women's community that subtly dominates the story. The story opens on the narrator and her superintendent, Miss Hemphill, who also happens to be her mother's distant relative (CS 52). "[B]ig," "strong," and "resolute," Miss Hemphill's practical nature contrasts to Margaret's overactive imagination (52). Her diffident exterior, we come to realize, results not so much from the "impersonal" quality Margaret remarks as from the necessity of surviving in a world that requires that she suppress the fullest expression of any nurturing instincts, an ironic requirement, given her profession. Margaret says to Miss Hemphill: " 'I can't help putting myself into my cases. I suppose one ought not to?' " Miss Hemphill's reply to Margaret's stereotypically feminine response to her "cases" is an assessment of what happens to a woman in the public world of work where her assets are devalued: "It isn't a question of what one ought to do, but of what one must. When you are drained of every bit of sympathy and enthusiasm, and have got nothing in return for it, not even thanks, you will understand why I try to keep you from wasting yourself" (53). One assumes that Miss Hemphill mothers the other nurses as she does Margaret; the images in the first few pages are of a female community of nurses sporadically intruded upon by male doctors, including Maradick.

Margaret's infatuation with Roland Maradick gives way to allegiance to his wife. Ultimately, this alliance weaves a matrifocal web made up of Mrs. Maradick, her ghostly daughter Dorothea, and Margaret herself, who becomes a surrogate mother to Dorothea. Margaret forms a sympathetic emotional bond with Mrs. Maradick even before they meet; just hearing the story of Mrs. Maradick's thwarted inheritance makes her feel "too emotional." Intuiting Mrs. Maradick's "pathos" (CS 55) beforehand, Margaret forms her attachment immediately when they meet: "I liked her from the start, and I think she must have seen it. . . . There was something about [Mrs. Maradick]—I don't know what it was—that made you love her as soon as she looked at you" (59).

That the narrator is meant to be seen as a double for Mrs. Maradick connects the story to its Gothic tradition, where such imaging is a staple, and makes a feminist statement about female identity. Translating her initial allegiance to Roland Maradick into identification with his wife marks Margaret's shift from a mediated self to a more directly perceived self. That is, Margaret refuses Maradick's "charming way . . . with women" (CS 57) and instead embraces the community formed by intuitive recognition among Mrs. Maradick, her daughter, and Margaret. In doing so, Margaret signifies her willingness to accept a female identity formed by the "too emotional" ties Miss Hemphill warned her not to succumb to, because they do not fit into the patriarchal world of professions. When Margaret says early in the story that she "would have died for" Roland Maradick (57), she says much more than she realizes at the time: as a woman, she *would* have "died" for him, giving up her personhood for the objecthood he demanded of her. Mrs. Maradick later literally dies for her husband, as did Dorothea (whose illness Roland failed to cure, according to Mrs. Maradick). That Margaret emphatically does not die for him, but instead causes him to die for her, points to the lesson Margaret learns (as Glasgow was learning) by almost *becoming* Mrs. Maradick and then rewriting her story with a different ending: women must refuse objectification by men and insist on writing their own stories, forming their own selves.

The issue of writing or telling a woman's story takes on another layer of meaning in this short story as language becomes one of the pawns in the underlying power play between men and women. Early in "The Shadowy Third," it is Roland Maradick's voice that most attracts Margaret and signals his mesmerizing power over her: "Even more than his appearance . . . even more than his charm and his magnificence, I think, the beauty and sympathy in his voice won my heart. It was a voice, I heard someone say afterwards, that ought always to speak poetry" (CS 54). It is on his verbal authority that Mrs. Maradick is assumed to be unbalanced. By saying that " 'We wish to avoid, if possible, having to send her away' " (57), he both prepares for just that eventuality and removes himself as the primary cause of it, thus protecting himself from criticism or accusation. It is important that Margaret (like her precursor Virginia Pendleton) is literally struck dumb in his presence. Her response to him is merely to bow (reinforcing her willingness to play a subservient role): "To save my life I couldn't have spoken without blushing the redder" (57), she thinks. Margaret finds that she can "only murmur in response" (57) to Maradick's "carefully chosen words about his wife's illness" (57). Only after their initial interview does it "occur" to Margaret "that he had really told me nothing. I was as perplexed about the nature of Mrs. Maradick's malady as I had been when I entered the house" (57). His authority lay in his words and in his recognition that he does not have to "really" say anything to wield it.

Mirroring Margaret's experience (or, more accurately, mirrored by it), Mrs. Maradick's malady is partly symptomized by her symbolic loss of voice and the accompanying loss of authority to convince others of her story's truth. When Mrs. Maradick learns that Margaret has "seen" her daughter, she warns Margaret: " 'You must not tell him— you must not tell any one that you have seen her!' " (CS 60). Recognizing the defiance marked by her own telling, Mrs. Maradick wants Margaret to make sure no one is "listening" at her door (60). She recognizes methods used to render her verbally powerless: " 'There is no use telling people things that nobody believes' " (60). When Margaret asks why Roland Maradick would have killed Dorothea, as Mrs. Maradick insists he did, Mrs. Maradick's voicelessness indicates her inability to control her own environment against the superior power of her husband: "she moaned inarticulately, as if the horror of her thoughts were too great to pass into speech" (60). She is not allowed to speak about the very thing that others are using against her; her oppression has as its source her ineffectual attempts to give literal voice to her thoughts.

Margaret's wresting of power from the authority symbolized by Maradick, Dr. Brandon the "famous alienist" (CS 62), and the unnamed "second alienist" brought in for consultation (66), is figured, appropriately, in her assumption of verbal authority. Defying Roland Maradick, Margaret narrates the confrontation in which she assumes her authority verbally. When Dr. Maradick asks her if Mrs. Maradick had "allude[d] in any way to her—to her hallucination," his hesitancy to name what he sees as his wife's problem is countered by Margaret's assured and calculated response:

> "She talked quite rationally," I replied after a moment.
> "What did she say?"
> "She told me how she was feeling, that she missed her child, and that she walked a little every day about her room." (63)

In choosing to "take sides" with Mrs. Maradick against Dr. Maradick, Margaret also defies Dr. Brandon, who has just recommended Mrs. Maradick's commitment to an asylum. Unlike Margaret, who fuses personal and professional personae in her emotional attachment to her "cases," Brandon "deals instinctively with groups instead of with individuals" (62). In verbally asserting her own authority, Margaret assaults the male bastions of medical and marital wisdom represented by Roland Maradick and Brandon and substitutes her own diagnosis.

During this confrontation Margaret responds to "invisible waves of sense-perception" warning her that she "must stand either with Mrs. Maradick or against her" (CS 63). These "waves" also describe the difference in the story between the women's intuitive (even supernatural) bonds of connection and the rational (scientific) and power-mongering bonds that connect the men. Margaret weighs carefully her answer to Roland Maradick's final challenge to her, and she feels the pull of his literally captivating charm even as she realizes it must be resisted: "the man held me captive even while I defied

him." Her answer?: " 'I believe that your wife is as sane as I am—
or as you are' " (64). Once Margaret has assumed responsibility for
telling Mrs. Maradick's story in defiance of the men's version of it,
"Mrs. Maradick seemed to grow stronger" (64). The competition for
authority returns as verbal power play when the moment arrives for
Mrs. Maradick to be taken away. Significantly, Dr. Brandon's announcement is evasive; he says she's going to "the country for a fortnight or so" (66). Mrs. Maradick, too late, tries defiance by naming
her destination: " 'You are going to take me to an asylum' " (67). For
a moment, Margaret seems to succeed at staying Brandon's hand. She
gains time by—what else, now that verbal authority seems the avenue
to control—beseeching him to wait because " 'There are things I must
tell you' " (67). But Margaret loses what little power she had gained
when, seeing the apparition of Dorothea, she subsequently cries out:
"After this can you doubt?' " She "threw out the words almost savagely" (67), but they are merely thrown back to silence and subdue
her as Dr. Brandon sarcastically repeats her very language (68). Brandon triumphs over Margaret just as Roland has defeated his wife: by
turning her source of power against her. As she leaves, Mrs. Maradick
asks that Margaret almost literally become her by assuming a role as
mother to Dorothea. When Mrs. Maradick dies "several months" later
in the asylum, the named actual cause of death is as vague (if pointedly
metaphorical) as the cause of her incarceration: "heart failure" (68).

However, though Margaret stays in the house as Maradick's office
nurse, she ceases to see Dorothea, as her bond with Mrs. Maradick
weakens. Mirroring the critical readings that emphasize Glasgow's
love affairs, critics have assumed that Margaret's jealousy over Maradick's approaching remarriage causes her again to turn on him.[19] I
read Margaret's change as one result of her realization that she has
allowed herself to be duped again, that she has forgotten the lessons
taught her by the life of subordination that Mrs. Maradick led, that
the new wife will lead, that Margaret is leading. She had let her "me-
thodical" (CS 69) life as Dr. Maradick's nurse crowd out memories
of Mrs. Maradick until she "had scarcely a minute left in which to
remember" (68) her. She had even begun to "persuade" herself that
Dorothea had only been "an optical illusion" (68). Just after learning
of the impending marriage and, what seems much worse, the impend-

ing destruction of Mrs. Maradick's house, Margaret, while sitting alone, "[a]lmost unconsciously" repeats a bit of verse Mrs. Maradick had once quoted to her. As she does so, Margaret sees Dorothea playing in the outside garden Mrs. Maradick had been excluded from, and knows the child to be "as real to me as the ground on which she trod" (70). Speaking *as* Mrs. Maradick, Margaret again evinces the oneness between the women and the child, and reestablishes a power born of female community.

The ending demonstrates the frightening potential power in women's community. As Margaret literally calls to Dr. Maradick, summoning him to a medical emergency, she "distinctly" sees the child's jump rope that will cause him to trip and fall three flights of stairs to his death. Language is power: Maradick's humming changes to "a cry of surprise or terror" as Margaret's "scream of warning died in [her] throat" (CS 71). The verbal power that could have saved him becomes instead an instrument of his death. He falls "at [her] feet," killed, not by a "misstep in the dimness," as "the world believes," but by "an invisible judgment" at the "very moment when he most wanted to live" (72). Just when Maradick had successfully disposed of his wife and her child, inherited her money, planned the destruction of her home, and become engaged to her replacement, he was killed. The invisible judgment is that of a spirit of female community represented by just those things he thought he had gained control over: his wife, her child, her house, and her nurse. Maradick's mistake was in overestimating his own power over women and underestimating the power of women in community. His masculine power had depended on feminine compliance; his "charm" relied on a willingness to be charmed, just as a tradition of submissive womanhood had often conformed to a male definition of it. But in the end, Margaret refuses to play. By "becoming" Mrs. Maradick and making Roland Maradick "die" for her instead of the other way around, Margaret is left in the house with the ghost of the child, thereby reclaiming the matrilineal heritage he had worked so assiduously to undercut. Ironically, Maradick has become the "angel in the house," presumably presiding powerfully over it but actually defeated by it; and he is as dead—and as powerless—as other such "angels" have been. Margaret's retrospective narrative of these events is testimony that while her "scream of warning" may have died before its utterance, she regained the verbal authority manifest in her very telling. Like Ellen Glasgow herself, Margaret as storyteller found the voice to tell the women's story that had been suppressed.

The Struggle for a Female Voice: "Dare's Gift"

The subject of women finding the voice to articulate their own experience is even more prominent in "Dare's Gift," published a year later, in 1917. As in "The Shadowy Third," language is a medium through which women gain power, and the necessity of women's united efforts in telling their own stories is evident even across historical boundaries. The horror of Massé's "Gothic repetition," manifest in the story's two-part structure and the doubled female protagonists, is that Mildred Beckwith "wakes up" metaphorically to the recognition that Lucy Dare's nightmare is still true in the reality of her own life half a century later. Both tales within the story tell of the women's betraying the men they love: Lucy Dare her Union lover, Mildred her attorney husband. The parallel structure of "Dare's Gift" reproduces the identification of Lucy Dare and Mildred Beckwith across the barrier of time, as the latter reenacts in the present the Civil War story of the former. But the women do not tell their own stories. Rather, they are encased in versions of them told by male narrators. Further, as Lynette Carpenter has observed, the story's placement in *The Shadowy Third and Other Stories*—between narratives by women sympathetic to their female protagonists—makes us question the veracity and reliability of the masculine point of view in "Dare's Gift."[20] As the story opens, the male narrator's limited perspective suggests a problem with women's stories told by men: even though it will be wrong, Harold Beckwith will tell the story that really belongs to his wife (as later Dr. Lakeby will tell the same story that belongs to her precursor, Lucy Dare), making "truth" even harder to get at than it is anyway. Both Lucy and Mildred are inscribed in some male's version of events that should be of the women's own telling.

The doubled structure also serves as a commentary on the historical progress of women, especially their forays into the traditionally male public world, a subject that by 1917 had received (and would continue to receive) much attention.[21] The competitive male spaces represented by war in Lucy Dare's life and by corporate law in Mildred

Beckwith's are accessible to women, if at all, only on terms already set in place. Lucy and Mildred can only enter those worlds through disruptive behavior—here, through betrayal—that directly threatens the men who set the terms and establish the discourse within the public sphere. In accepting a version of the "battle of the sexes" that Gilbert and Gubar in the first volume of *No Man's Land* see as paradigmatic in the culture and literature of the early twentieth century, "Dare's Gift" reveals men's anxiety over women's perceived threatening entry into their public world and women's anger at continued powerlessness and at the male anxiety that exaggerates women's progress. That Mildred's story is essentially the same as Lucy's expresses a distressing truth: the history of women's experience does repeat itself, and progress can seem merely chronological. Indeed, if anything, Mildred's case represents regression; though historically recent, her power seems lessened. She is physically displaced at the will of (male) others, and she may be emotionally unstable as well.

It is evident as the story opens that Harold Beckwith is a confused and unreliable narrator, and this becomes even more apparent as his retrospective narrative unfolds. From wondering a year after the events whether "the thing actually happened," to asserting that "every mystery" ("I admit it readily!") has its "rational explanation," to believing with equal assurance that "the impossible really happened" (CS 90), Harold's Poesque vacillation from near-hysterical assertion to quavering doubt destabilizes both the reader and Harold's narrative from the start, and seriously undercuts his ability even to tell his own story, let alone someone else's.

We learn early that the story will be about his wife. Harold reveals that the narrative's "impossible occurrence" concerns "the erratic behaviour of Mildred during the spring"[22] they spent at Dare's Gift, their rented country house, and that a year before the story's events Mildred had had her "first nervous breakdown" (CS 90). As in "The Shadowy Third" (and, as Carpenter notes, *The Yellow Wallpaper*), the solution named by "Drayton, the great specialist," is to send Mildred to live in the country, isolated from the frenetic activity of Washington, D.C. This familiar prescription for women under male medical care around the turn of the century required that Mildred be relegated to the private, domestic sphere, away from a man's world of public enterprise. While Harold "as a busy man" can only afford to be away "once a fortnight" (90), Mildred should be sent "away from Washington until she recovered her health" (90). The subtle message from the men (who presumably understand these things) is that Mildred need only be reminded of her proper place, and emotional health will follow.

However, Mildred clearly knows her place only too well, and it is more likely adhering to it, not fleeing from it, that has brought on any emotional instability. Dare's Gift, as the location that represents Mildred's assigned place as a woman—that is, her separate domestic sphere—constantly reinforces her undeserved secondary status. A friend's statement, which Harold takes as a compliment to the Beckwiths' marital happiness—" 'As if Mildred's final word would be anything but a repetition of yours!' "—testifies not to the "perfect harmony" that Harold sees in his marriage but to the subordination of his wife. The same friend "classified wives as belonging to two distinct groups—the group of those who talked and knew nothing about their husbands' affairs, and the group of those who knew everything and kept silent." Mildred, of course, belonged to "the latter division" (CS 95). Mildred's wifely perfection is thus described in terms of her silence; the quality that defines success in a wife inscribes her inability to speak for herself. In contrast to "The Shadowy Third," both the structure and the narrative point of view of "Dare's Gift" give the story its main thrust: the insufficiency in the telling of women's stories by anyone other than themselves.

Clearly, Harold shares his friend's valuation of self-effacement in a wife. He praises Mildred's unwavering devotion to *his* "enthusiasms" (CS 95), which leads him to rehearse regularly his cases with her "because," he says, "it helped to clarify *my* opinions" (98; emphasis added). At one point when Mildred "returned with irritation to some obscure legal point" (98) Harold had omitted, one wonders if it is only the spirit of the place that is making Mildred—whose legal astuteness at times surpasses her husband's—feel irritable. Despite the perfect accord between Harold and Mildred that is supposed to be a given, their relationship is clearly asymmetrical. When, the night after he has told his legal secrets to Mildred, Harold hears the "thousand voices" spoken by "the old house" in the country, he does not realize that they are giving voice to his "quiet" Mildred, trying to tell the stories that she cannot (99). Significantly, when she betrays him it is by telling *his* story to the newspaper, revealing the damaging evidence he had covered up. The exposé, headlined in "one of the *Observer*'s sensational 'war extras' " (101), highlights the extent to which Harold and Mildred's relationship has become a battle zone of sorts. Instead of "news of the great French drive," he reads Mildred's version of his confessions to her, a declaration of war by Mildred on Harold through her appropriation of his story and through her public telling. After her betrayal, a sign of Mildred's presumed instability is that "She talks as if she were quite out of her head" (102). When the reader, along with Harold, sees her, we behold *not* a woman "out of her head" but a calm and determined one: "In her chamber, standing very straight, with hard eyes, Mildred met me. 'I had to do it, Harold,' she said coldly— so coldly that my outstretched arms fell to my sides. 'I had to tell all I knew.' " Repeating her statement that she " 'had to do it,' " she also denies remorse: " 'I would do it again' " (103). Harold reasons that if she defied him and would do so again, she must be crazy: "I knew that Mildred's mind was unhinged' " (103).

Part two moves from Mildred's betrayal of her husband to Lucy Dare's of her fiancé. As in part one, Lucy's story is told not by Lucy but by Dr. Lakeby, the local physician called in to look after Mildred. The failure of men in general and of professional men in particular to understand and articulate women's experience calls into question Lakeby's trustworthiness as narrator of a woman's story. Drayton, Mildred's physician in Washington, had prescribed a peaceful rural existence for Mildred's recovery from her nervous breakdown; in fact, she only became more agitated. Lakeby's treatment contradicts Drayton's: " 'Dr. Lakeby says she will be all right again as soon as she gets back to Washington" (CS 103). The conflicting prognoses by the two doctors undercut the reliability of Lakeby's narration and should make us question his authoritative tone. But he easily offers Lucy's experience as evidence that the house is "saturated by a thought. It is haunted by treachery" (104). If that is true, then of course Mildred is exonerated for her betrayal; the house made her do it. The problem with Lakeby's interpretation is that it removes as a motive Mildred's simple assertion of will; it denies her the agency that she had finally found. It also denies Lucy Dare the same active will; the earlier (and later) betrayals in the house (briefly revealed but not developed) only reflect some spirit of place and not female anger or frustration or sheer determination. Lakeby's assessment of Lucy's "one instant of sacrifice" (106) captures in essence the historical version of the silencing of women. "Lucy Dare," he says, "has not even a name among us to-day." Misplaced historically because "the thing she did, though it might have made a Greek tragedy, was alien to the temperament of the people among whom she lived," Lucy Dare is "one of the mute inglorious heroines of history" (106). Lucy is "mute," Mildred "quiet"; both are inscribed in and circumscribed by male versions of the stories they are not empowered to tell. Lucy is as exiled from the public realm of war as Mildred is from the world of corporate law, and Lucy's only recourse, like Mildred's, is in the heroics of betrayal.

Lucy is still alive, and her continued existence confirms the story's sense that not much has changed from Lucy's story to Mildred's, from the conditions of life during the Civil War to World War I and the concurrent gendered battles waged in individual homes. Lucy, "never much of a talker" (*CS* 117), sits in her nursing home and knits mufflers for the war effort. In parodic reminder of a woman's natural place in the domestic sphere, Lucy "gravely" comments on her knitting: " 'It gives me something to do, this work for the Allies. It helps to pass the time, and in an Old Ladies' Home one has so much time on one's hands' " (117). No sentimental belief in the good of self-sacifice keeps Lucy monotonously "knitting—knitting—" (117), but the boredom of a woman's life—of an old *lady*'s life—still confined to domesticity.

That Lucy and Mildred in their betrayals speak the same words suggests some hope in women's united voices. At least *their* stories overlap in the direct quotes that reveal their own words and not someone else's, Glasgow seems to imply. Their use of identical language can suggest a lack of progress in women's lives, but the act of shared storytelling offers the glimmer of promise that we saw in "The Shadowy Third" and that has become a steady star in the constellation of Glasgow's hopes for finding a comfortable place in the women's traditions she found so problematic. The problem remains, however, in the male telling that isolates women from their stories, as mirrored in the structural representation of that isolation in "Dare's Gift." Mildred never even hears Lucy's story; only Harold learns it, in company with his male friend and as told by Dr. Lakeby. The two women speak the same language quite literally, but they are never allowed to know that. And Harold, early in his retrospective narrative, reveals his continued ignorance of his wife, of Lucy, of women, when he confesses a year later that "for my part, the occurrence remains, like the house in its grove of cedars, wrapped in an impenetrable mystery. I don't in the least pretend to know how or why the thing happened. . . . Mildred's share in it will, I think, never become clear to me" (CS 96–97). Moreover, Harold doesn't "talk over" the betrayal with his wife; he never gets her version of events: "What she felt, what she imagined, what she believed, I have never asked her" (97). The difficulty, of course, is precisely as Harold unwittingly describes it: he does not know or understand Mildred's "share" in the events, because Mildred's story is always subordinated to his. The problem on a personal level reproduces the larger one that Glasgow saw with increasing clarity: until the Mildreds of the world are given a voice, the Harolds of the world will never know their stories. Worse yet, perhaps, Glasgow argues, the Mildreds of the world cannot transmit their stories to one another, and are even in danger of not understanding their own.

The next few years bring important transformations in Glasgow's life. In 1916 and 1917 she had been confused about her relationship with Anderson and probably with Bennett as well, but by 1920 much of Glasgow's ambivalence had been resolved, as she abandoned any serious marriage plans. There is a marked shift in the tone of Anderson's letters—and in the relationship itself—beginning in late 1919, about the time Anderson permanently returned from Europe and the war. The letters are less warmly personal, the conflicts less important, the visits, one infers, less regular. Personal differences between Glasgow and Anderson are still evident, especially around late summer and early fall of 1920, but Anderson seems more exasperated than distressed at them, more tired than angry. Saying that Glasgow is reading unintended insults into his letters, Anderson enjoins her to "throw all this abstract discussion aside" and enjoy her trip to Maine. A sense of wanting to put their difficult relationship in the past and try something lighter comes through in Anderson's final advice to himself and to Glasgow: "We have both been serious so long, that we have almost forgotten how to smile, and should learn again." [23] At least according to her retrospective account in *The Woman Within*, Glasgow agreed. As the "grasp" of the "bond" between her and Anderson "weakened and relaxed," she says, she felt "at last free. If falling in love could be bliss," she discovered, "falling out of love could be blissful tranquility." Her sense of the humor in their relationship exceeds Anderson's; she says that the "unruly spirit of comedy has insisted upon breaking into the tragic mood of this episode." The freedom she associates with the shift in her relationship with Anderson is tied philosophically to the larger freedom from marriage. According to Glasgow, "The obscure instinct that had warned me, in my early life, against marriage, was a sound instinct." Her sigh of relief is nearly audible as she elaborates: "Yes, it was true. I was free from chains. I belonged to myself" (*WW* 243–46).

Anne Virginia Bennett's return to live in Glasgow's house at One West Main by November of 1920 is one marker of the change in Glasgow's life. Though the situation was not as simple as shifting her loyalty from Anderson to Bennett, I think that Glasgow increasingly recognized the larger implications of her relationships with those two people. Anderson had come to represent marriage and the unwelcome restrictions it brought; Bennett meant freedom to work and develop creatively and personally. In *The Woman Within* Glasgow describes Anderson as fundamentally interested in his own life and career and Bennett as the person who, Glasgow says, "[m]ore than anyone else" since her sister Cary's death, "has had my interests at heart" (*WW* 216). Seeing Bennett's companionship as facilitating her own self-development and Anderson's as hampering it enables Glasgow in her next two stories to focus on her newly re-visioned acceptance of the concept of female identity formed in context, particularly in affiliation with other women. Both "The Past" (1920) and "Whispering Leaves" (1923) consider self-definition shaped in relation to a female other (or others), past and present.

Contesting Women's History: "The Past"

In "The Past," Glasgow's ideological battle with her (personal) past—with a woman's (cultural) past—takes the form of a struggle between a deceased former wife and a present wife, the two Mrs. Vanderbridges, over their husband, Roger Vanderbridge. That they are so obviously doubled—both have the same name, the same husband, the same house—is complicated by the fact that the narrator, Miss Wrenn, a newly hired secretary to the second Mrs. Vanderbridge, is also a double for her employer. (As Meeker observes, it seems likely that Glasgow would have been thinking of Bennett, her own "secretary," as a model for Miss Wrenn.) The intertwining of female identity thus forces the issue of connection and separation and highlights questions Glasgow had been addressing in her own life. How does a woman both connect and separate from her past, accept a place in a woman's tradition but reject its self-destructive qualities? How does a woman delineate the boundaries of self without inviting isolation, or, conversely, how does she connect with (female) others without giving up on the idea of a separate self?

"The Past" is appropriately titled not only for its obvious accuracy in describing a story in which a past wife's haunted and haunting memory is defeated but also because Glasgow herself rejects a personal past of anxiety about men, women, marriage, and the traditions that describe and circumscribe them. It is a story more about the potentiality of horror safely circumvented than about horror's continuing threat. Anxiety about marriage is less palpably present here than in either "The Shadowy Third" or "Dare's Gift." Ambivalence about marriage and its implications gives way to triumphant certainty about the positive value of women's relationships, though Glasgow resists any simplistic formulation of sisterhood (a resistance whose importance Betsy Erkkila has emphasized in *The Wicked Sisters*): the primary adversary in the story is also a woman. Here, in the most optimistic of Glasgow's Gothic stories, the haunted past is safely overcome, the strength rather than the weakness of the women characters is emphasized, and cooperative rather than competitive relationships among women are privileged. In a fine essay, Gayle Greene discusses women's relationship with the past as a central concern of contemporary feminist fiction. "Memory," she argues, "is especially important to anyone who cares about change, for forgetting dooms us to repetition";[24] hence the obvious significance of memory and the past for feminist fiction that envisions a restructured cultural order. Glasgow, appropriating the naturally unsettling world of supernatural occurrence to mirror her theme of unsettling a patriarchal order, uses in her story an abrupt break with the past to represent metaphorically her substituted new reality, one based on cooperative female friendship. She thus resists the repetition that Greene believes should be changed and that Massé sees as central to Gothic horror.

Appropriately for a story that takes as its subjects the blurred distinctions between past and present and between women as they define themselves in connection with other women, "The Past" is obsessed with boundaries, the divisions between them, and the violence that accompanies their transgressions, subjects that Eve Kosofsky Sedgwick has addressed perceptively in *The Coherence of Gothic Conventions.* Glasgow's story revolves around the boundaries between past and present, dead and living, self and Other, male and female, art and life, language and reality, reality and illusion. The story's title immediately announces the boundary between past and present, soon to become fluid as Miss Wrenn discovers that the ghost of the first Mrs. Vanderbridge, who died fifteen years earlier, still inhabits the house. When Miss Wrenn first arrives at the Vanderbridge residence, "one of those big houses just off Fifth Avenue" (CS 119), what Sedgewick calls the Gothic quality of "within" presents itself in the distinction between the world outside the house and the enclosed world inside it.[25] Standing outside, Miss Wrenn notes the house's "magnificence" and then moves to an imprisoning interior: "when the black iron doors swung together behind me, I felt as if I were shut inside a prison" (119).

That the boundaries between past and present, outside and inside, extend to include uncertainty about the separation between self and self is soon evident. Mrs. Vanderbridge has hired Miss Wrenn because of their resemblance: the "remarkable similarity of our handwriting," their shared Southern origins, their education at the same "little academy for young ladies in Fredericksburg." Between them, in Miss Wrenn's view, there was "a bond of sympathy" (CS 119). Boundaries and their transversal are suggested by Mrs. Vanderbridge's name, "bridge" signifying an attempt to construct a way to penetrate boundaries, to move across to the other side. Miss Wrenn first realizes that the other woman she has observed in the house is a ghost when she sees the maid walk "straight through the grey figure and carefully place the log on the andirons" (130). This literally permeable ego boundary most dramatically illustrates a problem for women in defining a self as separate from others. The immediate attraction between the women, like that of Margaret Randolph and Mrs. Maradick in "The Shadowy Third," defines the doubling of the two characters as a mirroring of similarity rather than difference. This is not the case of a self and a threatening other, but of a "second self."[26]

There is a threatening other, however, in the person—or rather, in the apparition—of the first Mrs. Vanderbridge. She is even called "the Other One" (CS 128). In a story about the importance of cooperative female friendship, why include this woman as a vindictive, threatening other? For one thing, Glasgow is obviously aware of the foolishness of romanticizing female friendship and thereby eliding discord between women. More importantly, however, the answer lies in a recognition—the reader's as well as Glasgow's—of the destructiveness of *some* women's traditions, the kind, Glasgow had come to discover, that had been shaped by men's definitions of women and by women's willingness to accept the mediated selves formed in light of those definitions. The "Other One"—the former Mrs. Vanderbridge—defined herself, and continues to do so, in relation to men. Her relationships to other women thus necessarily depend on competition, on jealousy, on possessiveness, on territoriality. *Her* boundaries, in contrast to the ideal of female cooperation represented primarily by the relationship between Miss Wrenn and the present Mrs. Vanderbridge, must be precisely delineated—he is mine; he is not yours; I draw the line here. The Other One's acceptance of a male-defined self is particularly well illustrated by the fact that she owes her very presence to Mr. Vanderbridge: " 'She is really a thought, you know. She is his thought of her—but he doesn't know that she is visible to the rest of us' " (132).

But it is "really" more complicated than that, as demonstrated by Mr. Vanderbridge's ineffectual attempts to banish his first wife simply by changing his mind about her, a solution that would logically follow from the fact that his thought brings her about in the first place. Early in the story, Miss Wrenn picks up a photograph of Mr. Vanderbridge. As she studies not the man himself but the self represented in the Florentine frame, she has "an uncanny feeling of familiarity" (CS 121). The source of this sensation is her "memory of an old portrait of a Florentine nobleman"; Mr. Vanderbridge's "photograph might have been taken from the painting" (121). In this fascinating display of successive removals from what Miss Wrenn would call reality (it is a current photograph resembling an old painting though the photo looks older; the painter's name may not have been known; the photographer, not the person, may be responsible for the "arresting" features of the face) lies a clue to the story's solution to the problem of the Other One. Though he is represented as a good man, Mr. Vanderbridge is solidly associated with an outdated past, and he is therefore incapable of imagining ways to effect change. What's more, the confusion of his ego boundary points to the limitations of defining the self in isolation. Frozen in his Florentine frame just as he is isolated in his self-absorption, his only contact is with the past and his very self is difficult to know. Any change in the story must be brought about, as ultimately it *is* brought about, by the women acting in concert. Any larger change in social perception about women, Glasgow further suggests, is the responsibility of women themselves.

In a statement that Raper uses to ground his argument that Glasgow in her short stories develops a new psychological theory of projection,[27] Miss Wrenn observes that she "has dealt so long with external details" that she has "almost forgotten the words that express invisible things" (CS 134). Miss Wrenn's assessment of her limitation is also a reflection on language as another boundary to be broken through in order to express any new reality. Here she sets up the opposition between this material world and another, intangible one, and implies the inadequacy of the language of one to articulate the other. Anticipating feminist theories of language that argue that language itself *is* patriarchal oppression, Glasgow here sees the necessity for reconfiguring not only the world but the words we use to describe it. In recognizing the problem that even arguments for the necessity of a new language must be made in the only language available, the old one, Glasgow does not really propose an answer. But she does suggest that the solution is as radical as a verbal confrontation with a ghost. From the initial similarity of Miss Wrenn's and Mrs. Vanderbridge's handwriting to the latter's intuition that she will "get on beautifully" with Miss Wrenn because she "can talk" to her, to Mrs. Vanderbridge's choice to challenge verbally the apparition of her predecessor, to the solution of the story in the burning of letters that condemn the first wife— all are reminders of the importance of language in "chang[ing] the thought of the past" (139). What Miss Wrenn has presumably learned in the very act of narrating her retrospective account is the necessity of recognizing that language is limited, that she must re-member (in an almost Lacanian sense of a lost world of connection to the mother) the "words that express invisible things."

Miss Wrenn learns that that lost world of connection is recaptured in cooperative relationship with other women. When she discovers letters from the first Mrs. Vanderbridge's lover and shows them to the present Mrs. Vanderbridge, she assumes the same competitive attitude that the first wife exhibits. As Mrs. Vanderbridge realizes what the letters represent—" 'She wasn't faithful to him while she lived. She wasn't faithful to him even while he was hers' " (CS 137)—Miss Wrenn's initial response is to fight back in kind: " 'Then you can save him from her. You can win him back!' " (137). However, Mrs. Vanderbridge refuses to enter into competition that requires her to "win" her own beloved husband; rather, she directly "confront[s] the ghost of the past" and announces that she will not "fight" her except with goodness. Miss Wrenn observes that Mrs. Vanderbridge "was looking directly at the phantom and there was no hate in her voice—there was only a great pity, a great sorrow and sweetness" (138). In recognizing female self-identity as reliant on cooperation and connection, Mrs. Vanderbridge "had triumphed over the past in the only way that she could triumph. She had won, not by resisting, but by accepting; not by violence, but by gentleness; not by grasping, but by renouncing" (139). Though "At the moment" Miss Wrenn "did not understand" (139), her retrospective narrative marks her subsequent comprehension. Miss Wrenn's description of her almost mystical sense of oneness with Mrs. Vanderbridge and the spiritual triumph she effects attests to the powerful message of the possibilities for female friendship, especially united in the cause of change. The narrator senses that Mrs. Vanderbridge had transformed the "curse" of competitiveness into "a blessing" of spiritually charged cooperation: "I had a curious sensation of being enfolded in a kind of spiritual glow and comfort," she tells us, while remarking the inadequacy of language to do so. "It was light without heat, glow without light—and yet it was none of these things. The nearest I can come to it is to call it a sense of blessedness—of blessedness that made you at peace with everything you had once hated" (138).

Miss Wrenn bonds with Mrs. Vanderbridge at a moment when the latter's behavior could be construed as traditionally feminine and subservient—she accepts rather than resists, is gentle rather than violent, renounces rather than grasps. Instead, however, her behavior indicates the complexity of Glasgow's own battle with "the past": the traditions of womanhood she wrestles with, as I have argued, entail embracing qualities that have been used to keep women in their places, but that Glasgow revises as strengths. The conclusion of "The Past" revolves around the narrator's coming to a similar understanding.

Matrilineage Reconceived in "Whispering Leaves"

If the past encroached upon the present in "The Past," insisting to be reconciled, in "Whispering Leaves" the narrator actively seeks her past, directly associates it with gender, and constructs an identity within the gendered traditions of her foremothers. As the story opens, the narrator, retelling events of fifteen years earlier (the same amount of time that had elapsed since the death of the first Mrs. Vanderbridge in "The Past"), as much as announces that she went to Whispering Leaves, her mother's childhood home, to find her place in a matrilineal heritage. That the story is a female bildungsroman (in addition to the Gothic tale that it becomes) is evident from the narrator's introduction. She travels to a South that has existed previously only in the heritage passed down from her mother: "Though I was never in Virginia before, I had been brought up on the traditions of my mother's old home on the Rappahannock" (CS 140). That she never has her own name, but is only called by her mother's—"Miss Effie"—suggests that Glasgow regards the narrator's feminized quest as universal. Even critics identify the narrator's own name as Miss Effie, glossing over the fact of her namelessness and therefore ignoring the implications of assuming her mother's name, just as Glasgow at some unknown point in her life began to sign her name by adding her mother's family name "Gholson." For Glasgow, "Miss Effie" is Everywoman, searching for her identity through her mother. The narrator's name—her *mother's* name—further signifies the importance of her heritage over even her individuality, or, perhaps more accurately, the importance of her heritage *to* her individuality.

As the narrator travels to Whispering Leaves at the story's beginning, her experiential unfamiliarity with the region, the house itself, and her "unknown cousins, the Blantons" give her a "delightful sense of expectancy and adventure" (CS 140). Her clear association of gendered upbringing with her quest is evident as she implicitly contrasts her male cousin, who now owns the house, with herself. In contrast to her own search for selfhood within the context of matriarchal history, the middle-aged Pelham Blanton, the present owner of Whispering Leaves, is "without a history" (140). The only facts known about him revolve around gendered experience: his first wife died giving birth (of course!) to their son seven years ago, and shortly thereafter Pelham married a neighbor. In contrast to the ahistorical perspective with which Pelham Blanton is satisfied (in spite of his living in the ancestral home, to which he seems to have no sentimental attachment), the narrator wrote "asking permission to visit the house in which my mother and so many of my grandmothers were born" (140). The lessons that the past will teach her—*has* taught her, since the story took place in the past—define her place in a matrifocal herstory of nurturing and female connection that, she learns, exists separate from marriage and actual childbearing. She discovers at the home of her mothers and grandmothers that literal wifehood and motherhood are unnecessary for a life of nurturing affiliation that can also incorporate independence and self-determination.

As the narrator begins to situate herself in the traditions of her foremothers, her affinity with nature forms a bond that she shares with many of the women of Whispering Leaves.[28] It is an affinity that at the same time separates her from those who work against that female heritage, such as Pelham and his second wife, Hannah Twine. The narrator's recollections indicate that she is attuned to her natural surroundings even away from Whispering Leaves. In the opening sentence she says that though she went to Whispering Leaves "fifteen years ago to-day," she can "still see that road stretching through vine-like shadows into the spring landscape" (CS 40). In some ways it is her memory of the expectancy and anticipation inherent in the renewal of spring that makes possible her own rebirth in the present as she searches through the past of her mother and many grandmothers: "The spring came early that year. When I descended from the train into the green and gold of the afternoon, I felt almost as if I were stepping back into some old summer" (140).

Glasgow's frequent association of birds with women makes the discussion between Uncle Moab, the driver, and the narrator about the abundant birds at Whispering Leaves resonate with implications about a woman's place, particularly as the birds quickly become associated with Mammy Rhody, who had come to Whispering Leaves with Clarissa, Pelham's first wife. There are so many birds that Uncle

Moab pronounces it a "bird year" (CS 142), saying that the birds are "never quiet" at Whispering Leaves (143). Though Uncle Moab finds the constant call of the birds annoying, the narrator thinks to herself: "Well, I liked birds! If there were nothing more dangerous than birds at Whispering Leaves, I could be happy there." Her observation that she "never saw so many redbirds" (142) soon blends into the figure of Mammy Rhody, darting from "the underbrush" in a noticeable red turban. Though the narrator does not know it yet, Mammy Rhody has been dead some two years; the narrator will soon learn that she and Pell, Pelham's only child from his first marriage, are the only ones who see Mammy Rhody. Pell says that Mammy Rhody, who "could tame anything going from an eagle to a wren," "tamed" these birds for him (146). When the narrator first sees Mammy Rhody and describes her face as "brown and wrinkled as a November leaf" (144), her association with the natural world is complete. Always out of doors, Mammy Rhody is one with the birds, with the foliage, and finally with the narrator herself: "Wherever the shadows crowded more thickly, wherever there was a sudden stir in the underbrush, I peered eagerly into the obscurity. . . . Though I had had only the briefest glimpse of her, I had found her serene leaf-brown face strangely attractive, almost . . . as if her mysterious black eyes . . . had penetrated to some secret chamber of my memory. I had never seen her before, and yet I felt as if I had known her all my life" (147).

The narrator's bond with Mammy Rhody through an association with nature introduces a complex network of women's connection: Mammy Rhody had been Clarissa's surrogate mother; Clarissa had been Pell's mother; the narrator, through her mother and called by her mother's name, is searching for her own place as a maternal figure. As she does with Mammy Rhody, the narrator also shares her love of nature with Clarissa. Mammy Rhody had promised to take care of Pell after Clarissa died. As Hannah Twine Blanton escorts the narrator to her upstairs room (a Brontëan "red room" that also reinforces her association with the redbirds and Mammy Rhody's red turban), she discerns a garden "framed in the open back door." Commenting on this lovely "vision of spring," the narrator receives an "indifferent" response from Hannah. Hannah tells her that the thickly planted narcissus the narrator described as making the garden seem "carpeted with moonlight" were planted by Clarissa; Hannah views the garden as something to be "got rid of" (*CS* 149). When the narrator later observes that the "garden is charming" because its informality "expresses itself, not some human being's idea of planting," Pelham notes, " 'That sounds like Clarissa' " (153). The child Pell's association with the outdoors, especially the garden, with the birds—his hand is "like a bird's claw" (152)—and with both his mother and Mammy Rhody, implicitly connects him to the narrator as well, as she becomes more and more associated with the two women who have cared for him in the past. When Richard K. Meeker complains that the excessive "horticultural detail" in "Whispering Leaves" is awkwardly symbolic, he ignores the importance of nature in emphasizing the almost metempsychotic connections among the women characters past and present.[29]

Our sense that the narrator is increasingly connected to Clarissa and even more to Mammy Rhody is also effected through language, as in Glasgow's other Gothic stories. In "Whispering Leaves," however, language as a theme is most important in a seemingly oxymoronic relation; it is as positive absence rather than as needed presence that language functions. The silence through which, paradoxically, the women characters communicate points to their intuitive affiliation positively (that is, seen as the presence of silence rather than the absence of speech) through the medium of some unrecognizable language they use with each other. Perhaps as a way of making possible a form of communication with the women of an earlier time, Glasgow shifted her focus away from the frustrations of searching for a place in a tradition comprised of foremothers with whom she could not communicate directly and toward an intuitive communication that she could feel as she redefined their heritage. Clarissa speaks to the narrator of "Whispering Leaves" most notably through the medium of nature, especially by way of the flowers that are her legacy and to which the narrator is strongly drawn. Seduced outside by the beauty of the flowers and their "provocative fragrance" (*CS* 150) and reaching the end of the garden walk to find herself in a "flowery space," the narrator realizes, "Never until that moment had I known what the rapture of smell could be" (150). When the narrator speaks the words about the garden (quoted above) that provoke Pelham to say she "*sounds* like Clarissa," we know that she is speaking *as* Clarissa, as her double.

Just as the nonverbal communication in "The Past" marks deeply felt communion between women, it is in Clarissa's outdoor world that the most important silent communication takes place: that between the narrator and Mammy Rhody in the implied spiritual presence of Clarissa. The narrator begins to understand that Mammy Rhody is the key to the mystery of her quest for her place in a matriarchal tradition. The narrator's first view of Mammy Rhody prompts her to wonder if Mammy Rhody had "nursed my mother and my grandmother" and if she perceived the narrator's "resemblance" to them. She intuitively perceives Mammy Rhody's role in her search for matriarchal teachings; she thinks that Mammy Rhody not only recognizes her, but also possesses "some secret which she wished to confide to me, that she was charged with a profoundly significant message which, sooner or later, she would find an opportunity to deliver" (CS 147). Later, Mammy Rhody's eyes are "fixed" upon the narrator "with a look of entreaty like the inarticulate appeal in the eyes of the dumb" (150). The narrator, returning the "gaze," feels that Mammy Rhody "was speaking to me in some inaudible language which I did not yet understand, that she bore a message to me which, sooner or later, she would find a way to deliver" (150). At a third encounter, the narrator feels that Mammy Rhody, foregoing common language and substituting some direct heart-to-heart communication, "gazed directly into my heart" "for one miraculous instant" (155). A fourth time, Mammy Rhody looks at the narrator with "that long deep look so filled with inarticulate yearning." The narrator again perceives that Mammy Rhody is "charged with some message she could not utter. While her eyes met mine I was smitten—that is the only word for the sensation— into silence" (158). At that moment realizing that she is the only one besides Pell who actually sees Mammy Rhody, the narrator learns an important lesson: silence may communicate whole speeches between some, but silence must necessarily block communication between her and those with whom she feels no intuitive connection. Silence, that is, can be a facilitator or a barrier to communication, and must be manipulated accordingly. Having once nearly revealed that she too sees Mammy Rhody, this time she echoes Mrs. Maradick of "The Shadowy Third" in her recognition of others' tendency to misunderstand: "I kept silent, for the first thing one learns from such visitations is the danger of talking to people of things which they cannot understand" (159).

The narrator's silence in the presence of those who "cannot understand"—her cousin Pelham and his wife—indicates her increasing awareness that she must separate herself from the domesticity they represent, and instead align herself with a model of nurturing motherhood based on Mammy Rhody and Clarissa. An outdated model of domestic traditions, figured architecturally in the house's "last-century fashion" and absence of indoor plumbing (CS 149), is precisely the one lived by the current Blantons, and the one at least partially lived by previous generations in the house too, making the house itself representative of, among other things, self-effacing womanhood in the absolute service of men and children. It is that model that the narrator must first define and then redefine for herself. Hannah Twine's easy transition from paid housekeeper to wife at Whispering Leaves (145) serves as a pointed reminder of the insignificant distinction between servant and wife. Lacking humor, imagination, and sensitivity, Hannah's only conversation with the narrator (in stark contrast to the silent but complete communication between the narrator and Mammy Rhody and even Clarissa) consists of discussing "such concrete facts as wood and stones and preserves" (155). Suited to his second wife, Pelham is "a man who had ceased to desire anything intensely except physical comfort" (148). "Vain, spoiled, selfish, amiable as long as he was given everything that he wanted" (152), Pelham requires a servant/wife who provides for his comfort and raises his many children; Hannah, "a woman who was proficient in the art of making a man comfortable" (149), fits the bill. Her name, "twine," marks her inseparability from husband and children. Like Mrs. Twine in *The Ancient Law,* who would rather keep her abusive husband than risk having none, Hannah's very identity is more dependent upon the existence of her husband and children than upon her own.

Hannah's two sets of twins and an infant born a few months before the time of the story force the narrator to reckon with Hannah's model of motherhood alongside her model of wifehood. Glasgow's portrayal of Hannah's cold—at times even bordering on cruel—maternity gives the lie to the usual picture of cooing Victorian motherhood and serves as a reminder that to demand that women find complete fulfillment in serving husbands and children is to invite them, even to require them, to see themselves as nothing more than keepers of household order and peace. Hannah, intent on her role as provider of meals and physical satisfaction for her husband and as the shaper of future citizens, is more like the housekeeper that she was and the harsh disciplinarian that she resembles than the loving wife and mother. Besides guaranteeing dinner at a certain hour and dutifully producing five children in the approximately five years that she has been married, Hannah also sends Pell to bed terrified because she wants to "break him" of his fear of the dark "or he will be a baby all his life." At home with patriarchal standards, she explains: " 'It would be dreadful for his father's son to be a coward' " (CS 154). Her treatment of her own children would not differ, we are told; her tone with Pell "was no sharper indeed than the one she used to her own children" (153).

The most important message of the story and the one the narrator senses that Mammy Rhody is trying to convey is delivered through the silent, intuitive language established between these women. This communication envelops them in a sense of shared purpose that simultaneously excludes those who represent the wrong tradition. The message is this: the ideal of domesticity to which Pelham and Hannah Blanton adhere, defined as it is through marriage and motherhood, must be replaced by broader responsibilities for nurture that go beyond the literal definitions of marriage and motherhood. The woman's tradition that the narrator set out to find when she went to Whispering Leaves, that is, must be reconfigured to allow for independence and self-determination as well as for nurturing metaphorical motherhood. It must also expand to allow for close relationships between women who may share the care of themselves and of children, rather than insisting on marriage as the only legitimate domestic potentiality.

The narrator's lesson partly consists of learning not to reject nurturing simply because she rejects literal motherhood, and this is where we see Glasgow examining her feminized heritage and meshing old with new rather than rejecting completely the way of life of her foremothers. It is not so much motherhood as Hannah Twine's version of motherhood that she must reject, substituting instead a more all-encompassing ideal of nurture that is not limited to a husband (or even, perhaps, to men) or to children one has actually given birth to, and that does not require self-denial. When the narrator awakens to smoke as Whispering Leaves burns, she looks for Pell but does not find him, then rushes out to save herself. The others have not saved him, either, and as the house is consumed she alone sees Mammy Rhody carry Pell from the fire and silently transfer him to her arms, "safe and unharmed" (*CS* 163).

Though Mammy Rhody never speaks a word, at the story's conclusion the narrator has translated her message: "Her eyes found me at last, and I knew, in that moment of vision, what the message was that she had for me. Without a word I stepped forward, and held out my arms. As I did, I saw a glory break in the dim features. Then, even while I gave my voiceless answer, the face melted from me into spirals of smoke" (*CS* 163). Mammy Rhody literally gives Pell to the narrator, and communicates her message that the care of the child has now passed to her. Presumably the narrator does take Pell with her when she leaves, as Pell had said Mammy Rhody told him she must, and raises him herself, acting out a new version of domesticity that makes room for nurture and independent selfhood at the same time, and that circumvents dependence on patriarchalism or even heterosexual union. The destruction of the house by the fire from which Mammy Rhody rescues Pell signifies the necessary destruction of the domestic ideal personified by the Blantons, and the rebirth from its ashes of a new definition of domesticity and womanhood.

The doubling that is omnipresent in "Whispering Leaves"—two Miss Effies, twins, two Mrs. Blantons—mirrors Glasgow's own life too, as she uses the story to sort out her relationship to her own mother, her own Mammy Lizzie, her mother's Mammy Rhody. Glasgow's use of such doubling also demonstrates her difficulties in making boundary distinctions between self and other, especially a nurturing, motherly other. The ambiguity inherent in doubled characters—Am I myself or am I my twin self? is a question each twin must ask— demonstrates a problem in identifying one's self by both separating and connecting with an other, particularly a female other, a doubled female self. Scholars have argued that this issue of separation and connection is at the heart of female self-development; it is certainly an issue that Glasgow felt keenly, as "Whispering Leaves" and other female Gothic stories show. As she examines her past relationships with her mother and with her surrogate mother, Lizzie Jones, and as she contemplates her own potential status as a wife and a mother and then redefines *motherhood,* she works toward a notion of selfhood that includes both independence and dependence. When, at the conclusion of "Whispering Leaves," Mammy Rhody literally crosses the boundary of flame that consumes the house and the outmoded domesticity it symbolizes, the female other who crosses racial boundaries assumes a new importance that prefigures the women's relationship in *Barren Ground* two years later.[30] As "Whispering Leaves" ends, the matrilineage passes on to the narrator as she becomes "mother" to Pell. The property is not the definer of meaning; the property doesn't even exist any more. The woman's true heritage passes through nurturing relationships between women—and between races—who pass along the responsibilities for children to each other.

The Angel in the House: "Jordan's End"

Patriarchal lineage and its power to circumscribe is the subject of Glasgow's final Gothic tale, "Jordan's End," published in 1923 for the first time in Glasgow's only short story collection, *The Shadowy Third and Other Stories* (published as *Dare's Gift* in England). Unlike the other four, this one has no supernatural elements. Its setting is a patriarchal home and family; "Jordan's End," referring both to the house itself and that of its male line, also foreshadows the demise of both. The house as patriarchal metonym and the house as dwelling, haunted by insanity and the imprisoning of its inhabitants, combined with the subversive possibilities within the character of Judith Yardly Jordan, its Gothic heroine, place the story in the tradition of the female Gothic. As in "Dare's Gift," Glasgow uses a male narrator here as a reminder of women's entrapment in the men's stories that signify male entitlement within patriarchal traditions. And "Jordan's End," even more than "Whispering Leaves," is suffused with patriarchy and women's oppression within it. When considered apart from its (masculine) narrative viewpoint and at its most basic, "Jordan's End" is the story of a male heritage of inadequacy and a female tradition of covering up that inadequacy; of women trapped in a house (in both its literal and its familial form, as a family name they must assume at marriage) that they did not create; of men (including the two doctors in the story, one of whom is the narrator, and the aged Father Peterkin, who fills in pieces of the story) who escape from the ravages of the house and leave the women to do their best with a situation not of their making.

Judith Jordan's subversive potential exists as just that—potential. That subversiveness is subtle in this story, largely because, as in "Dare's Gift," its male narrator's sympathetic character makes it difficult to read through his perspective skeptically. But that difficulty is precisely Glasgow's point: Judith's tragedy lies in part in our recognition of the near hopelessness of her plight, mirrored in the difficulty of breaking out of the masculine perspective that shapes our vision as well as her life. Our sympathy for the unnamed country doctor who tells the story should not blind us to his gendered limitations or to the story's involvement with questions of separate spheres for men and women. Although the lens of the story focuses on the male heritage of the Jordans, the female heritage is equally and oppressively well defined: stay in the house, shoulder domestic responsibility, protect the men, and do not tell your own story. Even when Judith presumably kills her husband with an overdose of medication, the act is a form of protecting him: earlier, she says, she had "made him wait" to die, holding "him back by a promise" (CS 215). The story's conclusion holds out the dim hope that a distant future might be different: Judith vows to get away eventually and make her own life. But even so, limitation reigns; she can only leave after those who need her, the old women in the house and her nine-year-old son, are no longer dependent. Self-determination may be possible, but it remains improbable.

In some ways, the story is a fearful male fantasy (or, more accurately, Glasgow's fantasy of a male fantasy) of what happens when women gain too much control, and as such, it is a demonstration of the deeply felt fear on the part of many men around the turn of the twentieth century that scholars such as Gilbert and Gubar, Showalter, and Smith-Rosenberg have documented.[31] Despite the fact that the world of Jordan's End is still largely a man's world, it is a man's world crippled by various kinds of masculine inadequacy. The narrator is a doctor, but rather than exhibiting the scientific detachment his gender and his profession would ask of him, he is overly excitable and apprehensive. As he says, after being "visited" by a "superstitious dread" of the second story of the house, where the surviving adult male Jordan, Alan, spends his mindless days, he "gave up medicine . . . and turned to literature as a safer outlet for a suppressed imagination" (CS 210).

Following Alan's wife, Judith, up the stairs, the doctor's reaction is not one that he, or Glasgow and others in the 1920s, would have seen as typically male: "The apprehension, the dread, or whatever you choose to call it, was so strong upon me, that I was seized by an impulse to turn and retreat down the spiral staircase. Yes, I know why some men turn cowards in battle" (210). Old Father Peterkin, who leads the doctor to Jordan's End, is not only "very old" but "dwarfed" by a "hunched back" (203). After Peterkin briefly describes the dilapidated house and the "addle-brained" "old ladies" who live in it, the doctor asks, " 'Is there no man of the family left?' " (205), implying, of course, that a "man" around the house would put it to rights. Though at one time, according to Peterkin, "old Mr. Timothy Jur'dn was the proudest man anywhar aroun' these parts" (205), now the facts rehearse a frightening tale of male vulnerability. There are five surviving male Jordans: a grandfather and two uncles who are confined in an asylum; the present inhabitant, Alan, who has recently begun to sit and silently, incessantly, braid the fringe of a shawl that wraps him no less inexorably than the insanity that has evidently passed to him, too; and Alan's nine-year-old son, Benjamin, who is, unfortunately, "the very spit an' image of his pa" (205).

The narrator is clearly uneasy around—even afraid of—women's power, especially Judith Jordan's. The "dread" that he feels upon first approaching the house "is not lessened by the glimpse" once inside the house "of a scantily furnished room, where three lean black-robed figures, as impassive as the Fates, were grouped in front of a wood fire." The wives of Alan's incarcerated grandfather and two uncles are, he notices, "doing something with their hands. Knitting, crocheting, or plaiting straw?" (CS 210). Their manual activity replicates Alan's, as the doctor soon sees, but with an important difference: like the Fates to whom they are compared, they control not just their needlework but life itself. Alan's is the mindless repetition of mental inadequacy, the meaningless activity of powerlessness. The doctor is horrified shortly thereafter to see that one of the women crochets an "infant's saque"; when he returns on a subsequent visit to find Alan dead and veiled by a yellowed linen heirloom burial shroud placed there by the old women, his fear of their power is understandable: they really do seem to control the woven fabric of birth, life, and death. At the scene of Alan's deathbed, surrounded by the old women, a "witch of a negress did not pause in the weird chant, an incantation of some sort, which she was mumbling" (213). The doctor-narrator is not in control of Alan's life, as a doctor properly would be. The women clearly preside over the rituals of life and death, a powerful position that the doctor-narrator fears.

But the doctor does have the narrative power of the story he tells and the ability as author of that story to recreate Judith in a non-threatening image of femaleness. Gilbert and Gubar's now classic *Madwoman in the Attic* (1979) discusses the power inherent in the patriarchal authority to kill women into a "perfect image,"[32] to write women in the version most satisfying (or, perhaps, most manageable) to men. The narrator, though sympathetic to Judith and her plight, participates in oppressive patriarchy by viewing her not as herself but as idealized woman (an oppression in which the editor of Glasgow's stories in turn participates, as he repeats and extends the narrator's comparison of Judith to Antigone, a classic tragic heroine).[33] The doctor-narrator imprisons Judith in his image of her no less than the Jordan men are imprisoned by their insanity or he by his fear of female power. The terms of his redefinition astonish as they reveal his need to fix Judith, to immobilize her into inactivity, or into activity only as he circumscribes it. Eerily reminiscent of Poe's simultaneous idealization and denigration of women—the most poetic subject, according to Poe, is the death of a beautiful woman—the narrator similarly describes Judith.[34] Just as Judith seizes her literal power over life and death by killing her husband, the narrator—fearful of that actual power—responds by metaphorically killing Judith into ideality. His description as he contemplates her act of mercy killing illustrates his persistence in making her over into his image of frail feminine manageability: "Could she have killed him? Had that delicate creature nerved her will to the unspeakable act? It was incredible. It was inconceivable" (CS 215).

The narrator's memory of his first view of Judith reveals much more than his admiration of her beauty, and the language as he describes that memory re-creates her as an ethereal but dead (and, disturbingly, desirable) angel in the house: "I have been in many countries since then, and looked on many women; but her face, with that wan light on it, is the last one I shall forget in my life. Beauty! Why, that woman will be beautiful when she is a skeleton, was the

thought that flashed into my mind" (CS 207). The seemingly incongru-
ent thought that a Judith long dead ("a skeleton") will be a beautiful
Judith seems less unusual in light of the narrator's subsequent observations about her spirituality. He describes her as "so thin that her
flesh seemed faintly luminous, as if an inward light pierced the trans-
parent substance. It was the beauty, not of earth, but of triumphant
spirit." She seems to him not to belong "in this world" but to "have
stepped straight out of legend or allegory" (CS 207). Despite the narrator's obvious admiration, there is nevertheless a serious problem
here. Judith as a skeleton and Judith as a legendary perfect woman
are really the same Judith: in either case she is not a real person, but
a dead icon of perfection. Already expressive of the fixity she represents later in the story, when her impassiveness at the deathbed of
her husband causes the narrator to describe her as "motionless as a
statue" (213), we see that it is the *narrator's* wish for her static, statu-
esque self that is revealed. She is a skeleton; she is not of this world;
she is spirit rather than matter; she is a heroine of legend; she is the
static/statuesque symbol of allegory. And more, observing that the
"contour of her face" is "Italian in its pure oval," the narrator stabi-
lizes her in a frame no less than Leonardo's or Raphael's Madonnas
are fixed in theirs. She is Woman as Idea, not *a* woman. In such a
role, she is far less threatening than the Judith who kills her husband
and banishes the doctor forever. That her motive for mercy killing is
sympathy makes the fact of her "unspeakable act" no less frightening
to the narrator, just as our sympathy for him makes the fact of his
participation in patriarchal domination no less frightening to us. Ob-
jectified as an ideal in various terms, Judith becomes manageable. She
also becomes explainable; the otherwise "inconceivable" murder of
her husband can now be attributed to her deadness as a human being.
The narrator believes that Judith, cold within, "felt nothing" in the
cold air, and moved "like one who had all eternity before her"—in
other words, like a ghost, "divided from her kind" in the loss of her
humanness (214).

The irony is that Judith's supposed power, the power that so awes
the narrator, cannot save her from the undeniable heritage of her past.
In the tradition of the female Gothic's heroine, Judith remains imprisoned in the domesticity that provides her only sphere. Responsible for
the "old people" (CS 215) who yet live, Judith also cannot circumvent

the probable degeneration of her son, who is so like his father. She is inescapably riveted to the crumbling house, to the legacy of the Jordans for whom it is named, to a domestic life tied to taking care of its inhabitants. And any act that moves toward freedom from that domestic prison results only in the prison created by the narrator's definition of her. At the story's conclusion, Judith turns from the narrator and drops the shawl that is reminiscent of the women's needlework and of the repetitive plaiting that signifies her husband's madness. Yet she is not free from either. Far from the isolated and transcendent heroine of legend that the narrator describes, she is woven into the lives of the Jordans as tightly as the wool of the shawl she does not bother to pick up. And the narrator's idealization of her denies her the right to redefine her heritage in her own terms just as surely as it suggests his fear of her—or any woman's—ability to do so.

In many ways Glasgow used her stories in the female Gothic tradition to exorcise ghosts in her own past and present and to substitute her definition of a satisfying life for herself. Bitterness toward her father and sympathy for her mother, anxiety about men and marriage fostered by her relationship with Henry Anderson, doubts about artistic worth as she worked in an undervalued genre (the short story, especially as Gothic), tension at her increasing realization that she found the companionship of women more congenial, and uncertainty as she rejected the traditional ideal of woman's separate sphere of domesticity, redefining it to include female connectedness without self-denial—all were subjects she explored in her female Gothic tales at a time in her life when questions of gendered existence seemed especially pressing.

It would be nice to say that the female Gothic tradition provided the backdrop for Glasgow's complete liberation into a re-created world that left no room for ambiguity about gender or sexuality or professional self-doubt. But it was not that simple. The contemporary reviews consistently praised highly *The Shadowy Third*, which contains these five stories.[35] Yet even as she worked successfully in a genre that provided her with the materials for questioning and subverting the traditions of female subordination to men, and even though she frequently carried through many of those questions and subversions, she often stopped short of recognizing the revolutionary potential inherent in the female Gothic tradition she adopted only to abandon before using it to full advantage. For one thing, she regularly questioned the legitimacy of both the short story and the Gothic, associating the former with superficiality, the latter with sensationalism, and both with literary hack work executed solely for crass financial gain.[36] She thereby devalued her own work and undermined her own artistic integrity, leading the way for the critical neglect of her stories that has followed their initial success.

More important, Glasgow did not fully introduce in her Gothic fiction what was in many ways the most radical act of her own self-definition: the exchange of men and the marriage plot for women and a life of affiliation with women. I do not want to suggest that all writers must somehow incorporate their actual experience into their fiction (though I am at the same time not sure how to completely avoid doing so). Glasgow's female Gothic tales move toward not only rejecting men's denials of women's subjectivity in the form of patrilineal property succession or the doctrine of separate spheres, but also of accepting in place of those male denials a reconstituted notion of property as matrilineal or of public agency as the equally legitimate sphere of women. And, most significantly, in her Gothic stories that redefinition promises fulfillment in the company of women acting independently of men. Nevertheless, in three of the five stories, the woman or women whose companionship made possible the break with patriarchy disappear (through either natural or supernatural causes), leaving at the conclusion a woman alone without her enabling companion. Margaret Randolph of "The Shadowy Third," Mildred Beckwith of "Dare's Gift," and the unnamed narrator of "Whispering Leaves" all lose the female friends who facilitated their own subversion of male power: Mrs. Maradick, Lucy Dare, and Mammy Rhody. In "The Past," the two women presumably remain together, but the husband also remains; in a way, Miss Wrenn "loses" her friend Mrs. Vanderbridge through Mrs. Vanderbridge's rededication to her marriage. In "Jordan's End," female companionship has been transformed into the strange relationship between Judith and the three old women, and Judith's complete isolation reinforces her lack of connection and her need for it. Despite the female agency—especially in companionship with one another—that Glasgow imagines in her stories, ultimately the stories often emphasize the difficulties in restoring female subjectivity rather than the empowering possibilities realized, for a time, within them.

In contrast, Glasgow's own life during these years demonstrates an increasing commitment to her female friends and an ever-stronger belief that her life had no room for traditional marriage and heterosexuality. The decade of the twenties marked the end of Glasgow's Gothic experiment (except as it surfaces briefly in *Barren Ground* as the backdrop for the protagonist's fortunate escape from marriage, as it had briefly appeared earlier in the Haunt's Walk of *The Miller of Old Church* in 1911, or as her own backdrop in her autobiography) and the end of her ambivalence about men as sexual partners and marriage as a viable option. What the twenties initiated was a newly conscious turn to women for the sense of connection Glasgow sought, and a new sense of being liberated from the need to define herself according to male standards and prerogatives. The time was right for *Barren Ground*.

FIVE

Female Companionship II: The Serpent of Freudianism

For more than fifty years Louisa had understood her more absolutely than any man could understand the woman he loves. Beautiful as this long association had been, it was fortunate, Victoria reflected now, that it had come to flower before the serpent of Freudian psychology had poisoned the sinless Eden of friendship.

Glasgow, *They Stooped to Folly* (1929)

DORINDA OAKLEY, THE protagonist of Glasgow's favorite and best-known novel, *Barren Ground* (1925), speaks the final, confident words of her story: "Dorinda smiled, and her smile was pensive, ironic, and infinitely wise. 'Oh, I've finished with all that,' she rejoined. 'I am thankful to have finished with all that.' "[1] To her stepson's hint that she might remarry, Dorinda, for at least the tenth time since her failed love affair thirty years earlier, repeats that she is "finished" or "through" with "romance," with "love," with "all that."[2] With *Barren Ground,* Glasgow builds on her renewed commitment to a tradition of women's self-definition through female community rather than through heterosexual union, and solidifies her commitment to women's rejecting masculine narratives and telling their own stories. In this novel—her "vehicle of liberation," as she termed it[3]— Glasgow announces not only her heroine's liberation from the demands of youthful heterosexuality, but her own liberation from the personal and narratological expectations of the conventional marriage plot. Neither Glasgow nor Dorinda succumbs to the usual "end"—

marriage or death—of the heroine's text as discussed by Nancy K. Miller; both emphatically reject marriage as the conclusion to their life stories. In contrast to Glasgow's earlier novels, the ending of *Barren Ground* does not even hint at heterosexual possibility. "Finished with all that" articulates Glasgow's newfound freedom from the love plot of Dorinda's *and* of Glasgow's lives, and from a literary tradition that dictates women's self-definition through men and men's stories.

In terms of fictional practice, however, Glasgow's realization was destined to be short-lived. In *Barren Ground* she shows her awareness of the possibilities of female friendship and concludes the novel by confidently, if unobtrusively, substituting female companionship for heterosexuality. In this way, she uses "woman-to-woman . . . bonds," one example of a strategy discussed by Rachel Blau DuPlessis for "writing beyond the ending," as DuPlessis terms the practice of envisioning plots that see beyond conventional textual definitions for women. But, particularly during the 1920s, the "modern principle of association," as Frances Cobb had called women's bonding in 1862,[4] came increasingly under attack in both medical and popular circles. Popular culture in the 1920s was permeated by the psychosexual theories of Freud, Havelock Ellis, and others.[5] As scholars have argued, under the influence of these "sexologists," female friendships were reinterpreted, viewed no longer as the innocent, almost quaint, relationships of an earlier time but as sexually threatening and even deviant.[6]

By the 1929 publication of *They Stooped to Folly,* as the epigraph to this chapter indicates, Glasgow was fully aware of the much-touted dangers of women's exclusive friendships. Her understanding of the negative interpretation placed on female friendship by the popular sexologists made it impossible after the time of *Barren Ground* to write unselfconsciously of women's homosocial relationships. The pervasiveness of these theories, to which Glasgow frequently alludes, made it more difficult to enjoy the narratological freedom Glasgow had discovered in writing *Barren Ground*. They disallowed rejecting heterosexuality, particularly when female companionship was offered as an alternative, and made it difficult, especially for novelists who sought popularity, to avoid the heterosexual romance plot. In *They Stooped to Folly* in 1929, Glasgow subordinated her potentially explosive female friendships to the novel's more obvious (and more acceptable) theme of romance and marriage. By the time of *The Sheltered Life* in 1932, Glasgow portrays the sexologists' homophobic and misogynistic view of female companionship as deviant, but uses that portrayal to comment on the destruction caused by such labeling. In *The Sheltered Life,* what previously might have been a redeeming female friendship becomes instead a neurotic, unsatisfying obsession. Cultural imperatives that prevent anchoring a female self to a tradition of women's community, the novel argues, destroy the women *and* the men of that culture.

Glasgow's frequently expressed frustration with Freud (or, perhaps more accurately, with what she saw as the wholesale adoption of popularized Freudian psychology), reveals a larger frustration with her own inability to shake off the restraints placed on her attempts to write freely, as she felt she finally had been able to do in *Barren Ground.* The brief seven-year period encompassing *Barren Ground* and *The Sheltered Life* recapitulates a move from experiential and narrative liberation to a renewed sense of confinement, imposed by expectations external to the self, which Glasgow had spent her career working against. No wonder the anger that Ammons finds characteristic of Glasgow is so apparent during this time.[7] In accepting, even if unwillingly and even if only publicly, a view of female friendship based on descriptions by Freud, Krafft-Ebing, Ellis, and others, Glasgow substitutes a new male tradition for the female traditions she had just begun to rediscover.[8] Under ideological pressure (and perhaps also reflecting her earlier ambivalence about traditions of womanhood), Glasgow acquiesces, even if angrily, to a male interpretation of female experience that unravels the fabric of a woman's tradition she had recently woven for herself.

Significantly, however, Glasgow does not simply return to her earlier impulse to reject outright a woman's tradition of community and friendship. Indeed, what complicates Glasgow's attitude toward women's relationships during the mid twenties and afterward is not so much her own doubt as her knowledge of a new public attitude toward women's friendships.[9] Glasgow's private commitments to other women strengthen, deepen, and broaden during the twenties and after, the same time that her fiction first openly celebrates those strong friendships and their narrative implications (*Barren Ground*), portrays the public view of them as unhealthy (*The Sheltered Life*), and finally abandons them altogether (*Vein of Iron* and after). Glasgow's correspondence during this time reveals that she solidified existing relationships with Mary Johnston, Amélie Rives Troubetzkoy, and especially Anne Virginia Bennett, and gained important new close women friends, many of whom were also professional women of letters—Radclyffe Hall, Clare Leighton, Marjorie Kinnan Rawlings, and Signe Toksvig, for example. Because many of these letters, which remain unpublished, have gone unexamined, it has been difficult for scholars to recognize that Glasgow's fictional rejection of a woman's plot emphasizing women's friendships does not parallel her life story.[10]

Marriage Plots and Other "Great" Traditions: Barren Ground

For the brief space of *Barren Ground,* at least, Glasgow enjoyed her newfound freedom from male-defined personal and literary traditions. That Glasgow conceived of this liberation as affecting her own story as well as her protagonist's is evident in the language Glasgow uses to describe the evolution of Dorinda Oakley as character. Recalling Dorinda's imaginative birth, Glasgow, in her Virginia Edition Preface (1938) to *Barren Ground,* fuses her personality with her character's, seeing herself and Dorinda as almost the same person. In the ten years between imagining Dorinda and realizing her in *Barren Ground,* Glasgow says, she and Dorinda had "changed and developed together." Feeling "connected" to Dorinda "by a living nerve," Glasgow says she "knew the look in her face, the tone of her voice, the high carriage of her head, the swift gestures that obeyed a thought or an impulse." She was intimately aware, even, of the "secret labyrinth of her unconscious motives." Author and character fuse as Glasgow acknowledges that their voices and "behaviour" were the same; "I was aware, through some sympathetic insight, of what she would say or do in any circumstances" (*BG,* xvi).

Glasgow says she first visualized Dorinda a decade before the novel itself, or not long after the publication of *Virginia* in 1913 and in the midst of writing *Life and Gabriella,* published in 1916. In her 1938 Preface to the latter, Glasgow described these two earlier novels as "companion" pieces, the first concerned with "woman as an ideal" and the second with "woman as a reality." *Life and Gabri-*

ella, she further explained, marked "the complete and final departure" from the Victorian idealization of women—that "great tradition" that forms the backdrop for *Virginia*.[11] In linking Virginia, Gabriella, and Dorinda (and thus herself), Glasgow emphasizes her imaginative reconstruction of women's responses, including her own, to the so-called great traditions that have been handed down to women.

Glasgow's feeling of being "connected" to Dorinda physically ("by a living nerve") and psychologically (knowing "her unconscious motives") underscores Glasgow's sense of connection between women that, as I have argued, strengthened over time until, in *Barren Ground,* it presented a genuine alternative to heterosexual relationships. One critically overlooked revelation by Anne Virginia Bennett to Marjorie Kinnan Rawlings is consonant with the heightened theme of female companionship that pervades earlier novels and reaches its apex in *Barren Ground.* In an interview, Bennett told Rawlings that "many" of the names in *Barren Ground* have as their source Bennett's own family. In her notes, Rawlings wrote that "Dorinda's mother Eudora was A.V.'s mother's name."[12] The novel's very origin traces a matri-centric genealogy that connects author, companion, and protagonist (and even biographer, if we include Rawlings), and simultaneously reasserts the centrality of mother-daughter relationships.[13]

Appropriate to Glasgow's continued reassessment of women's traditions, *Barren Ground* opens with a discussion of Pedlar's Mill's traditions, focusing on an original matrilineal heritage in her home-town that Dorinda will have to regain.[14] The initial image of the novel, striking in its visual concreteness, emphasizes Dorinda's isolation and also objectifies her. Such an introduction announces the desolation not only of the town and the landscape against which she poses, but also the difficulty of female self-definition against a cultural backdrop that provides few models. Her "orange-coloured shawl" stands out against the white snow; her motionlessness gives her "an impression of arrested flight." The "bare, starved, desolate" landscape "close[s] in about her," and the last train has gone (*BG* 3).

As many readers observe, Dorinda is intimately tied to the landscape. The connection between Dorinda and the all-consuming wild broom sedge is made explicit as the text opens. On the first page of the novel's text, Dorinda's orange shawl has its visual parallel in the broom sedge that, in the autumn, catches "fire from the afterglow and blaze[s] out in a splendour of colour," the only hint of color other than Dorinda herself (*BG* 3). When we are told by the folk philosopher Matthew Fairlamb that "Broomsedge ain't jest wild stuff. It's a kind of fate" (4), Glasgow suggests that both land and protagonist are entrapped in an (agri)cultural ideology guided by a supposedly natural biological determinism. Once, when Dorinda announces that "No man" will be allowed to "interfere with my work," one of her farm workers remarks that Dorinda's attitude may be "sassy," but it "ain't natur'!" (325–26). According to Lucinda H. MacKethan, Dorinda's triumph is that she "lives to change nature," as represented by her reclamation of the family farm. Her triumph is actually even more far-reaching: Dorinda lives to change what *masquerades* as nature, and in so doing unmasks the Victorian ideology that defines "natural" according to that era's own cultural imperatives. As Catherine Rainwater has argued, in *Barren Ground,* "nature predominates and emphasizes how the very concept of will is predicated on resistance to circumstances perceived as extrinsic and given." [15]

In fact, the larger significance of the first chapter is the narrator's condemnation of cultural imposition, here as practiced by the settlers of Pedlar's Mill in order to preserve those cultural imperatives and convince others that their status is natural. This heritage of intolerance, disguised as religious righteousness and a fatalistic belief in the natural landscape's inevitable triumph over the "human invader" (*BG* 4), is revealed through the narrator's patently ironic introductory history of the area and its settlers. Heightened class consciousness led the settlers of Queen Elizabeth County to distinguish "good people" from "good families," the latter designation reserved for the "superior pioneers" with "blue blood in their veins" and "the fear of God in their hearts" (4–5). Among the early settlers is Dorinda's great-grandfather, John Calvin Abernethy, who bought a "thousand acres of land and fifty slaves" (6). Glasgow's irony (evident, for example, in naming the ancestor for Calvin) condemns the staunch Presbyterian forebear whose belief in predestination enabled his easy transition to the determinism that designated his superiority as natural. Abernethy sold his slaves farther south, the narrator recounts, "and the price of black flesh he devoted to the redemption of black souls in the Congo" (7). As the narrator says, "To a thrifty theologian . . . there are few points of ethics too fine-spun for splitting" (7). The doubly oppressive tenets of slaveholding and missionary zeal, which enables a view of others as needing "redemption," form part of the heritage of Pedlar's Mill. Though a distinction is made between aristocratic "good families" and middle-class "good people," both are ironized. The "good families" have passed along "custom, history, tradition, romantic fiction, and the Episcopal Church," whereas the "good people . . . have preserved nothing except themselves" (5). There's not really much difference, Glasgow suggests: both traditions emphasize the self-righteousness of those doing the preserving.[16]

The cultural imperatives worthy of preservation, according to the time and place, certainly do not include encouraging the development of women. The already "benighted" 1890s, the narrator asserts, were even more benighted in the "thinly settled part of Virginia" where Dorinda's story takes place. Just as no "modern methods of farming" nurtured the land, no modern attitudes provided the fertile imaginative soil necessary to nurture the New Woman of Pedlar's Mill. The judgmental narrator notes that occasionally a new settler would cultivate the land successfully "for a season or two," but the "surrounding air of failure" eventually would defeat such efforts. Not coincidentally, the "settler" Glasgow profiles is a "German Catholic" trying to survive in a "staunch Protestant community" (*BG* 4). Thus, the newcomer to the region succumbs to failure induced, in part at least, by the intolerance of the region toward outsiders, including women. With the post–Civil War demographic shift to the towns, "The old men stayed by the farms, and their daughters withered dutifully beside them" though their "sons" successfully fled (5). The stultifying approach to cultivating the land extended to cultivating the women. These sons, newly empowered politically, "proceeded immediately to enact their preferences, prejudices, habits, and inhibitions into the laws of the state" (5). Whether the object is the land, immigrant settlers from an alien culture and religion, or daughters whose duty in life is to "wither" beside their fathers, maintaining the hegemony of the "old men" and their unenlightened "sons" is the inheritance of Pedlar's Mill.

The daughters, it is made clear, will have to be responsible for changing the patriarchal traditions of the place and the age. Dorinda's mother, Eudora, inherited her own father's land, though through marriage it effectively became her husband's. Perhaps in a sly reference to her own father's failure to perpetuate in his children what she calls his "rock-ribbed Calvinism" (*WW* 16), Glasgow gives John Calvin Abernethy "but one son" who dies while felling a tree, thus leaving the inheritance to the granddaughter, Eudora.[17] It is not Eudora but her "ineffectual" husband, Joshua Oakley, who fails to cultivate the land successfully; he "worked hard . . . to lose everything that was left" of Eudora's inheritance (*BG* 8). Likewise, it will be not the equally ineffectual Oakley sons but the daughter, Dorinda, who reclaims the land. "Kinship with the land was filtering through her blood," Dorinda thinks at one point (260). Though her father had worked to "lose" Old Farm, at his death it reverted to his wife, enabling a return to matrilineage through the farm itself. Glasgow seizes the chance to make her point that, within a patriarchal structure, Mrs. Oakley's ownership can only be allowed with male approval: "The farm had always belonged to Mrs. Oakley; but in order that her authority might be assured, Joshua had made a will a few months before his death and had left her the farm implements and the horses" (255).

It is partly through Dorinda's relationship with Fluvanna Moody, the black woman who works with her to establish the dairy farm, that Dorinda is able to overcome the heritage of intolerance and determinism in Pedlar's Mill. Fluvanna's race, her gender, and her close relationship with another woman make her centrality in Dorinda's life a challenge to Pedlar's Mill's racism, misogyny, and heterosexism; Fluvanna's aid in Dorinda's agricultural scheme to overcome the fateful broom sedge makes her a partner in standing up to the town's deterministic view that broom sedge, a metonymic substitute for the whole cultural landscape, is "a kind of fate." When Dorinda is able to create for herself a contented female life by simultaneously substituting female companionship for heterosexuality, racial diversity for segregation, and innovative agricultural methods for the outdated farming practices common in Pedlar's Mill, she threatens the hegemonic traditions that try to define her. She asserts herself against cultural tradition, and in so doing also asserts her creator's challenge to traditional narrative.

Glasgow's readers, however, conditioned to expect the heterosexual marriage plot, have complained about the very thing that makes Dorinda and her story so important. They have seen her as bereft of *human* (read heterosexual) companionship and argued that Dorinda herself *is* the barren ground of the novel, a view Linda Wagner has tried to correct.[18] Such an approach ignores Dorinda's contented domestic arrangement with Fluvanna and forgets that Dorinda lives not alone but with another woman. In an assumption all too familiar to feminist critics—women are incomplete without men—these readers interpret Dorinda's rejection by Jason Greylock early in her adulthood, her subsequent decision to marry Nathan Pedlar only on a condition of celibacy, and her final, settled contentment with Fluvanna as signs of her "barren" unemotional and unfulfilled life.[19]

The novel itself, however, leaves no question of the importance in Dorinda's emotional life of her relationship with Fluvanna, although fully appreciating the two women's companionship requires some reading around the silences and omissions about it. Though it takes up little prose space, their friendship is an established daily fact. As in Glasgow's life, especially in her domestic relationship with Anne Virginia Bennett, we would do well to remember that behind the brief descriptions of Dorinda and Fluvanna lies a relationship that exists constantly, every day and for years. Dorinda muses that her "best years . . . were shared only with the coloured woman with whom she lived. She had prophesied long ago that Fluvanna would be a comfort to her, and the prophecy was completely fulfilled. The affection between the two women had outgrown the slender tie of mistress and maid, and had become as strong and elastic as the bond that holds relatives together. They knew each other's daily lives; they shared the one absorbing interest in the farm; they trusted each other without discretion and without reserve" (*BG* 297). To describe Dorinda Oakley as "a mechanized human being totally drained of humanity," as Godbold does, is to ignore passages such as this one. To assume that Glasgow, as a means of "survival" after her "painful relationship with Henry Anderson," creates through Dorinda a "philosophy of life so without feeling, so without emotion, that its adherent might as well be dead,"[20] is not only shockingly offensive, it ignores other events and other people—often female—in Glasgow's personal life. Such readings also unmask critics' assumption that emotional fulfillment through a woman-to-woman bond is necessarily inferior to a heterosexual one, that this "affection between the two women" can be murderously interpreted as so devoid of "feeling" and "emotion" that both Dorinda and Glasgow "might as well be dead."

Recent feminist critics have recognized both the revisionary potential of Dorinda's and Fluvanna's relationship and its problematic implications. Taking a cue from Adrienne Rich's general condemnation of Glasgow's racism in her 1983 poem "Education of a Novelist," Elizabeth Ammons charges Glasgow with "benevolent racism" because Glasgow ignores "the tremendous imbalance of power built into the completely unequal relationship" between Dorinda and Fluvanna.[21] In a study of interracial women's friendships in American novels, Elizabeth Schultz similarly sees the "strength" of the relationship between Dorinda and Fluvanna as "undermined" by Glasgow's failure to confront her own stereotyped image of the "cheerful" Fluvanna.[22] Such examination of racial attitudes provides essential material for understanding the history of racial oppression as it is manifest in fictional form.

Focusing primarily (or even exclusively) on Glasgow's blindness to subtleties of her own racism, however, can in turn blind us to Glasgow's criticism of a generalized oppression that gives rise to its more specific forms, such as racism. Schultz, for example, discusses the sentence that immediately follows the passage I quoted above: "Fluvanna respected and adored her mistress; and Dorinda, with an inherited feeling of condescension, was sincerely attached to her servant" (*BG* 297).[23] Highlighting Dorinda's "inherited feeling of condescension," Schultz concludes that Glasgow "reinforces" the racism she had temporarily "transcended" in the two women's relationship. If we shift the emphasized word in that phrase from "condescension" to "inherited," however, the conclusion changes. Given the clear condemnation of inherited oppression in the opening chapter of *Barren Ground*, it seems likely that Glasgow here distances herself from Dorinda and in fact *criticizes* Dorinda for condescending to Fluvanna. The weight of the paragraph, both before and after the qualification that Dorinda can't entirely escape her inheritance, is on the "strong and elastic" bond between them. Indeed, Glasgow suggests, the nurturing tradition of female community formed by the two women must be a substitute for the tradition of oppression Dorinda and Pedlar's Mill have "inherited": "Sometimes on winter nights, when the snow was falling or the rain blowing in gusts beyond the window, the two women would sit for an hour, when work was over, in front of the log fire in Dorinda's room which had once been her mother's chamber. Then they would talk sympathetically of the cows and the hens" (297). Dorinda and Fluvanna inside, the storms "beyond the window"— Glasgow recognizes the pull of the "inherited" traditions that Dorinda and Fluvanna together must resist from their fortress in Dorinda's mother's chamber.

Dorinda's "inherited condescension" syntactically occupies the approximate center of the paragraph describing Dorinda's and Fluvanna's companionship. For the reader, therefore, it also occupies the temporal center. The entire paragraph, indeed, is filled with references to the passage of time. Its first words ("gradually, as the years passed"); its reference to "Dorinda's youth"; its conflation of both past and present in Dorinda's earlier "prophecy" of friendship with Fluvanna; its recurring reference to the relationship between past and present—all suggest that this friendship contains within it the "sense of time" that Glasgow in her Preface terms one of the "invisible protagonists" of the novel (*BG* xiii).[24] Their friendship, both actually and symbolically, can build, can overcome "inherited condescension," can envision a future setting of recurring winter nights' sympathetic talk. In Dorinda's mother's chamber, the transformative power of Dorinda's relationship with Fluvanna can revise a patriarchal heritage of "condescension." In the maternal space that Dorinda now occupies, she must amend her legacy of racial intolerance through a healing, racially mixed female friendship.

Dorinda's negotiation of conflicting patriarchal and matriarchal inheritances comes together in two dreams, one her mother's and one hers.[25] Significantly, Eudora's dream itself rewrites Dorinda's great-grandfather's active racism, as if Eudora had attempted to change the inheritance of her grandfather but failed, leaving it to Dorinda to continue the revision. This patriarchal ancestor, John Calvin Abernethy, assuaged his meager conscience by selling his newly bought slaves down the river and "devot[ing]" the "price of black flesh" to "the redemption of black souls in the Congo" (*BG* 7). Later, his granddaughter Eudora's "missionary lover" "died of fever in the Congo" on the eve of their wedding (15). One result of Eudora's grief is her recurring "missionary dream," "a dream of blue skies and golden sands, of palm trees on a river's bank, and of black babies thrown to crocodiles" (38). Dorinda retains a childhood memory of her mother's behavior following her dream: after "flitting barefooted over the frozen ground" on winter nights, Eudora would be rescued by her husband just before she attempted suicide. Then, sitting bewildered beside the fire, Eudora would only repeat "over and over," " 'I am lost, lost, lost' " (38). She admits to Dorinda that her dream returns "sometimes" (104).

Eudora's dream stems in part from a religious fervor that took the place of "romance" in her life following her lover's death (*BG* 37); she "lost" both her lover and the chance to share his missionary work. But she is also lost to the possibility of changing the inheritance of her grandfather, whose moral hairsplitting allowed him to believe that donating money to Congo missionaries exonerated his traffic in slavery. Eudora's dream eerily imagines not the salvation of Congo souls but their destruction. Her dream also imagines the horrors of maternal helplessness: she cannot save the "black babies" and so is "lost." Likewise, she cannot pass on a legacy of power and self-determination to her daughter Dorinda, but can only imagine that she needs to do so. When Dorinda returns home determined to "make something out of the farm" (229), Eudora, like other mothers who found themselves possessed of newly independent daughters after the turn of the century,[26] can only gaze in openmouthed wonder at the daughter she has somehow produced. Eudora, "awed and impressed" by Dorinda's "air of worldly knowledge and disillusioned experience," wonders to herself: "Was it possible that she had created this superior intelligence, that she had actually brought this paragon of efficiency into the world?" (231). Eudora can see that her patriarchal heritage is insufficient; she cannot imagine beyond that realization and see what to do about it.

It falls to Dorinda to dream a different dream and to change the reality her mother could only escape in the bewilderment of unsatisfying marriage, nightmares, and suicide attempts. Dorinda's relationship with Fluvanna realizes her mother's desire to rewrite the racism of John Calvin Abernethy's legacy. And Dorinda's dreams chart her course from her mother's helplessness to her own renewed matriarchal vision of female agency. While in New York after Jason's betrayal, Dorinda literally dreams of the obstacles to gaining control. During her dream, she imagines herself behind a plow in an endless field of broom sedge. In the midst of the broom sedge that signifies a deterministic world that defines women as subordinate, Dorinda sees a field of tenacious "prickly purple thistles," all "wearing the face of

Jason." Jason and the destructive sexual passion he represents replace the broom sedge in a determined universe that Dorinda must try to overcome. In her dream she thinks to herself: " 'I am going to plough them under, if it kills me' " (*BG* 208).[27] It is upon waking that she decides to return to her family farm, inherited through her mother, and thus begins the long process of reclaiming the land. In doing so, she will replace both the fateful broom sedge and Jason, and reclaim her right to self-determination. The agricultural metaphor that informs Dorinda's dream—plowing under—describes her desire not to defeat Jason personally, but to use the seemingly fated heterosexuality he represents as fodder for her new growth toward self-definition. Jason plowed under becomes a metaphor for using patriarchal structures in order to subvert them, a gesture Glasgow often repeats. Barren ground can become fertile soil.

Much later, two nights of dreaming recall Dorinda's mother's powerlessness and point the way to Dorinda's rebirth. In the first instance, a dream years after Dorinda's return to Old Farm, images of flight and captivity echo her mother's "missionary dream." Upon awakening, Dorinda stands before an open window "shivering in the frosty air" as the dream recedes and the "ice [freezes] again over her heart" (*BG* 302). Though she has successfully begun the farm's reclamation (she has triumphed over the broom sedge of her dream and the actual broom sedge), she still has not reclaimed herself from the fate Jason represents: a system of values that allows Dorinda no selfhood apart from her sexual relation to a man. She still fails to realize that she has worth apart from him (and apart from the fate that he stands for), and accepts the interpretation that because she has rejected heterosexuality, her heart is frozen.

Yet a final night of dreaming leads to her rebirth, not to her captivity and repeated oppression as her mother's cyclic dreaming did. For a time, Dorinda's story threatens to conclude after Jason's death, as she laments on the day of his funeral that "the only thing that made life worth living was the love that she had never known and the happiness that she had missed" (*BG* 447). She spends much of the stormy night awake, and just before sleeping concludes that love, "irrevocably lost to her" was "the only thing that made life desirable" (449). But once "the storm and the hag-ridden dreams of the night were over," Dorinda emerges reborn: "Within herself also the storm was over."

In a Thoreauvian moment she wakes, bathes, and goes outside into the "clear flame of the sunrise" (449). The landscape, "emblazoned in gold," brings Dorinda to her "permanent self": "The spirit of the land was flowing into her, and her own spirit, strengthened and refreshed, was flowing out again toward life." Now, Dorinda reinterprets in a positive manner her dark conclusion of the previous night that "love was irrevocably lost to her," and instead focuses on the permanence of nature and the spiritual truth it engenders. "Yes, the land would stay by her," she concludes. And as her expansive vision takes in "far horizon to horizon" (449), she feels "the quickening of that sympathy which was deeper than all other emotions of her heart, which love had overcome only for an hour and life had been powerless to conquer in the end,—the living communion with the earth under her feet. While the soil endured, while the seasons bloomed and dropped, while the ancient, beneficent ritual of sowing and reaping moved in the fields, she knew that she could never despair of contentment" (449–50). For Dorinda, in contrast to her mother, dreams ultimately function as life-saving and life-renewing. Dorinda recognizes that to have "lost" her absorption in an ideology that privileges only "love" in a woman's life signals, not defeat, but victory. Though Dorinda's life had been culturally overdetermined before she had a chance to live it, in her triumph over nature—both in her successful farming and in her rejection of the love plot that masquerades as nature and overwhelms a woman's "permanent self"—she has managed to defy the determinism of her supposed rightful inheritance. She tills the barren soil that presumably nourishes neither crops nor a female self, and, reclaiming her subjectivity from the objectivity of the novel's opening, can end her story with her own words: "I am thankful to have finished with all that" (451).

In April 1925, the same month *Barren Ground* appeared, Glasgow also published a review of Carl Van Doren's *James Branch Cabell*.[28] Glasgow takes the opportunity to criticize Cabell for his lack of realism, especially for his portraits of idealized women. Cabell's female characters, whom Van Doren "praises" for a "glimmering quality," according to Glasgow "are less women than changeful, delicately-tinted aspects of 'the face that launch'd a thousand ships.' The world of chivalry, real or imaginary, is one where women have always presented an extravagant appearance, but where, or the tale does not tell, they have never expressed an authentic opinion" (VDC 204). The review, which appeared about ten days before *Barren Ground,* serves as a partial prescription for reading Glasgow's forthcoming novel. In *Barren Ground,* Glasgow creates a woman character who tells her own tale, who "expresse[s] an authentic opinion." Glasgow discovers, in Gayle Greene's words, the possibilities for "changing the story" expected of her and of her protagonist. Glasgow exposes the real "barren ground" of the novel. It is not Dorinda in her childlessness and coldness, as some have suggested. It is not even the actual land from which Dorinda at last succeeds in wresting a prosperous living. Rather, the "barren ground" is the patriarchally controlled and transmitted *figurative* landscape—the ideology and the culture—against which Dorinda and other women are forced to define themselves and envision their destinies. As Dorinda thinks to herself as she flees Pedlar's Mill for New York City: "life" itself is "just barren ground" where people must "struggle to make anything grow" (*BG* 165). At a crucial point in the novel, after she has left Pedlar's Mill, Dorinda says to herself: " 'I've finished with love, and until I find something else to fill my life, I shall be only an empty shell' " (195). It is this equation of romantic love with a woman's worth that Glasgow works against in *Barren Ground.* Women must learn—both Glasgow and Dorinda argue—to discover alternative stories for their lives and to work against inherited traditions that undermine them.

"Inventions of Desire": The Fallen Woman and They Stooped to Folly

In *They Stooped to Folly* (1929), published four years after *Barren Ground,* Glasgow continues to protest against man-made traditions of womanhood, this time in the form of the "ruined" or "fallen" woman. In a well-established paradigm, a tradition of close female friendships provides at least a partial solution and an alternative plot to conventional male-inscribed women's stories. But with the heightened awareness of popular sexology by the end of World War I, offering close friendships between women as an alternative to heterosexually centered stories was increasingly fraught with social, cultural, and sexual risks. Carroll Smith-Rosenberg has observed that, "By the 1920s, charges of lesbianism had become a common way to discredit women professionals."[29] The example of *The Well of Loneliness*, by Glasgow's friend Radclyffe Hall, which had been censored in England in 1928 for its explicit portrayal of lesbianism, bears witness to the effect on women writers of such charges. Glasgow, always sensitive to actual and potential slights to her and her work, certainly would have been reluctant to jeopardize her hard-won professional reputation. As a result, though the friendship between Louisa Goddard and Victoria Littlepage in *They Stooped to Folly* in many ways remains unequaled for closeness in Glasgow's fiction, Glasgow draws attention away from the relationship between the women by incorporating it into the novel's more generalized exploration of men's and women's romantic behavior, marriage, and tradition.

The epigraph to this chapter, taken from *They Stooped to Folly*, with its reference to Freudian psychology as "poison" to "friendship," demonstrates the extent to which Glasgow was aware of the potential implications of Louisa's and Victoria's friendship—as Donovan has also argued.[30] Glasgow had treated earlier female friendships, such as that between Laura and Gerty in *The Wheel of Life*, without defensiveness. But, as many scholars have argued, a casual attitude toward what Glasgow terms an "Eden of friendship" between women was impossible by the time turn-of-the-century discussions of homosexuality had entered popular culture's common parlance.[31] In *They Stooped to Folly*, Louisa Goddard is unmarried, physically uninspiring to men, and engaged in intellectual activities and reform movements. She is dangerously close to the stereotyped sexual "invert," who, according to Chauncey, simultaneously questions cultural and sexual norms and therefore threatens stability, or to the "mannish lesbian" who, for Smith-Rosenberg, represents the "disorderly conduct" that challenged conservative middle-class values at the turn of the twentieth century. By having Victoria—the married partner in *They Stooped to Folly*'s female friendship—think forthrightly that "it was fortunate" her friendship with Louisa "had come to flower before the serpent of Freudian psychology had poisoned the sinless Eden of friendship" (*TSE* 185), Glasgow meets these two women's friendship directly, thus deflecting any impulse to overread its sexual implications. By centering her novel's attention on myths of fallen womanhood created by men, Glasgow can suggest female friendship as an alternative female tradition without allowing an interpretation of "deviance." Female friendship becomes part of her larger aim: to expose masculine mythologies of womanhood—not women's actual behavior and experience—as "folly."

This objective becomes more explicit when Glasgow incorporates most of her 1928 essay "Some Literary Woman Myths" into the Virginia Edition Preface to *They Stooped to Folly* in 1938. Anticipating the content of her novel, Glasgow refers to masculine "woman myths." The title of her novel alludes to Oliver Goldsmith's *Vicar of Wakefield,* and the epigraph is from the song in chapter twenty-four of Goldsmith's novel of virtue ultimately rewarded, if not always protected.

> When lovely woman stoops to folly
>   And finds too late that men betray,
> What charm can soothe her melancholy?
>   What art can wash her guilt away?

Glasgow completes her frame of reference to male inscriptions of women's stories by dedicating her novel "To James Branch Cabell . . . in acknowledgment of Something About Eve . . . this book that commemorates the chivalry of men" (Glasgow's ellipsis). In 1927, Cabell had dedicated *Something About Eve: A Comedy of Fig Leaves,* "To Ellen Glasgow—very naturally—this book which commemorates the intelligence of women." Glasgow's novel no more celebrates chivalry in her fictional men than Cabell's celebrates the intelligence of his women. The allusions to Goldsmith and Cabell set up a complex sexual mythology where men define and categorize women as foolish in their endless pursuit of men, and where such foolish women are obstacles to male ideals. It is through such masculine constructs of femininity that Glasgow directs us to read her novel.

For Glasgow's clearest expression of the perspective through which we are to view her novel, let me return in some detail to "Some Literary Woman Myths," the 1928 essay that later became a major part of the Preface to this novel. In the earlier essay Glasgow traces a history of "literary woman myths" that have been "invented by man," ("SLWM" 36), from male views of "woman as an inspiration" to "woman as an impediment."[32] Her point is that women's plots, devised by men, tell much more about men than about women. Using *Clarissa* as the exemplum of inspirational woman, Glasgow points out that the portrayal of Clarissa "is more remarkable as a reflection of man's sentiment than as an analysis of woman's mind" ("SLWM" 39). Though twentieth-century writers have shifted to a view of women as an "impediment," Glasgow observes, little else has changed; the stories are still not really about women. As she says here of Cabell's work: "When we read his books, and especially his latest one, which tells us something about Eve but more about Adam, we are almost persuaded that to pursue the infinite and attain the finite has been the disillusioning career of man alone" (42). Though male modernist authors purport in their writing to be true to the experience of the independent New Woman (Glasgow mentions specifically Hemingway's Brett Ashley), in fact, Glasgow says, most of these women characters "are merely inquisitive little boys trying to be outrageous in their elder sister's clothes" (44). That is, the Brett Ashleys of the modernist fictional world are "merely" male versions of women—adolescent male versions, at that—dressed to look like women.[33] Further, in adopting a metaphor of cross-dressing to criticize male novelists' limited understanding of female character, Glasgow uses popular culture's most common symbol of what was threatening about the New Woman. The demand for equality outwardly represented by her "mannish" clothes made the physical manifestation of fashion a question of large import, as Smith-Rosenberg and Gilbert and Gubar argue.[34] Glasgow double-crosses, to adapt Elizabeth A. Meese's term, and makes the male modernists the cross-dressers. In so doing, she subverts their own metaphor and exposes its limitations.

Most damaging to women, Glasgow asserts, the "myth of woman as an impediment" has firmly taken hold in fiction, making it difficult to rewrite "woman myths" from a female perspective. Without some "reversal," she concludes, "we may cheerfully assume that an obstacle rather than an ideal will be the arresting feature of our novels" ("SLWM" 45). The sarcasm of "cheerfully" combined with the ambiguities of "arresting" drives home her point. "Little boys" who think they can understand women by dressing in the outward trappings of their "sister's clothes" are victims of arrested development, she implies; male versions of women's stories are the salient (or "arresting") features of fiction and therefore have the force of something widely accepted; and male versions of women's stories "arrest" or imprison women in men's perspectives, and make it impossible to progress beyond the point at which they are "arrested." A goal of *They Stooped to Folly* is to release women from their arrested state in modern American fiction.

Glasgow attributes the "reversal" from woman as ideal to woman as obstacle in large part to Freudian psychology—"the Freudian perils of the postwar years" ("SLWM" 37). Significantly, she attempts in *They Stooped to Folly* her own reversal away from the ill effects of Freud and the sexologists on women. Along with Goldsmith and Cabell, then, Freud and those who followed become part of a male bastion of mythmaking that Glasgow wants to undercut. She realized the difficulty of achieving such a reversal. In an essay published in *Harper's* in December 1928, not long before *They Stooped to Folly* first appeared,[35] Glasgow observed that writing "protest" literature is difficult because "expression belonged to the articulate, and the articulate was supremely satisfied with his own fortunate lot as well as with the less enviable lots of others."[36] Her list of possible protesters is interesting in light of *They Stooped to Folly*'s subject: "Only the slave, the 'poor white,' or the woman who had forgotten her modesty may have felt inclined to protest." And besides, she asks, "even if they had protested who would have listened?"[37] *They Stooped to Folly* gives "the woman who had forgotten her modesty" a chance to tell her own story, or, at least, to expose that story as a masculine construct and have it retold. The novel reveals that the woman of "folly" has been convinced by men's stories about her and has accepted them: she believes that she has "fallen" from inspiration to impediment, from angel to demon, from virgin to prostitute, from Mary to Magdalen.[38] Glasgow's epigraph—and her revised story—omits the second verse of Goldsmith's song of women's folly:

> The only art her guilt to cover,
> To hide her shame from every eye,
> To give repentance to her lover,
> And wring his bosom, is—to die.

Refusing the literal death that presents the alternative to marriage in the heroine's text, and refusing the centrality of the betraying lover to whom giving "repentance" is the woman of folly's sole object, Glasgow revises the story and offers new ones, including that of women's friendships to replace the heterosexual imperative.

Appropriate to Glasgow's iconoclastic purpose, *They Stooped to Folly,* set in the 1920s and, in flashbacks, to U.S. involvement in World War I, is a novel about a shifting and confusing world. The war in Europe rumbles beneath the surface of the conventional world of Queenborough (based on what Glasgow saw as her equally conventional hometown of Richmond). Glasgow's male narrator, the Victorian patriarch Virginius Littlepage, is befuddled by the world's disorder. "He had respected convention; he had deferred to tradition," and yet he finds his ground no longer firm (*TSF* 3). Partly because the novel begins with his narration, often we are sympathetic toward Virginius. But his controlling point of view in the novel's first section, "Mr. Littlepage," serves a different primary purpose: as often in Glasgow's Gothic stories, it circumscribes the story of the novel's women, especially "they" who "stooped to folly." We have *his,* not *their,* point of view, just as Glasgow has argued.

Virginius's sense that people have "lost [their] way in the universe" in part results from his relationship with his young secretary, Milly Burden, who initially attracted him enough to threaten the "stable equilibrium of his emotions" (*TSF* 5). But, preferring "severe virtue in women," Virginius is safe from Milly after all, for nothing "could blind him to the fact that she had once forgotten her modesty" (5). Milly belongs to the third generation in Virginius's genealogy of women who forgot their modesty; he places her in the tradition of "poor Aunt Agatha" (whose name is rarely separated from its descriptor, "poor"), and of his "attractive, if unfortunate neighbour," Amy Dalrymple. Agatha, after giving birth to a child forty years earlier (192), accepted others' interpretation of her as "ruined" and "had fallen like a perfect lady" (74). We are never told what happened to the child except that it was "taken . . . away" (192). Agatha "immured herself for forty years in a third-story back bedroom" and appeared— "flitted" into view—only at family meals. Amy Dalrymple, a generation after Agatha, was divorced by her husband for her infidelity and then deserted by her lover. Her subsequent residence in Europe further damns her in the eyes of Queenborough residents. Milly Burden— yet another generation later—like Aunt Agatha, bore a child (which subsequently died) while the father was in Europe during the war.

Agatha and Amy, the two older women, attempt to live according to the standards others have set for them; they accept their "fallen" status and behave accordingly. But it is this acquiescence that ultimately condemns them, suggesting the self-destructiveness that results when women accept others' interpretations of their experience and of right behavior. "Perfect lady" that she was, Agatha first had accepted her role as passive (but guilty) recipient of a man's indecorous attentions, then accepted with equal placidity the silence expected of her: "No persuasion, no threats, not even the sinister one of an asylum, had compelled her to divulge the name of her seducer" (*TSF* 74). Agatha, clinging to "that last obligation of honour, which had impelled an erring woman to screen her betrayer" (144), silently retreated to her third-story prison. Her lover, meanwhile, "had lost three faithful wives" and "never missed a Christmas cotillion" (74). Glasgow also hints that Agatha's retiring and guilt-ridden persona masks an intelligence that she felt obligated to hide. Victoria, who sees through much of the shallowness of her culture, upon meeting "poor Aunt Agatha's sharpened glance," reflects: "I sometimes think [Agatha] might have had a mind if she had ever been allowed to use one" (230–31). Though Agatha is described as having a "still and shallow mind" that "seldom" thinks "about anything," in fact, Victoria's belief in Agatha's intelligence is validated when Agatha wonders, for example, "if the women of her generation had ever realized what the passing of Queen Victoria had meant to them?" (139), or when she asks herself, "how can religion be cruel if God is a loving Father?" (140). Rather than pursue her thoughts, however, Agatha succumbs to patriarchal definitions of a woman's capacities: "Well, all that is too deep for a woman's mind. Father used to say that a woman's mind is like a flower, designed to shed fragrance, not sense." Only briefly does Agatha doubt her father's truism: "I wonder..." (14; Glasgow's ellipsis).

Like Agatha, Amy Dalrymple accepts stereotypical femininity, though hers is characterized by physical beauty and selflessness, rather than the passivity and silence exacted of Agatha's generation. Not perfect lady but womanly woman, Amy has merely lived up to others' expectations that her physical appearance welcomes male sexual advances and that her feminine selflessness encourages those advances to fruition. Amy "might have remained as virtuous as Louisa had her figure been less pronounced or the field of woman's activities more varied" (*TSF* 86). But her "deceptive bosom, which inspired hope in men, and a naturally kind heart, which hesitated to dispense disappointment, had been, if not the occasion, at least the original cause, of her frailty" (86–87). Not a desire for men, but generosity and kindness led to Amy Dalrymple's "fall," and she certainly does not view her relationships with men as rousing conquests: "It is true that when men were deceived by her ripe mouth and rich bosom, her kind heart had made but a feeble show of resistance; but these episodes, after they had happened, invariably seemed to her to have occurred in her sleep" (87). Glasgow emphasizes the unfairness of Amy's circumscribed options by making her a war hero. Her "queenly figure" "subdued" by her war uniform and her "renown for easy virtue" transformed into "a reputation for heroic exploits" (87), Amy had saved wounded soldiers, rescued patients from a burning hospital, and been decorated for her service. The novel argues that given a proper setting, women triumph. Ironically, it is the same concern for others that damns Amy in an uncongenial cultural climate and praises her in the topsy-turvy world of war. Glasgow's pointed criticism of the hypocrisy of genteel American society is difficult to miss.

Whereas Agatha and Amy are condemned for trying to succeed in the terms others have set for them, the modern woman, Milly Burden, is condemned for her refusal to accept others' guidelines for her behavior. Like many of her actual historical counterparts, Milly insists on her "right" to sexual freedom and to a career (though she does not examine the limited range even within those rights),[39] and perhaps, had her baby lived, to single motherhood. An older generation's strict adherence to conventional forms, including her mother's narrow theology, do not allow for the "rights" that Milly demands (*TSF* 22, 34), but only for privileges. Virginius, whose perspective dominates our view of Milly, expresses his frustration at Milly's refusal to play the wronged woman: "So little . . . had she resembled the proverbial lost woman that Goldsmith himself would scarcely have known her for what she was" (33). But it is Milly's new tradition of womanhood—one that refuses to be victimized, refuses to be wronged (a term whose passive voice reveals its limitations), refuses to accept others' expectations of her—that triumphs in the end. Milly's contemporary, Mary Victoria, the seemingly capable daughter of Virginius and Victoria, proves to be as outdated as her virginal and queenly name. Near the novel's conclusion, Milly expresses not her bitterness but her realistic expectations from life as she plans to move to a new city and a new job and to look, not for love with a man, but for "something worth loving" (302, 303). She not only defines her life but also correctly characterizes Martin Welding, who has betrayed both her and Mary Victoria. In contrast to Milly's confident, "defiant" pronouncements, Mary Victoria wilts in her father's arms: "all her gallant spirit . . . was oozing slowly away. Her erect figure appeared to shrink and falter beneath a burden that was too intolerable to be borne" (301, 302). Milly learns to define herself apart from men, while Mary Victoria's very selfhood, though literally upheld by her father, "oozes" away because her husband has left her.

It is Virginius, however, more than any of the women characters, who must rethink the suppositions upon which he has based his life and opinions. In answer to Glasgow's point (reinforced by the structure of her narrative) that male perspectives have dominated the interpretations of women's experience, the novel demands that Virginius (or men), more than women, must change. Though he is, by his own admission, convention itself, Virginius shows occasional promise in self-reevaluation. Early in the novel he observes to himself that "even the Southern gentleman . . . was beginning to suspect that the ruined woman is an invention of man" (*TSF* 18). At the conclusion of part one, named for him, Virginius thinks: "The truth is that the world has never been fair to women. Men have never been fair to women" (120). On both occasions, however, his flitting realizations are undercut by what immediately follows: his desire for Amy Dalrymple, a desire born of his physical attraction to her sexuality. He never pushes his brief conclusions to their logical ends: he has "invented" Amy's "ruin" and, in his desire for the very female sexuality for which he condemns her, he remains unfair. Glasgow condemns Virginius at her novel's conclusion for his irredeemably clouded vision: "his troubled gaze" looks across the river only to be "smothered by the darkening drift of the twilight" (304). At the end, he sees nothing.

In contrast to Virginius, the women in *They Stooped to Folly* see plenty, though as characters in male mythological fictions, they cannot always act upon their clearer visions. Glasgow's answer to Virginius's maundering is the solidity of female friendship, even when it is only imagined. Indeed, women's happiest moments in the novel are with one another, their saddest when they are alienated from each other.

In a wistful moment, Amy Dalrymple realizes that by centering her life on men, she has denied herself the saving companionship of other women. " 'I suppose you would call me a man's woman,' " she tells Virginius. " 'That may be the reason,' she added gravely, visited by a flash of penetration, 'why I had so few friends when I needed them' " (*TSF* 262). Toward the end of the novel, however, Amy finds her friend as she begins to enjoy the company of Aunt Agatha. When Victoria objects to Agatha's newfound companion by hinting that Amy is "rather a pushing person" (145) who more properly should have "waited . . . for the first advance to come from us" (146), Agatha retorts: "I suppose it didn't occur to her that she could harm my reputation" (146). Agatha thus reminds Victoria that if she must accept her male-centered role as a fallen woman, she can certainly still define her own relation to women who share her "ruined" status. Agatha and Amy "go to every moving picture together," and Agatha, in her fondness for Amy, once touchingly "pause[s] for a last glimpse of her friend" after getting out of Amy's car (157). Glasgow leaves us with a growing female friendship both women have previously missed by having their lives defined solely in relation to men.

Glasgow offers the friendship between Victoria and her lifelong friend Louisa Goddard as the potential ideal relationship between women. In a section added to the original essay for her 1938 Preface, Glasgow says that the friendship between Louisa and Victoria marks "the highest point" of her "narrative." Virginius, of course, thinks of the single, intellectually energetic Louisa (Virginius calls her "an admirable spinster") as deficient in "charm" (*TSF* 27). To him, there is "something masculine in her prominent features and her pronounced opinions upon public affairs" that keeps her from appealing to men (39). Implicitly linking Louisa's unmarried state to asexuality and intellectuality, Virginius thinks of her as "frigid, no doubt, in temperament" (39), and is mildly puzzled that Louisa, living her life without regard to male expectation, can be "the happiest and most industrious woman of his acquaintance" (39).

For Glasgow, it is precisely Louisa's refusal to be defined by and in relation to men that makes her happy and industrious, and her defiance is demonstrated in her close relationship with Victoria Littlepage. Louisa has "admired and loved" Victoria "since childhood," and the two women share "every event in life" (*TSF* 123) with one another. They have not allowed men to come between them: "Even as children they had been inseparable, and marriage, which destroys so many earnest friendships, had only sealed their devotion into an indestructible bond" (44). Even Virginius eventually wonders aloud to Louisa: "Yours has been a wonderful friendship, and it has made me ask myself, now and then, if men really know anything about women" (240).

However, "the new psychology" (*TSF* 45) that Louisa Goddard studies disallows an emphasis on the women's friendship, and Glasgow's exasperation at having to apologize for her female characters (it's "fortunate" that their friendship "had come to flower before the serpent of Freudian psychology had poisoned the sinless Eden of friendship") is evident. In her Preface, she notes that modern fiction "seldom" allows "friendship between two women" to occupy "a prominent place." Even though "such an association appears to be not uncommon in life," because the author "is usually a man," he usually "has found the relationship to be deficient alike in the excitement of sex and the masculine drama of action." However, Glasgow concludes, "more and more, in the modern world, women are coming to understand their interdependence as human beings; and without an example of this, a picture of our time that denied the place and permanence of any such friendship would be wanting in complete veracity" (xxiii–iv). Glasgow protests against male-defined plots and asserts her right as a woman novelist to an alternative realism. But her tone is also defensive as she justifies including a central same-sex relationship, and perhaps wishful as she characterizes the "modern world" as one in which "women are coming to understand their interdependence." The truth may be closer to that which historians of women have described: the tradition of female bonding that Glasgow has discovered for herself, which had reached its peak in *Barren Ground*, was being replaced with the sexologists' reemphasis on heterosexuality. Sexual freedom for women often meant, as the cases of Agatha, Amy, and Milly in *They Stooped to Folly* suggest, a returning to relationships with men.[40] The novel's surprise revelation of Louisa's lifelong love for Virginius, the death of Louisa's compassionate friend Victoria, Virginius's transformation of his late wife into an impossible ideal, and Milly's triumphant but isolated flight all lament the passing of a tradition of sisterhood and its replacement with "modern" narratives that revise rather than subvert the heterosexual romance plot.

Playing on the phrase describing women who have "forgotten themselves," Glasgow in *They Stooped to Folly* reminds us of its various meanings. One, Goldsmith's definition, describes women who "stoop to folly": women who have, presumably, lost their moral grounding and indulged sinfully in extramarital sex. Milly tells Virginius that her mother's rigid Calvinism allows a woman to be hanged for murder, "but you are still an honest woman as long as you haven't forgotten yourself" (*TSF* 254). Another meaning encompasses women whose selfless devotion to others has led to their forgetting themselves, as when Virginius realizes his wife's concern for her family overrode her concern for herself in the fatal illness she hid from them: "Faced with that discovery of her mortal illness, she had forgotten herself, she had thought only of him and her children" (277). A final meaning is Glasgow's: women and their stories, unless we retell them, are in danger of being "forgotten."

In part, Glasgow may represent her personal experience, especially as evident in her correspondence, in her statement that women were "coming to understand their interdependence." In her own life, certainly, the late twenties was a time during which she solidified her close relationships with women friends, and she continued to cultivate important new friendships with women for the remainder of her life. Most of Glasgow's surviving letters to Anne Virginia Bennett date from the late twenties to the late thirties; familiar letters to Amélie Rives Troubetzkoy continue throughout this time as well. Glasgow met other women who became close companions, even if mostly (sometimes exclusively, as in the case of Toksvig) as epistolary companions: British writer Radclyffe Hall; illustrator Clare Leighton; Marjorie Kinnan Rawlings; and the Danish writer Signe Toksvig.

In the letters between Glasgow and all of these women, there is a distinctly familiar, personal tone that is usually missing in her professional letters, most of which were written to men in powerful literary positions. One could say that this tone argues for the letters' insignificance, presumably a reason that Blair Rouse chose not to include them in his edition of Glasgow's letters. One could say, on the other hand, that it argues precisely for their importance: Glasgow's ease, her vulnerability, indicate her closeness to and her trust of the recipients.

To her "dearest A.V.," Glasgow writes long (often more than fifteen autograph pages) and newsy letters during her travels, remarking on the scenery and her shopping sprees and asking after Anne Virginia and their pet dogs. Twice in England she orders special coats for Anne Virginia, and from Italy she "keep[s] wishing that you could see and smell this place of flowers."[41]

Other new friendships at the time were professional as well as personal. Radclyffe Hall, in addition to receiving Glasgow's professional support for her work,[42] also received books from Glasgow, often jointly addressed to Hall and her longtime companion, Una Troubridge. Glasgow visited the two women in England in 1930, and Glasgow's correspondence with Hall is substantial. Glasgow met the illustrator Clare Leighton on New Year's Day 1936, and began a friendship marked by warm letters. In their correspondence, the two women discuss marriage, men, divorce, and their work, exchanging inscribed books. Clare's devotion is often apparent. In 1940, when Glasgow was in the hospital, Clare sent her two original engravings. One is a forest scene; the foreground shows a pitchfork in a dirt mound. Its inscription reads: "For Ellen in hospital, that she may walk in the woods. With love from Clare." The other, a rural scene with trees, a stream, and a farm against the distant hills, is inscribed: "For Ellen with love from Clare Leighton" "to open her hospital doors." As with other women friends, a shared reverence for nature marks this friendship. So does a willingness to express feeling; Clare does not shy away from telling Glasgow that she is "one of my warm glowing things in life" or from saying: "I love you so much."[43] Signe Toksvig, the Danish-born writer married to critic Francis Hackett, never met Glasgow personally, but the two women corresponded for the last two years of Glasgow's life. Toksvig, the author of a biography of Hans Christian Andersen and a study of Emanuel Swedenborg, shared with Glasgow an interest in mysticism and a characteristic willingness to express affection. She writes Glasgow that when a mutual friend spoke "about the delight of being in your actual presence, [it] made me feel lonely for you! But, you know, I often feel in a kind of communication with you." Later in the same letter, Toksvig says: "I do feel near to you. Actual fleshly presence is not necessary. Still I do send you a kiss."[44]

Glasgow's sense of the centrality of other women in her life, a sense that had settled into conviction by the mid to late twenties, came at the same time that the new psychology was questioning the nature of women's friendships. Social discourse reinterpreted a former "female world" of closeness as sexually deviant just at the time that Glasgow confirmed and accepted the importance of women friends in her own life. The tension that results—a sense of self at odds with its culture, forced to adhere to a strict divergence between public and private, robbed of comfort just as it is found—makes its way into the theme of Glasgow's next novel, *The Sheltered Life,* and eventually into her self-characterization in the autobiography she began writing in the mid-thirties.

The Sheltered Life *and*
Post-Freudian Female Development

Glasgow may have realized in 1933, when she wrote her Preface for the Old Dominion edition of *Barren Ground,* the extent to which that novel marked an isolated moment in her career. That novel's confident assertion of narratological and personal freedom from patriarchal textual imperatives allowed Glasgow to write beyond convention (to borrow Wagner's apt phrase) and to substitute a tradition of female companionship and feminist independence from men and male constructs. But in describing *Barren Ground* in 1933 as her "vehicle of liberation," Glasgow included a modifier that critics usually omit: *Barren Ground* "became for me," Glasgow says, "while I was working upon it, *almost* a vehicle of liberation."[45] Almost. For if *Barren Ground* liberated Glasgow to substitute for the marriage plot a narrative of female friendship, *They Stooped to Folly* required her to defend women's friendship as "sinless." And *The Sheltered Life* (1932), even while it exposed as destructive a tradition of women's self-abnegation in seeking marriage, could not go as far as to offer an alternative female solidarity. The novel's anger—and it is a very angry novel—targets a cultural norm that, as it elevated heterosexuality, negated a tradition of female bonding Glasgow had discovered for herself as much as it criticizes what she elsewhere calls the "evasive idealism" that critics often stress in this novel, and that Glasgow had long held in contempt.[46]

The structure of *The Sheltered Life* loosely adheres to a Freudian notion of personality development, in itself a capitulation, on the surface, to the new masculine tradition of Freudian psychology. The novel opens with the protagonist, nine-year-old Jenny Blair Archbald, on the verge of developing into the young adult self she will be by the novel's end. Jenny Blair's journey toward maturation depends, the novel suggests, upon transferring her allegiance from a maternal world of connection to the world of men and heterosexuality— or, in Freudian terms, on successfully negotiating the Oedipal stage. Hence, in this model of development, sexuality is inextricably linked to issues of affiliation and separation-individuation, as psychologists since Freud have discussed. Glasgow, having earlier discovered for herself a need for a nurturing female tradition of connection, especially connection between women, but one devoid of an insistence on female self-abnegation, found herself in a post-Freudian culture that made renewed demands for a separate, independent ego. And Freudian "independence" meant heterosexuality. Though Glasgow's experience denied a wholesale adoption of the Freudian model of separation as the mark of a healthy ego and of healthy sexual development, she nevertheless lived within a cultural discourse saturated with psychosexual theory. *The Sheltered Life* reveals her tension as she angrily denounces a culture lacking in human cooperation and obsessed with heterosexuality, but the novel is no longer able to offer female companionship as an alternative plot.

The opening chapter of *The Sheltered Life,* set in Queenborough in 1906, emphasizes the separation between generations represented by Jenny Blair Archbald and her mother. The novel begins with Jenny Blair reading Louisa May Alcott's *Little Women,* not for pleasure, and not, as her mother had, to "form her character," but, in mimicry of turn-of-the-century acquisitiveness, for materialistic gain: her grandfather will pay her a "penny a page" and she wants new roller skates.[47] Glasgow's theme emphasizes the danger in rejecting affiliation in personality development; Jenny Blair emphatically separates herself from her mother's world and from the text that formed her mother's "character."[48] Rather than seeing them as inspirations, Jenny Blair finds Alcott's Meg and Jo March "poky old things" (*SL* 3), ironically echoing Jo March's own denunciation of her resemblance to a "poky old woman" because she is forced to knit socks for the Civil War effort.[49] "Mamma may call the Marches lots of fun," Jenny Blair continues, "but I'm different. I'm different" (3). Her mother, asking whether Jenny Blair is "getting on" (6) with the book, tells her: "I could never have too much of *Little Women* when I was a girl. I remember I tried to form my character on Meg—or it may have been Jo" (7). Again turning her mother's beloved Jo's words against her, Jenny Blair replies: "Oh, Mamma, it is so dreadfully poky" (7). Jenny Blair seeks to form her own character, based, not on a maternal model of connection, but on a model that defines her as distinct, as "different."

Cora Archbald's confusion about whether her childhood female role model was the independent Jo or the more womanly Meg March underscores the deficiency of spiritual mothers in Jenny Blair's life, and serves as a reminder of the vast distance marked by the single generation between Cora and Jenny Blair Archbald. This era, as many critics have perceived, often led to tension rather than communion between actual and symbolic mothers and daughters.[50] Whereas Cora Archbald had been provided with the very different options represented by both Meg and Jo, Jenny Blair has neither. Ironically, so separated is she from the female models of her mother's generation, Jenny Blair fails even to recognize her own resemblance to the independent and outspoken Jo, including their shared regret over being born female (*SL* 14; *LW* 3). Alienated from the mother text represented by *Little Women,* Jenny Blair's generation finds itself without literary foremothers. Indeed, though she rejects the female text, she pauses at one point to "decipher the hieroglyphics left in chalk on the board fence by horrid little boys" (37). Even if she finds the boys horrid now, Jenny Blair is intent on discovering textual meaning in male hieroglyphics. Intriguingly, Jenny Blair discerns her resemblance, not to Jo or Meg or to any "little women," but to Alice in Wonderland— a book first published in 1868, three years after Alcott's novel. Alice, whose text is the story of male-imagined female development, learns to define herself in sublime separation from the world of familiar everydayness and from other people. Jenny Blair looks "gravely at her face in the mirror" and sees not Meg or Jo but Alice; she wonders "if she would always, even when she grew up, remind herself of Alice in Wonderland" (78–79). Jenny Blair cannot read herself into female existence through female texts as her mother could.

Instead, Jenny Blair must try to define herself independent of her mother and independent of female community, literary or otherwise.

When we first meet her, she is "discovering her hidden self" (*SL* 3) in a refrain that she "croon[s]," as if replacing a maternal lullaby: "I'm alive, alive, alive, and I'm Jenny Blair Archbald" (3). In a freighted cluster of images, Jenny Blair perceives in herself a "fragment of personality" that becomes "detached" from some "warm mother-of-pearl vagueness within" until "all she knew was, 'I am this and not that'" (3). Rejecting a maternal ("mother-of-pearl") core in herself, Jenny Blair defines her new self through separation, asserting her new selfhood in opposition to others ("this and not that").[51] Significantly, Jenny Blair associates her song of self with her father, who died in a foxhunting accident when Jenny Blair was five. She keeps her song, which is "all her own," "hidden away with her chief treasure, the gold locket in which somebody had wound a tiny circle of her father's hair" (4). When "alone and happy," Jenny Blair sings her song "aloud," but in the midst of the maternal figures in her family, she does not communicate it: "alone with her mother or her aunts, the words dissolved into a running tune" (4). Her mother, symbolically separated from her daughter by the song of a separate self, does not understand the words ("would never, never understand," Jenny Blair thinks): "What are you saying, Jenny Blair?" she asks (4).

These opening pages introduce the conditions under which the rest of the novel's problems develop, problems in defining a female self (or, in Jenny Blair's mother's words, forming a female character) without the benefit of female affiliation. Instead of a community of women, whether of actual or symbolic mothers or female friends, Jenny Blair and her post-Freudian generation of young women must define a female self in the context of an exaggerated heterosexuality. Educated in the assumption that the only healthy female self is one conjoined in heterosexual relation, Jenny Blair is separated from the tradition of female bonding that her mother's generation had enjoyed and that Glasgow herself had come to embrace. Bent on pursuing men and marriage, Jenny Blair and her contemporaries reject the female friendship that sexologists had defined as deviant. On this level, *The Sheltered Life* is the story of overemphasized heterosexual pursuit and the damage it does to human relationships, particularly relationships among women.

Indeed, the women in *The Sheltered Life* are separated from one another largely because each must pursue her heterosexual role. Not only does Jenny Blair reject her mother, but her aunt Isabella attempts to redeem her "reputation"—"tarnished" (*SL* 13) when her fiancé breaks their engagement after Isabella took a carriage ride with another man—by seeking another, more accepting, male. Jenny Blair's other aunt, Etta, sobs that "the only thing in the world" she wants is to be loved (*SL* 63). Eva Birdsong, the town's reigning beauty since her youth, devotes herself so exclusively to her philandering husband, George, that she can still say to Jenny Blair that men and women who truly love one another "ought to be sufficient to themselves." Someday, she promises, Jenny Blair will understand that "a great love doesn't leave room for anything else in a woman's life. It is everything" (55). The "sinless Eden of friendship" that Glasgow earlier celebrated, even if guardedly, has disappeared, and each woman's story seems isolated from that of others.

In fact, however, as Glasgow makes clear, those stories impinge upon one another in subtle ways. The destructiveness of separation from a female tradition of companionship and mutual nurturance is most evident in the stories of Eva Birdsong, Etta Archbald, and Jenny Blair Archbald. Our first view of Eva signals her isolation from other women; the reader joins Cora, Jenny Blair, and Etta in observing Eva through a window as she walks past the Archbald house. This physical distance as a metaphor for the psychic distance not only from other women but even from herself is one that turns upon Glasgow's use of female friendship as a symbolic second female self. As the three women at the window watch unperceived, Eva, "thinking herself alone in the street," briefly "permitted her well-trained muscles to relax." Her artificial smile disappears, "her step" loses "its springiness," and her body sags down "into the stiff ripples of taffeta" (*SL* 16). Eva, consistently described as ideal, allegorical, legendary (15), momentarily lets slip the veil of her hypocrisy and willed self-deception. In a 1930 review, Glasgow complained that Cabell's unrealistic women characters were merely "inventions of desire."[52] Glasgow's objection is echoed by *The Sheltered Life*'s narrative comment that Eva's features seem "woven less of flesh than of some fragile bloom of desire" (17). As Eva's nephew John Welch says, Eva's problem is "not facing things" (273). That is, Eva does not show an honest "face," and refuses to confront (or "face") not only others but her real self, her own needs and desires.

Jenny Blair, who throughout the novel tries to maintain allegiance to Eva but instead transfers her adoration to Eva's husband, George, precipitates the murder at the novel's conclusion, when Eva finally "faces things" with such force that violence results. Rather than the companionship for Eva that she might have provided—and, indeed, tries to talk herself into providing—Jenny Blair acquiesces in a sexual relationship with George and thus pits herself against Eva in a love triangle. Though as a child she had rushed to the window to watch in adoration as Eva walked by, Jenny Blair aligns herself with George at her first sexually charged encounter with him. After falling down and passing out in a forbidden area of town, Jenny Blair is taken into the home of Memoria, the kind black woman who is "kept" by George. As in *Virginia*, racial oppression here is tied to gender as Jenny Blair's "forbidden" territory is a racially segregated neighborhood in which George can safely hide his adultery. Memoria and her neighborhood are effectively invisible to others, allowing George his hypocrisy. Jenny Blair perceives without understanding the ease with which George fits into the setting of Memoria's home (*SL* 40), an ease that reveals his racial and sexual domination.

Substituting heterosexuality for female bonding, Jenny Blair experiences the "exquisite torment" and "yearning rapture" of heterosexual awakening when George urges her to secrecy about their day's adventure. Treating Jenny Blair, who's not yet ten, as a sexual being, George takes advantage of her, just as he does of Memoria, of his wife, and of all women. He tells her she will probably be "one of the prettiest girls in Queenborough" and compares her eyes and hair to those of a "wood-nymph" (*SL* 44). George hints that she may become a "beauty" (44), tells her that she seems old enough to keep a secret (45), threatens emotional blackmail if she tells of their meeting at Memoria's house ("I'd feel, of course, that I could never trust you again") (46–47), and praises her for being "plucky" (47). "Intoxicated" (47) by his words, Jenny Blair thinks: "Until this evening, she had always loved Mrs. Birdsong best, but now, she told herself, Mr. Birdsong was first of all" (49).

Once Eva begins to "face things," the novel moves inexorably toward its powerful conclusion, where Eva murders her husband. After her hysterectomy, a symbolic stripping of Eva's femaleness according to an ideological construct that defines her by her status as wife and mother, Eva's nervous breakdown marks her separation from her former self. But rather than the destructive events that they seem to be, the surgery and the breakdown that follows it are constructive: however painful the process, Eva *needs* to be separated from that false self she has become, in order to recover her true self. Her "desperate flights into the street," Eva tells Jenny Blair, function as the means to "get away from myself—or the part of myself I leave in the house" (*SL* 284). The self Eva leaves in the house is the self that revolves around the pretense of domestic bliss with the adulterous George. As Eva says, "Unless I go alone, I can never find myself. When you've never been yourself for forty years, you've forgotten what you are really" (285). "I'm worn out with being somebody else—with being somebody's ideal," Eva continues; "I want to turn around and be myself for a little while before it is too late" (285). Eva's "flights" connect her to the dead ducks George has just brought home from his hunting trip: they're "beauties" who were "superb in flight," he says (283). Scattered around the library and labeled by George with "bits of narrow green ribbon" that Eva had torn from her "old dress," the dead ducks look "decorated, as if for a wedding feast" (287). Literally dressed in Eva's clothes and representing her as a bride, the ducks' message seems clear: marriage has symbolically killed Eva. In order to be reborn to herself, she must literally kill her husband. When Jenny Blair finally works up the courage to look at Eva after the murder, Eva's face is "vacant," her features are "like wax," and "her skin was as colourless as the skin of the dead" (290). But Eva's deadness is quickly revised as Jenny Blair forces herself to look at George; now it is he and not Eva who resembles the dead birds. She sees the "blood on his lips" (291), just like the "drops of blood" that remain "in the beaks" of the ducks (290). Cora Archbald's assertion early in *The Sheltered Life* that George is so "devoted" to Eva that he would "pour out every drop of his blood for her if she needed it" (19) is turned on its head at the novel's conclusion. Eva needs for George to pour out the drops of his blood for her; it is her only chance to save her self.

Jenny Blair's transferred love from female companionship, also evident in her relationship to her mother, to heterosexuality results in the emotional distance from others that causes her life to be shallow (and, as we shall see, ultimately, George's murder). This rejection of female bonding, Glasgow implies through Jenny Blair, is responsible for the floundering search for female selfhood that characterizes Jenny Blair's life and also results in the self-destructive tragedy of a life such as Eva Birdsong's. When Jenny Blair learns at an early age to desire George rather than to befriend Eva, she paves the path to her later cool detachment from the concerns of other women.[53] After concluding that "being sorry for people was the worst pain of all," Jenny Blair prays, first, that she won't feel too sorry for others (*SL* 63), and then, that "Aunt Etta's unhappiness" won't "come too near me" (67). As she grows to young womanhood, Jenny Blair's self-centeredness leads to her surface existence concerned only with appearances: she wants to become an actress, wonders if it's possible ever to be "pretty enough" (129), is glad people "love" her for her attractiveness (254), and avoids facing the truth of her flirtation with George (251). Her disregard for others' feelings and her refusal to accept the consequences for other people of her actions nourishes her years-long flirtation with George, even though she professes to care for Eva. Most seriously, this disregard allows Jenny Blair to repeat her favorite statement that she "didn't mean anything" (echoing Jason Greylock's words after he has jilted Dorinda) even though she instigates the passionate embrace with George that causes Eva Birdsong to kill her husband. Jenny Blair's words—"I didn't mean anything in the world!" (292)—conclude *The Sheltered Life*.

The story of Etta Archbald's alienation from the female companionship she obviously desires is both bizarre and painful. Glasgow invests her characterization of Etta with the destructiveness she sees in a culture conversant with sexological theories of female friendship as deviant. Aware that her power as a woman depends upon a sexual attractiveness to men that she lacks, Etta bewails her limited access to heterosexuality even while she seems to desire female companionship instead. Her "neuralgia" serves as a metaphor not so much (except, perhaps, as it is internalized) for her own as for her culture's insistence on a single, adamantly heterosexual definition of love and the narrow range of female life stories such narrowness allows. As she "eagerly" invites Eva Birdsong into her house, Etta sighs, "with an emotion so intense that it was almost hysterical," that Eva Birdsong is "adorable" (*SL* 17). Announcing "I can't believe she was ever more beautiful," Etta's "greenish pallor" becomes flushed with "wine-coloured splotches" of emotion. Reminiscent of earlier female characters beginning with Mariana in *Phases of an Inferior Planet,* Etta had "transferred her emotion" to Eva "several years before, when she had lost faith in men and found it difficult to be romantic about God" (17). The trajectory of Etta's emotional life, in other words, opposes Jenny Blair's: Etta moved from male to female connection. When her sister, Isabella, warns Etta that if she "gush[es] over" Eva "too much," Eva will "grow tired" of her. Etta "passionately" denies it—"You know she will never tire of me"—then "burst[s] into tears" (17).

The companionship that Etta desires with Eva has its parallel in a relationship that is little more than hinted at. Jenny Blair overhears Etta sobbing in the night to Jenny Blair's mother, Cora, that "all" she wants "in the world" is love (*SL* 63). Later, when Cora tries to explain to Jenny Blair, she tells her that Etta "has plenty of people to love her. Even if men don't admire her as much as they admire Isabella, she has devoted friends among women" (65). Jenny Blair protests that these friendships "don't last": "It hurts [Aunt Etta] dreadfully, because she cried all the time after Miss Margaret Wrenn broke off with her" (65–66). When Cora "sternly" demands to know how Jenny Blair knew "that Margaret had broken off" with Etta, Jenny Blair tells her mother: "Oh, I heard it all when it happened. She broke off because she didn't like to be pinched, and Aunt Etta would pinch her until she was black and blue" (66). Cora, stunned at first, "recover[s] her authority" and tries to revise the story by saying that Margaret "was only making-believe" (66). Etta later confirms Jenny Blair's knowledge, however, revealing that Jenny Blair has captured the spirit if not the letter of her aunt's relationship with Miss Wrenn. Hoping to see Margaret Wrenn in the dressing room at a dance, Etta thinks to herself: "I will make her speak to me. She has never been near me since I bit her arm that evening until she cried. But it was only in play. I didn't know it would hurt her like that" (77). The relationship between Etta and Margaret fulfills the sexologists' dire predictions about female friendship gone awry, and Etta's constant illness lends weight to a diagnosis that such companionship is unhealthy and unnatural.

Glasgow's target is not Aunt Etta, however, but the ideology that has redefined her need for female companionship as deviance. Left without the kind of emotional fulfillment she desires, the novel asks, how can Etta do anything but retreat into hysteria as she is forced to desire the heterosexuality she has rejected? A victim of cultural discourse that has redefined her desire, Etta becomes a physical manifestation of the illness that results when one must adhere to social dictates that run counter to private ones. As such, Etta does not differ markedly from Eva Birdsong or Jenny Blair.

Glasgow abandons the narrative revisions she realized in *Barren Ground* by undercutting the traditional heterosexual plot and, at least on the fictive surface, subsequently accepts the neurosis of female friendships (acknowledged in *They Stooped to Folly* and actualized in *The Sheltered Life*). Such a decision testifies to the force of narrative. As Gayle Greene argues in *Changing the Story*, fictional narrative retains the capacity to change not only the terms of its own story but of actual life stories as well. That potential can facilitate positive change, as Greene stresses in her discussion of contemporary women writers. But when the rebellion against conventional narrative maintains only a tentative reality, as it does in the case of Glasgow's *Barren Ground*, narrative potential can also undermine the impulse to change. The very power of narrative is what makes it at once the vehicle both to challenge the status quo and to uphold it. It is, perhaps, the newness of Glasgow's realizations in *Barren Ground* that makes them so fragile. The dominant narrative—of traditional heterosexuality and female powerlessness—wins out after *Barren Ground* as Glasgow relinquishes her literary and narrative freedom from male conventions and traditions and chooses to hold on to private revisionary strategies only, evident especially in her letters. *Barren Ground* remains Glasgow's one unequivocal act of triumph over actual and narratological traditions, explaining, perhaps, why so many readers agree that *Barren Ground* stands alone in Glasgow's oeuvre.

Glasgow's 1929 reference to the "serpent of Freudian psychology" as the "poison" in the "sinless Eden of friendship" between women leaves no doubt as to her awareness of the new interpretation placed on the close connections among women that had been celebrated in her mother's generation. I think that Glasgow was frustrated by the power of men's words to reinterpret female experience, and the power of patriarchal tradition to reassert itself at will. She must have felt this frustration particularly keenly after she had succeeded in her own reinterpretation by transforming what she had seen as her mother's willingness to efface herself into an independence within female connection. The journey from *Barren Ground* through *They Stooped to*

Folly to *The Sheltered Life* is one from celebration of female connection, to recognition of its new meanings, to anger that she must capitulate to those interpretations. Indeed, I find *The Sheltered Life* Glasgow's angriest book, despite its place at the conclusion in a trilogy of so-called comedies of manners. *The Sheltered Life* finds those "manners" destructive to women, and soundly denounces the power of the patriarchy to substitute its own traditions, Freudian or otherwise, for the nurturing tradition of female connection that previous generations of women had enjoyed and that Glasgow had recently discovered for herself. Glasgow never really returned to her theme of female friendship in her fiction, though she wrote two more novels and left another unfinished. She turned her energies in this regard to letters to women friends and to the autobiography she wrote from the mid thirties until her death in 1945. For fictional representations of women's relationships with one another, she left us with her angry denunciation, in *The Sheltered Life,* of the power of ideology to redefine women's experience, and chose relative silence on the subject of women's friendships rather than engagement in a discourse ideologically gendered male.

SIX

The Woman Within: Rewriting and Rereading a Woman's Life

> The truth of the writer, the identity of the writer, the authority of the writer, all these are matters that are always questionable. . . . Of course I don't know who "I" am/is/are.
>
> Cixous, "Difficult Joys"

APHOTOGRAPH OF Glasgow's study in her home at One West Main Street in Richmond tantalizes with the objects that are clearly discernible.[1] Displayed among the many photographs on Glasgow's corner desk are two of Anne Virginia Bennett with a pair of the couple's favorite dogs. Other desktop photos, more difficult to identify with certainty, are mostly of women, it appears; one is probably a daguerreotype of Glasgow's mother and her sister Emily that Glasgow says was "always on my desk."[2] On the mantel just to the right of the desk is a picture of Emily Brontë, obviously a frequent source of inspiration. On the bookshelf still farther to the right, one title in particular caught my attention: *The Education of Henry Adams.*[3] In many ways, these objects in the room where Glasgow did most of her writing for over half a century are, for me, emblematic of her complex relationship with tradition. A jumble of reminders of personal, professional, and literary relationships, these artifacts make impossible (or at least irresponsible) simple conclusions or reductive statements about Glasgow's relation to them in traditions of friendship, of attitudes toward family, of literary history.

In thinking of Glasgow writing *The Woman Within* (1954) at that desk beginning in about 1934, I find particularly provocative the presence of Henry Adams and his *Education,* often considered the quintessential American autobiography, at least for this century. In a 1939 letter to Van Wyck Brooks, Glasgow, in the midst of writing her own autobiography, said of Adams: "I must confess to a secret sympathy with that malicious old demon, Henry Adams. His penetration was as narrow (and as fine) as a needle . . . ; but the most irritating thing about him is that he was so often right in his malice."[4]

Glasgow's dual response to Adams of sympathy and irritation, to borrow her words, also characterizes her ambivalent feelings toward tradition. And in the United States, especially for an author writing an autobiography, Henry Adams is, as Henry James might say, tradition itself. If Adams could feel oppressed and constrained at the heavy and omnipresent weight of a public past peopled with his famous forebears, Glasgow could feel the same of her own more personal history. Where Adams famously begins his autobiography "under the shadow of the Boston State House," Glasgow begins hers with flickering and vague images that offer no security. Rather than the solidly embodied Henry Brooks Adams whose birth gives meaning to the opening paragraph of his *Education,* the "amoeba"-like (*WW* 3) vagueness of an unnamed and disembodied Ellen Glasgow searches for meaning in the opening of *The Woman Within.* Whereas Adams must evaluate his place in a tradition ready-made to nurture him, Glasgow must first find the traditions that are hers. For Glasgow, wrestling with the notion of tradition and considering whether women's traditions are distinct, autobiography became yet another way of examining male traditions of writing and, simultaneously, of identity construction, that were available to her. Like the male-defined heroine's text that she explored through her fiction, here she faced a tradition potentially void of female meaning. In writing an autobiography, Glasgow uses a male-dominated generic tradition to explore patriarchal traditions (including the notion of tradition itself, perhaps) in order to rewrite them for herself.

In one sense, autobiography is itself about tradition. To write the story of one's life is to identify and engage the precedents, both cultural and personal, that make up the present "I" of the autobiographical narrative in a contemporary historical context. The autobiographer confronts the tradition of other autobiographers, as well. For the woman writing her life history, especially one who reached young adulthood before the turn of the twentieth century, both kinds of tradition—personal/cultural and literary—are problematic, as many critics have suggested. The literary tradition offered little narrative aid, nearly bereft as it was of known female presence, and the personal/cultural tradition had been founded on notions of a stable and coherent self, called into question particularly by postmodern considerations of the extent to which "selves" are shaped by cultural (including linguistic) systems.

As with much of her fiction, Glasgow's autobiography, *The Woman Within,* written during the last ten years of Glasgow's life and published nearly ten years after her death, serves as a springboard for her leap into an examination of tradition and her feelings about it. In looking back over her life—in rewriting her life the way she wants it to be perceived, or the way she wants to perceive it—Glasgow examines many of the markers of tradition that are familiar by now: her relationships with her mother and father; her attitudes toward men and marriage and the traditional romance plot; her friendships with other women; and her relationship to the literary traditions she engages. Once again, as with her fiction, Glasgow takes the materials handed down to her and reworks them, subverting patriarchal traditions and transmuting them into traditions of womanhood that she can live with.

Autobiography is also about selfhood or identity, and it is with the intersection of tradition and identity that Glasgow's autobiography concerns itself. The Western tradition of selfhood, or what Domna Stanton calls the "Western myth of subjecthood," especially as it has been transmitted through autobiographical accounts, has assumed certain stable definitions. Describing the "notion of the individual" that reached its apex in "metaphysical selfhood," Sidonie Smith succinctly summarizes this "self": "Its core is understood to be unitary, irreducible, atomic; its boundaries separating inner from outer, well-defined, stable, impermeable; its relationship to the world, unencumbered by alternative, absorbing roles. A Cartesian self, its vision is rational, totalizing, and appropriative, unshaken by the anarchies of embodiment."[5] In *The Woman Within*, Glasgow ends by rejecting the independent, stable ego of masculine selfhood and by reconnecting herself to a woman's tradition of affiliation, thus questioning at once long-standing androcentric assumptions about individual selves and the literary transmittal of those assumptions. *The Woman Within* temporarily subscribes to traditional standards of self-representation, only to demonstrate their inadequacy and thereby to subvert and rewrite them.

Glasgow chose a circuitous route to this conclusion, beginning with an account of her childhood, youth, and adulthood that at first glance often appears to reinforce rather than to reject masculine models of identity. A significant portion of *The Woman Within* describes a coming to self-knowledge based on the very models that Glasgow will denounce. Glasgow says in *The Woman Within* that in her despair following the death of her mother (in 1893, when Glasgow was twenty), she searched for some "hidden clue to experience, for some truth, or at least for some philosophy, which would help me to adjust my identity to a world I had found hostile and even malign" (*WW* 89). Lost without the mother in whom Glasgow grounded her "identity," Glasgow believes that she must "adjust" her self to fit the world's idea of what it should be. She accepts the inferiority of a female self that requires adjustment.

Thus, on the surface of her life's narrative, Glasgow accepted the traditions of what Sidonie Smith calls the "paternal narrative" as she adopted the "speaking posture of the representative man."[6] In reshaping her lived life by writing it, Glasgow sees her life in terms of binary oppositions, for one thing. Binarism suffuses *The Woman Within:* inner/outer; maternal/paternal; light/dark; victim/victor; male/female; imprisonment/freedom; exile/community; sound/silence, to name some of them.[7] Besides oversimplifying the complexity of experience, this categorizing of the world into easy opposites also implies hierarchies of meaning and supposes a stability against which one can measure something (or someone) else. To put it another way, it invites division into self and other, where self is superior and stable.

Many critics have suggested that precisely these kinds of divisions have allowed autobiography as a genre to remain characteristically androcentric.[8] The assumed equivalence of "male" and "universal" excludes female voices as a measure of selfhood no less surely than does the outdated supposition that notable public exploits are requisite for a worthwhile life's story. A woman who chooses to write her autobiography, therefore, walks a line between public utterance that is presumably masculine and the voice of her own experience. She must, Barbara Rose concludes, speak two languages; according to Rose, a "woman autobiographer needs to be a liar."[9]

Glasgow's "lies" commonly reside in her accounts of the selfhood she feels pressured to have, the "identity" she must "adjust" to fit the world's schema. Just as her fiction, especially in the years after the First World War, demonstrates her awareness of the sexologists' interpretations of close female relationships as abnormal, Glasgow's autobiography shows the influence of the new psychology, which often informs her search for selfhood in her autobiography.[10] And the new psychology, as others have also suggested, is itself male-centered. *The Woman Within* reveals its indebtedness to Freudian psychology in several ways: in overt references to Freud or principles of Freudian psychology; in its adoption of a formative but uncontrollable subconscious; in its acceptance of the inescapability of childhood experience in adult personality; in its adherence to a Freudian model of healthy ego development through separation-individuation; and in its assumption of a fundamental (hetero)sexual principle. This indebtedness is evident from the opening page. From the beginning of her autobiography, Glasgow *seems* to accept what Charlotte Perkins Gilman called "our androcentric culture," thus establishing a patriarchal standard by which to measure her female life.[11]

It takes no guesswork to conclude that Glasgow gave considerable thought to Freud and to the new psychology in which he was so central a figure: she readily expressed her opinion of both. Consistent with her lifelong habit of reading voraciously with an independent mind, Glasgow's library suggests that she formed many of her ideas about the early twentieth century's new psychology from the books she owned and annotated. Of the approximately three thousand volumes that went to her sister Rebe (Mrs. Cabell Tutwiler) when Glasgow died, many are important texts in that psychology, and they show Glasgow's sustained interest over many years. She owned Freud's *The Interpretation of Dreams* (1913) and *The Psychopathology of Every-*

day Life (1914); *Freud and His Times* by Fritz Wittels (1931); Jung's *The Integration of Personality* (1939) and *Modern Man in Search of a Soul* (1936); and Otto Weininger's *Sex and Character* [n.d.]. Glasgow's nephew, Carrington C. Tutwiler, Jr., who cataloged Glasgow's library, notes his aunt's "interest in psychology," which "started with Locke [and] continued to Jung and Freud." Tutwiler clearly associates this reading with Glasgow's advanced ideas: "her library was perhaps one of the few in Richmond to contain *The Psychopathology of Everyday Life*." Tutwiler makes the intriguing revelation that some books that had been in his aunt's collection were lost "or removed in an over zealous attempt to protect the writer's reputation." Among them was Havelock Ellis's *Studies in the Psychology of Sex.*[12]

Some of Glasgow's friendships, especially outside of Richmond, reflect a shared interest in the new psychology. Two friends, Joseph Collins and Pearce Bailey, were cofounders of the Neurological Institute in New York City.[13] Collins also was the author of popular books using psychological approaches, and Glasgow on at least one occasion consulted him about her characterization of Judge Gamaliel Honeywell in her 1926 *The Romantic Comedians*.[14] In *The Doctor Looks at Love and Life* (1926), Collins praises Glasgow for her "consistent" Judge, who "is a mirror held up to the amatory life of man," and commends her for featuring an "old man" in love.[15] Havelock Ellis had written the introductory "commentary" to her friend Radclyffe Hall's *Well of Loneliness*.[16] Other friends and acquaintances were novelists whose works depended heavily upon the new psychological theories, especially May Sinclair, who honored Glasgow with a tea when Glasgow was in London in 1909.[17]

Glasgow's explicit comments about Freud, Ellis, and psychology, of course, obviously demonstrate her continuing intellectual engagement with their ideas. Most significant for her own autobiographical undertaking, Glasgow heavily annotated the psychology books she owned with notes about self, ego, self-sufficiency, and aloneness,[18] revealing her special interest in notions of selfhood and identity that had developed, at least in part, out of contemporary psychological theories. Glasgow's comments most often discount Freud or Freudian psychology, often (along with other critics) holding Freud responsible for what she saw as an overemphasis on sex and for a related misreading of women. As a character in a manuscript that Glasgow never published said in 1921: "even sex is not the whole of human experience,"[19] a sentiment familiar to several of Glasgow's protagonists.

Though Glasgow speaks of the "dark labyrinth of human psychology" as one of her "favorite backgrounds in fiction," her tone toward the new psychology more often varies from mildly ironic to bitter. When the women characters of male postwar novelists such as Hemingway "grow up" and have a "thorough course, not a superficial dash, of psychology with their authors and Havelock Ellis," she says, they may realize they have more to learn about women. She notes that "popular fiction, ably assisted by Freudian psychology, has accustomed us to dark views of our ancestors." The "Freudian perils of the postwar years" brought us the "modern myth of woman as an impediment." Perhaps at her least generous, Glasgow holds Freud and the new psychology responsible for infantilism, adolescent behavior, and even lunacy. In 1928, she wondered whether modernism had "received the sanction of those humane impulses which have at last released psychology from its long imprisonment in the nursery and the asylum." She wrote in 1934, probably the same year she began *The Woman Within:* "Pompous illiteracy, escaped from some Freudian cage, is in the saddle, and the voice of the amateur is the voice of authority."[20]

Glasgow's brief comments on Freud near the end of *The Woman Within* capture the divided impulse, evident throughout her autobiography, that registers the complex relationship between acceptance and rejection.[21] She simultaneously acknowledges her own and others' debt to the new psychology, criticizes others for taking it "too far," categorizes it as a passing trend, and observes that, after all, it isn't so "new" anyway. She uses the new psychology to her advantage, observing that though she was "never a disciple," she was "among the first, in the South, to perceive the invigorating effect of this fresh approach to experience." But perhaps "the name of Freud may have been long, or perhaps latterly, discredited," she says, implying her own prescient doubts about the permanent usefulness of Freudian psychology (*WW* 269). This pattern of using patriarchal authority—in this case represented by the authority of the new psychology and the malecenteredness to which it subscribes—pervades *The Woman Within,* and enables Glasgow to adopt what is useful to her and to undermine it at the same time.

The title of the autobiography itself draws attention to a Freudian subconscious, to an inner life that is worthy of the telling, to a woman "within" who is separate from the outer woman and yet, perhaps, is nevertheless knowable and representable. In a remark from her 1931 address to the Southern Writers Conference at the University of Virginia, Glasgow shows her absorption of Freudian notions of the unconscious: "it is the unconscious, not the conscious, will that chooses for us our subject, and over the unconscious we cannot exert prohibitions."[22] In part one of *The Woman Within*, "The Child and the World," Glasgow binds the childhood discovery of independent selfhood to a future self, here connecting childhood trauma to later adult personality. At the time, the "terror" that pushes the child "into consciousness" is only a felt, rather than an articulated, experience of a "malevolent" face: "I have no words," she now recalls of that past that was once the present (*WW* 3–4). Lacanian theory, building on Freudian Oedipal theory, would emphasize that this preverbal experience occurs before the fall into the symbolic realm, where language itself becomes representative of the Law of the Father, an awareness that has led French feminist critics to call for a feminine language, *l'écriture féminine,* that defies and denies phallogocentric linguistic dicta. Glasgow says that this original "terror" never leaves her; "I cannot, even now," she says, "divide the aftergrowth from the recollection" (4).

However, though Glasgow accepts the basic Freudian constructs that demand a recognition of individual selfhood, of an active subconscious, and of an inextricably linked childhood and adulthood, she also exposes their inadequacy for explaining her female *person*ality (the latter, common term itself inscribing the conflated notions of "male" and "person" in its exclusion of women). For one thing, Glasgow associates her memory of "terror" with the anxiety of separation, especially from her mother (and from her substitute mother as well), that is pervasive throughout the early pages of *The Woman Within*. As she is "rocked in [her] mother's arms," Glasgow says, she opens her eyes only to see "a face without a body staring in at me, a vacant face, round, pallid, grotesque, malevolent." Gripped by fear, she rehearses the moment as an awareness of her individuality: "One minute, I was not; the next minute, I was. I felt. I was separate. I could be hurt. I had discovered myself. And I had discovered, too, the universe apart from myself" (*WW* 3–4). The unidentified face tears her from her mother's comforting arms and replaces security and warmth with fear.

This "bodiless apparition" (*WW* 4) hovers over Glasgow and her autobiography. Poised at the beginning of Glasgow's story of her self, it points not only to Glasgow's fear of separation from her mother but also to her fear of what Sidonie Smith calls "embodied selfhood," the figure of woman as other that, as Smith argues, has been necessary to male self-definition because it reflects and thus "guarantees" masculine identity.[23] Simultaneously, the bodiless figure signals Glasgow's fear of her own disembodiment. Afraid of an "embodied selfhood" imposed on her as a woman, and equally afraid of disembodied selflessness, Glasgow begins *The Woman Within* with the classic dilemma of woman autobiographers: she must try to be her self and not her self at the same time. That is, she must reject the familiar "metaphysical selfhood" of Western culture and reconstruct some other, unknown, perhaps terrifying, new female self.[24]

Despite her statement that she inherited from her parents' "union of opposites" a "perpetual conflict of types," in fact Glasgow undermines a belief in her parents' equal importance in forming her personality. She says that she "inherited nothing" from her father, whereas "everything in me, mental or physical, I owe to my mother" (*WW* 16). Glasgow's presentation of her parents reinforces her sense that a female tradition must connect her to her mother and separate her from her father. The Freudian family drama would reverse that formula.

As with her earliest "unconscious memory" (*WW* 8), Glasgow's portrait of her parents serves primarily to express the devastation of a female child who is supposed to adhere to Freud's Oedipal model but who really worries about maternal separation. Her father is not the desired future heterosexual partner, but the archetypal evil male. He functions in *The Woman Within* to symbolize the tyranny of men over women, and Glasgow goes so far as to imply that her father's "stalwart, unbending" and (to her) aggressively masculine personality actually killed her mother. The "severe shock" that "altered" her mother "so completely" that "her buoyant emotion toward life was utterly lost" was probably her mother's discovery of Mr. Glasgow's black lover(s), as Glasgow and others have suggested,[25] paralleled in Glasgow's fiction prominently in both *Virginia* and *The Sheltered Life* and more subtly elsewhere. In a draft of *The Woman Within* preserved in Glasgow's papers, Glasgow had originally written that this "shock" occurred as Glasgow's mother "entered her climacteric."[26] In the later, published version of her autobiography, Glasgow excised the reference to her mother's menopause and substituted "in a critical period" (61). She thus implicitly connects her father's flagging interest in her mother to her mother's presumed loss of femininity and sexuality. Glasgow attributes the "atmosphere of despair" caused by Mrs. Glasgow's unhappiness to Mr. Glasgow's sexual appetite, transferred now to his lover(s). Glasgow also clearly links her mother's declining health and death to the years she spent bearing and raising (and sometimes losing) ten children. Glasgow resents her father for what she sees as her mother's sexual victimization; he is responsible not only for the "emotional shock" that killed his wife, but for the strain on her "delicate physical constitution," weakened by years of childbearing, that made her unable to bear that shock (63–64). And with the death of her mother—a separation forced, as she sees it, by her father—a part of Glasgow died too, she says.

In describing the development of her personality, Glasgow appears to accept the Freudian model of the individuated, autonomous ego, which many feminist psychological theorists have associated with masculine notions of selfhood.[27] Just as Glasgow described her first coming to consciousness as an awareness of herself as "separate," Glasgow continues in The Woman Within to see herself as isolated. The working title of her autobiography was "The Autobiography of an Exile." When her black caregiver, Lizzie Jones, left when Glasgow was seven, Glasgow says she first felt "that sense of loss, of exile in solitude, which I was to bear with me to the end" (WW 30). She feels set apart as "different" and "outside the world" (48). As a professional writer, she views herself as an outcast. Seeking a publisher at age eighteen requires her "separation" from the group of young women she has traveled to New York with (95). Describing her relation to well-known literary figures of her time, she declines to "become a disciple": "I had no place in any coterie, or in any reciprocal self-advertising. I stood alone. I stood outside" (142, 144). Examples of Glasgow as the isolate self abound in The Woman Within.

But two formative memories in Glasgow's opening pages share an important feature: both associate cruelty with male violence against others, and thus with what Glasgow characterizes as a masculine failure to empathize. When she moves immediately from her father's oppressive house to her early memories of cruelty, Glasgow asks us to link a failure to empathize with a masculine sense of self as separate from others. In doing so, she criticizes the model of selfhood within which she feels she has been imprisoned and replaces it with a sense of self-in-context. In the first memory, Glasgow remembers watching from her carriage as "men and boys" chase a black dog, beat it with clubs, and catch it in a net (WW 9). When the dog stops briefly and makes eye contact with Glasgow, she, in contrast to the pursuers, feels that she herself is being pursued. In her second memory, Glasgow recalls the cries of an elderly black man, Uncle Henry, as he "fights off the men who hold him," in an attempt to resist being sent to the almshouse. A "group of little boys" joins in by jumping up and down. Uncle Henry's "mournful" plea is against the enclosure that Glasgow also fears: "Don't put me in! Don't put me in!' " (11). Later, this fear of enclosure recurs as Glasgow describes the end of her relationship with Henry Anderson in terms of a lucky escape from captivity: "I was at last free," she says. "Nothing . . . had changed—nothing, except that I was free."[28] Her final escape from Anderson is an escape from a literal marriage and from the expectation of marriage that traps not only Glasgow but other women in a predetermined plot: "I was free from chains. I belonged to myself" (244–45).

The isolated, autonomous ego that allows the separate self to exist in disregard of others comes under attack in less obvious ways, too. As we have seen, Glasgow associates male lack of consideration and even cruelty most strongly with her father. She further associates power with maleness. Her early memories of Uncle Henry's forced removal to the almshouse or of the dog captured in a net have their parallels throughout *The Woman Within* in Glasgow's own fear of enforced isolation by men through entrapment or imprisonment. Glasgow uses these recurring patterns of enclosure as a metaphor for her own feelings of entrapment in male traditions, including those that try to force her into equating separation from others with maturity, with a healthy adult ego,[29] and thereby implicitly demand that model for her autobiography as well. Her father's house has a "black iron fence enclosing the yard" and an "iron gate"; the house itself is "narrow," the buildings comprising it are "divided" from one another. Even the plants suffer: nothing grows but a "stunted ailanthus" and a "blighted creeper or two." When Glasgow includes the details of her father's position of managing director of Tredegar *Iron* Works and his interest in "prison reform" (WW 6–8; emphasis added), she connects him to attempts to imprison.

Glasgow describes her increasingly serious loss of hearing in the language of imprisonment and separation. As the "slight trouble" (*WW* 96) with her ears that began as early as 1891 worsens, she refers to her encroaching deafness as "the shadow of the wall," and her final hearing loss as the "impenetrable wall" (137, 181). It "come[s] nearer," stalking her, "tracking [her] down, like a wolf waiting to spring" (181, 118). She feels her deafness "inevitably closing in" around her, and feels that "there was no breaking through" (182). As a result, Glasgow separated herself from others: "I stopped seeing my friends. I would go out of my way to avoid those I had loved rather than ask them to raise their voices." Her affliction, she says, keeps the woman who was "winged for flying" "wounded and caged." The wall of deafness that imprisons her becomes a "wall of deceptive gaiety" that she constructs, isolating herself from other people (137–39).

In emphasizing loss of hearing and loss of voice (as when she refuses to ask others to "raise their voices" so that she can hear them), Glasgow employs metaphors that Mary Field Belenky and her co-workers have identified as common to women when they describe their epistemological assumptions. The authors point out that where visual metaphors of absorbing knowledge, the most common in the history of Western intellectual pursuit, suggest passivity and distance, metaphors of hearing imply "closeness between subject and object" and dialogism.[30] When Glasgow describes her loss of hearing as responsible for her social isolation, then, she literalizes her separation from female selfhood based on reciprocity and close connection to others. Her imprisonment within a closing circle of silence is a metaphor for her alienation within a tradition of male selfhood, just as her association of her father with prison is symbolic of her entrapment within male institutions, literal and metaphoric.

Lois Rudnick observes that autobiography, particularly in the United States, "insists on the self."[31] In *The Woman Within*, with its seeming self-centeredness, Glasgow may appear on the surface to agree with such a requirement. But her opening pages establish a decentered self that refuses the notion of a fixed identity, asserting instead a disjointed self and a destabilized identity. Glasgow thus takes issue with the Freudian model of separation-individuation as the mark of the mature ego, autonomous and independent and concerned primarily with self-interest. She replaces that ego with a self-in-relation, defined (though unstable because constantly in flux) in relation to others. A female self, she suggests, dependent upon contextualization rather than separation, must resist the categorization and the fixity of a male-defined identity. In her two early preverbal memories, the dog and Uncle Henry become part of her, thus blurring the lines between self and other and complicating the idea of personal identity.

Glasgow makes use of Ammons's notion of "conflicting stories" when she fuses images of entrapment or imprisonment with a paradigmatic patriarchal romance or marriage plot. Her autobiography thus appears to conform to demands on women for traditional heterosexual love and marriage even while it subverts them through the symbolic language used in their descriptions. Her supposed first love affair with the married man she calls "Gerald B—" is an example. Saying that she "fell in love at first sight" (*WW* 153) with Gerald, and for seven years kept the relationship "intense[ly] secret" (160), Glasgow nevertheless expresses simultaneously her fear of being trapped. She had, she says, "a deep conviction" that she was "unfitted for marriage," and had no desire to "surrender" herself, knowing that she "could not ever be completely possessed" (153). Glasgow's descriptions of her relationship with Henry Anderson—the "Harold S—" of the autobiography—are filled with the language of imprisonment and the descriptions of the end of it with that of freedom. She wonders how she "could have remained, for almost twenty years, an unwilling *prisoner* of unreason" (emphasis added). She attributes the relationship in part to her desire for freedom from her "*inescapable* past," contrasting her former love for the "loneliness of the spirit in *freedom*" with the aloneness she wanted Harold to help her escape (221; emphasis added). Instead of escape, however, he offered the "possessiveness" of marriage (230). Glasgow recounts an episode of drug overdose— thinking more of sleep than of death, she says—in the midst of her affair with Harold. She describes her return to consciousness—and to her relationship with Harold—as life "tracking me down into prison." "Caught again," her "brief freedom" over, she returns to "life" feeling "like a small trapped animal" (240). "Free from chains" at the end of the love affair with Harold, Glasgow expresses wonderment that "love . . . should be so magnified in a life" (245).

Even though it devotes much of its surface narrative to heterosexual love, however, *The Woman Within* itself questions such "magnification." Her adamant refusal to idealize marriage and motherhood; her sense of release after love affairs; the instances of sexual aggression by men; and her clearly expressed distaste for heterosexual physicality all participate in the narrative's resistance to traditional romantic love with its subplot of motherhood. To the discouraging Macmillan editor who advised Glasgow early in her career to concentrate on producing not "the finest book" but "the finest babies," she responds in her autobiography: "I wanted to write books, and not ever had I felt the faintest wish to have babies" (WW 108–109). In telling of the agent who observed to Glasgow that she was "too pretty to be a novelist" (96) and then assaulted her, Glasgow details a narrative of male sexual entitlement that has its parallel in her fiction. Though she burned her first manuscript (Sharp Realities) in anger, in recalling Mariana's "nausea" from kissing, Dorinda's recoil from Bob Ellgood's bull-like neck and flushed purple face,[32] and many other instances in her fiction, Glasgow denounces the male presumption that women always desire them physically. Glasgow's autobiography writes the counternarrative to male assumptions about women's desire, replacing a traditional (male) story with an alternative female perspective.

Ultimately, Glasgow subverts her surface narratives of both exile and romantic love simultaneously, by returning to an emphasis on the significant role of female companionship in her life. Asserting in the penultimate chapter that she still, as always, "found it easier to break with tradition than to endure it" (WW 280), Glasgow sets the tone that characterizes her concluding chapter, "Epilogue: Present Tense." This final chapter's title neatly questions linearity in narrative by complicating traditional chronology: an epilogue succeeds a conclusion and often comments on the future; this one, rather, introduces and comments on the present and past. The Epilogue further disrupts chronology when we take into account the composition of the autobiography's "present tense." It was written over a period of approximately ten years, and dating individual sections is difficult to impossible; where is the "present"? Even before the epilogue, as Marilyn R. Chandler notes, Glasgow's frequent ellipses and her repeated statement that she is getting ahead of her narrative point to Glasgow's being "uncomfortably constrained by chronology." [33] The frequently unconventional narrative signals Glasgow's "break with tradition" as she continues her questioning of male constructs—whether for women's experience or women's personality development or women's narratives—that she began in her fiction.

In a revealing backward glance, Glasgow characterizes her youth as "the time when one's whole life is entangled in a web of identity," a time when "the soul drifts on the shallow stream of personality, within narrow borders." Imprisoned within the "narrow borders" of selfhood, of *personality*, Glasgow implies, young womanhood spends its energy trying to "adjust" itself, to use her earlier word, to the traditional definition of selfhood or "identity," as if it were a monolithic, stable, unified state of personhood rather than a construct. Only after age sixty, Glasgow says she learned, can one escape "that retarded channel" of narrowly defined identity and move "out upon the wide sea of impersonality" in order to "begin to live . . . with one's entire being" (*WW* 283). The Second World War, Glasgow felt, also necessitated relinquishing the myth of contained selfhood; it demanded multiple perspectives. This exploding of the myth of individual identity led, for one thing, Glasgow says, to her new understanding of narrative point of view in her own fiction. With *In This Our Life* (1941), whose events take place in 1939, Glasgow says she learned to approach her subject "not from the single or even the dual point of view, but from the diffused mental and emotional outlook of a whole community," thus "welding together" her earlier ideas (*WW* 286).

Glasgow's community perspective that both "diffused" and "welded" expression harkens back to an idea that I began this book with: selfhood within community, the "mature dependence" that Gilligan sees as an alternative feminine story to masculine psychological models that stress separation and autonomous selfhood. As I have suggested throughout this book, for Glasgow, rejecting that culturally constructed male identity and accepting a sense of female self-in-relation was accomplished largely through her relationships with other women. Appropriately, she returns to those relationships in the final pages of *The Woman Within*.

The second of the "two things" that Glasgow says had "never failed" her is the "gift of friendship" (*WW* 284). The first is laughter. Elsewhere she echoes this sentiment, at times changing one of the "two things" but always retaining friendship. As she wrote in 1935, "love may be a high adventure, but affection is a permanent shelter."[34] The final pages of *The Woman Within* extol the virtues of her friendship

with Anne Virginia Bennett, the "delightful and devoted nurse" who
spent her time with Glasgow in "heavenly rambles along the Indian
trails" in the Maine woods. During a severe heart attack, Glasgow
hears "the voice of Anne Virginia" "calling to hold me back" (288–
89). Earlier in *The Woman Within,* Glasgow described Anne Virginia
as the one who, "more than anyone else" since her sister Cary had died
in 1911, "had my interests at heart." The "compassion for all inarticulate creation" that Anne Virginia shares with her, Glasgow says, she
"even turns . . . upon me." Both in the published version and in a draft
of *The Woman Within,* Glasgow characterizes Anne Virginia Bennett
as someone who "has never really regarded writing as anything more
serious than 'a way' " (216), "or a pastime," she adds in her draft.[35]
"Few persons," Glasgow continues, "have ever felt less interest in, or
respect for, the profession of letters," and Anne Virginia has always
"looked with suspicion upon the 'people who write' " (216). Glasgow
harkens back to her earlier metaphors of voice and hearing to represent closeness in female friendships as she writes of Anne Virginia's
"voice" that calls her back to their shared world, and transforms herself into, not the articulate artist whose pronouncements from a cold
page distance her from her friend, but simply another "inarticulate
creation" that enjoys the benefit of Anne Virginia's loving attention.

Glasgow comments most extensively on her relationship with
Bennett in the section of *The Woman Within* that reports her father's
death and the beginning of her relationship with Henry Anderson,
both in 1916, a structural strategy that highlights the impermanence
of men in her life compared to Bennett's long-term presence. In a draft
of *The Woman Within,* Bennett, her "only companion" at that time,
is not "my secretary," as she is in the published version (*WW* 215)
but "my close friend." In the draft Bennett did not "volunteer" for
Red Cross Service in France; rather, she "left me" to become a nurse
for the Red Cross.[36] After Bennett departed for duty in France, Glasgow describes the "desolation" of her loneliness, "in which my mind
lay like a drowned corpse in my body" (234). She depended upon
the companionship and deep emotional attachment to Bennett, and
it is Bennett's "compassion" and concern for Glasgow that Glasgow
describes at the end of her life's story.

Besides Anne Virginia, Glasgow expresses affection for many
women, some whose names are by now familiar. In doing so, she con-

nects her childhood and her adult existence, just as she had in structuring her autobiography, but this time with an important difference:
it is not the trauma of fear, especially fear of men, but the nurture of
love, especially by women, that connects these two times in her life.
Able to see only "one or two" people at a time, Glasgow receives sick-
bed visits from Caroline Duke (the Carrie Coleman of her childhood),
who had stayed with Glasgow during the nights after Bennett left for
France (*WW* 234), and from Elizabeth Crutchfield, "the very Elizabeth Patterson with whom I had stayed in the immense old nursery
at Reveille" (292). Two other long-time friends visit: Julia Sully, who
had traveled with Glasgow to Colorado in 1909 and, as Glasgow says
here, "had wandered with me over Dinwiddie when I was in search of
a background for *Virginia*"; and Roberta (or Berta) Wellford, "who
had stood by me when Cary was dying" (293). Glasgow associates
these friends with times and places of female companionship: her
childhood nursery, her novel *Virginia,* her beloved sister Cary.

Glasgow includes a special new friend, too, one whom she might
address, as she did Louise Chandler Moulton in 1905, as a "dear
newly *found* but not new" friend: Marjorie Kinnan Rawlings. Glasgow's earlier friendship with Moulton and this later one with Rawlings are similar: both are nurtured primarily through letters; both
became immediately intimate; both are characterized by a mysticism
or spiritualism that recurs in other relationships between women in
Glasgow's actual and fictional lives; both involved a younger and an
older woman writer.[37] As Glasgow instructed, her autobiography's
Epilogue reprints a now well-known 1941 letter to Glasgow in which
Rawlings recounts a dream. In it, Rawlings leads Glasgow inside from
the cold outside, gives her coffee, and protectively encloses Glasgow's
hand inside her own. Rawlings announces in her dream that "from
now on I should take care of you."

In the dream, as the two women sit holding hands and talking,
James Branch Cabell "came into the room and asked what the two of
us were up to. (As of course he would!)" (*WW* 294). The letter from
Rawlings and the dream it conveys do more than express appreciation
to a comforting friend. They implicate the women in a nurturing community of two, united against the intrusion of the male who wants to
usurp their story and force himself into it—"as of course he would!"
The strength of the image and of the implied friendship carries the

final chapter of *The Woman Within*. "And all it meant," Glasgow says very near the end, "is that with faithful friends I had come over the last hill into the endless valley. The friends were faithful, and I can say little enough about them, who, like Carrie Duke and Anne Virginia, I could count upon" (295). Though Glasgow in her autobiography may break with tradition, she does so in order to substitute her own, woman-centered traditions. By the end of *The Woman Within*, she has created a world of loving female friends united in a woman's tradition of female community.

I'd like to read an additional set of documents as part of Glasgow's "autobiography": her will and final bequests. When Glasgow died on 21 November 1945, she left an estate of approximately $160,000 in personal property, not including the house at One West Main, which legally belonged to her brother Arthur.[38] Glasgow left $10,000 to Anne Virginia Bennett; $10,000 to her sister Rebe Glasgow Tutwiler; $5,000 to Caroline Coleman Duke, her lifelong friend; $1,000 each to her literary executors, Irita Van Doren and Frank V. Morley; small monetary sums to workers in Glasgow's employ; various distributions of paintings and porcelain figurines; and a trust fund of $100,000, to be supplemented by proceeds from publication of her works. Glasgow further expressed her wish that Bennett remain in the house at One West Main for as long as she wished, and bequeathed all income from the trust fund (except for fifty dollars a month to Glasgow's household employee, James Anderson) to Bennett.

Glasgow also left several letters to Anne Virginia Bennett and Rebe Glasgow Tutwiler expressing her wishes for the final distribution of several objects of personal property. Her carefully thought out requests mirror the close network of female companionship in her life, leaving personally symbolic objects to special friends and at times explaining (or implying) their significance. For example, Glasgow leaves "two miniatures" of Cary, her sister who died in 1911, to Roberta Wellford, who had been primarily Cary's friend. In doing so Glasgow reinforces the web of association among the three women. Similarly, to Julia Sully, another longtime friend, Glasgow leaves "the bronze image of Buddha." Elaborating on this request, Glasgow says that it "was given to me by Amelie, because, she said it was the finest thing she had left," thus connecting Julia, Glasgow herself, and her deceased close friend, Amélie Rives Troubetzkoy. Also to Julia, Glasgow leaves her "jade beads, which I bought, when Julia was with me from Mrs. Elihu Vedder, at Ogunquit." Glasgow often changed her mind about her bequests, deciding, for example, to give the Buddha to her "new friend, Signe Toksvig," and explaining again that the statue was given by Amélie. "It has always, since she gave it to me, stood on my desk, and the image will have a meaning for Signe."

Glasgow twice reminds Anne Virginia and Rebe to "give some remembrance to Agnes." On an envelope for a letter from Agnes to Glasgow dated 27 December 1941, Glasgow identified Agnes Reese as the "grand daughter of my mother's Mammy."[39] Glasgow had sent cards and flowers to Reese's husband in the hospital in Roanoke, for which the letter thanks her. A moving statement by Reese connects the mothers, grandmothers, and daughters that envelop Glasgow and Reese, and even suggests that female community as an antidote to a war associated with men: "When I read your beautiful card signed— 'with love from the 3rd generation,' it made me think what a lovely place this would be today—if nations had a little of that kind of love in their hearts for each other." As in Glasgow's friendships, her fiction, and her will and final bequests, the emphasis here is on connection, particularly with other women, even through time and across the boundaries of race and class.

Glasgow re-viewed and rewrote her own life in her last years, and even in her last months if we take into account the final documents detailing her wishes for passing on her personal property. In those final letters, Glasgow distributes the artifacts—metonymic pieces of herself—that will maintain her connection to others in the future. In writing her autobiography, she similarly connects herself to herself as she becomes both subject and object of her story; that is, she is both the "I" of the story and its "she" as she writes her life into a new kind of existence. Glasgow also connects herself to us, her readers, in a gesture of encompassing identity that recognizes something I think Glasgow was trying to articulate in *The Woman Within*: "selves," insofar as we can talk about them at all, are not single but multiple, not uniform but multiform. Her title for her autobiography, and often its dual structure, rather than overemphasizing her within-ness, attempted to point out that she was both the woman within and without simultaneously. Facile definitions of coherent selfhood need not apply.

Despite what seems at times its move toward a notion of unified identity, *The Woman Within* subscribes to the idea of multiple selves—what Marmaduke Littlepage, the artist-brother of Virginius in *They Stooped to Folly,* calls the "quadruple lives" of most people (*TSF* 179). Glasgow's protest, finally, aimed to recognize not only the multiformity of something we choose to call individual selfhood but the importance of recognizing two other forms of identity in particular: the self-in-context and the necessary tolerance toward the self-as-other. Working her way through a complex relation to the traditions available to her, whether through the personal perspective of women's community; the literary perspective of a predominately male autobiographical tradition and the definitions of selfhood that accompanied it; or the combined personal and literary perspective of the female Gothic, Glasgow argued for the authority to voice her own ideas and to write her own stories. Whether or not we always agree with her seems decidedly beside the point.

Notes
Works Cited
Index

Notes

Preface

1. *The Diary of H. L. Mencken*, ed. Charles A. Fecher, 49.
2. James Branch Cabell, *As I Remember It*, 228; Domna C. Stanton, "Autogynography," 9.
3. Mary Helen Washington, *Invented Lives*, xviii.
4. Margo Culley, "What a Piece of Work is 'Woman'!" 5; Florence Howe, "Introduction," 14; Elaine Showalter, *Sister's Choice*, 175.
5. Carolyn G. Heilbrun, "Non-Autobiographies of 'Privileged' Women," 62.

Chapter One

1. Simone de Beauvoir, *The Second Sex*, trans. H. M. Parshley (New York: Knopf, 1953); rp. (2 vols. in 1), with an introduction by Deirdre Bair (New York: Vintage, 1989), 267. Page citations that follow are also to this reprint edition. Though her original articulation in 1949 of woman as other was not new for feminists, as Moira Ferguson's *First Feminists* demonstrates, Beauvoir's perception that becoming a woman is accomplished through the "intervention of someone else" who establishes her as "an *Other*" (267) gave new urgency to a reemerging mid-twentieth-century concern with woman's place.
2. Particularly influential studies by critics from the United States followed Beauvoir. Betty Friedan in 1963 discussed the "problem that has no name" created by women's "adjustment to an image that does not permit them to become what they now can be" (*The Feminine Mystique* 300). In 1972, Adrienne Rich enacted the "re-vision" she calls for by appropriating her essay's very title from an Ibsen play ("When We Dead Awaken,"). Judith Fetterley accepts the shaping power of reading, insists on the necessity for resistent reading strategies for women readers of specifically American literary "classics," and describes her own book as a "survival manual for the woman reader lost in 'the masculine wilderness of the American novel'" (*The Resisting Reader* [1978], viii). Sandra M. Gilbert and Susan Gubar began with the controlling metaphor of "the Queen's looking glass" to figure the problem of women writers' "searching glance into the mirror of the male-inscribed literary text" (*The Madwoman in the Attic* [1979], 15). Annette Kolodny in 1980 continued to push for "rereading" as a way of understanding women's literary texts from "within [their] own unique and informing contexts" rather than from some misguided sense of universality that really describes masculinity ("A Map for Rereading," 60).

For more specifically linguistic approaches that see language itself as the patriarchal problem to be circumvented, see, for example, Hélène Cixous, "The Laugh of the Medusa," [1983], 279–97; Alicia Suskin Ostriker, "The Thieves of Language" (314–38); and Patricia Yeager, *Honey-Mad Women* (1988). A useful discussion of feminism and language, and of some distinctions between Anglo and French feminist approaches, can be found in Toril Moi, *Sexual / Textual Politics* (1988).

3. Nancy K. Miller, "Writing Fictions," 56, 59. See also Nancy K. Miller, "Arachnologies," chap. 4 in her *Subject to Change*, 77–101.

4. E. Stanly Godbold, Jr., *Ellen Glasgow and the Woman Within*, 200–201.

5. Amélie Rives Troubetzkoy to Ellen Glasgow, 25 August 1937, Glasgow Papers, box 18. Glasgow had written on 23 August to express her sorrow in advance of the day that she knew would be so difficult for her friend. Glasgow tries to prepare Amélie ahead of time, comforting her with happy memories the two women shared and reading both the past moment and the present sorrowful loss as holding a promise of existence "beyond time" (Blair Rouse, ed., *Letters of Ellen Glasgow*, 224).

6. Rives Troubetzkoy to Glasgow, 9 September 1937, 10 September, 26 September, and 6 October 1937, Glasgow Papers, box 18.

7. Carolyn Heilbrun, *Writing a Woman's Life*, 110. See also Margaret J. M. Ezell, *Writing Women's Literary History*, 35–36, for a provocative discussion of the (mis)use of nineteenth-century models in formulating the terms for evaluating earlier women writers.

8. Glasgow, *The Woman Within*, 108. Subsequent references to the 1954 edition of *The Woman Within* are cited parenthetically in the text to *WW*, with page numbers. The "new woman" comment is quoted in Godbold, 38.

9. Ellen Glasgow, *A Certain Measure*, 9.

10. "Vigor" and "dramatic" are from "An Iconoclastic Hero," *New York Times Saturday Review of Books and Art*, 17 April 1897, p. 7; "distinctly, almost audaciously, virile and vigorous" is from the *Literary World*, 28 (15 May 1897): 164; the last three are from "By the Great Unknown," *Chap-Book* 6 (1 April 1897): 403–4: all are reprinted in Dorothy M. Scura, ed., *Ellen Glasgow*; 5, 7, 4.

11. Though Linda W. Wagner in *Ellen Glasgow* (22), asserts that Glasgow was "delighted" to have her book attributed to Frederic, I am not aware of such a response on Glasgow's part. In her autobiography, Glasgow says that one critic at Harper "had insisted" that *The Descendant* "was an anonymous work by Harold Frederic" (*WW* 121).

12. Review of *The Descendant*, in *Bookman* 5 (May 1897): 368, 369; reprinted in Scura, *Ellen Glasgow*, 6.

13. Clarence Wellford, "The Author of *The Descendant*," *Harper's Bazar* 30 (5 June 1897): 458; the review, without the photograph, is reprinted in Scura, *Ellen Glasgow*, 8–10. The sketched reproduction was published in Christine Terhune Herrick, "The Author of *The Descendant*," *Critic*, n.s. 27

(5 June 1897): 383. See also Edgar E. MacDonald and Tonette Bond Inge, *Ellen Glasgow*, 3; Godbold, *Ellen Glasgow*, 42. The photo is in the Glasgow Papers, box 25, and is reproduced as this book's frontispiece, in Godbold, *Ellen Glasgow and the Woman Within*, following p. 130, and in the *Ellen Glasgow Newsletter*, Issue 9 (October 1978): 15. The photograph is misdated in the latter. My warmest thanks to Dorothy Scura for helping me to verify this information.

14. Isaac F. Marcosson, review of *The Voice of the People, Louisville (Ky.) Courier-Journal*, 21 April 1900, p. 8; reprinted in Scura, *Ellen Glasgow*, 35–37.

15. MacDonald and Inge (*Ellen Glasgow*, 42–43) quote a 1914 interview published in the *New York Evening Sun*. In it, Glasgow described *Virginia* as the first of a planned (but never fully realized) trilogy of novels about women increasingly "articulate" about the feminist "cause that effects women's happiness."

16. Frederic Taber Cooper, "Inconclusiveness and Some Recent Novels," *Bookman* 37 (July 1913): 537, reprinted in Scura, *Ellen Glasgow*, 168–69; E[dwin] F[rancis] E[dgett], "*Virginia:* Ellen Glasgow's Story of Old Fashioned Womanhood," *Boston Evening Transcript*, 19 April 1913, sec. 3, p. 6, partially reprinted in Scura, *Ellen Glasgow*, 158; "Views and Reviews of Current Fiction," *New York Tribune*, 22 January 1916, 8–9, reprinted in Scura, *Ellen Glasgow*, 178–80.

17. Louis D. Rubin, Jr., *No Place on Earth*, 13. In *Tomorrow Is Another Day*, Anne Goodwyn Jones—recognizing the antifeminism in this passage—quotes it to demonstrate the problem of Glasgow's "occasional failure" to make more emphatic use of her own experience as "a method for analysis" (233).

18. See Edgar E. MacDonald, "An Essay in Bibliography," 199–200.

19. Godbold, *Ellen Glasgow and the Woman Within*, 54, 55.

20. Ibid., 137.

21. Rubin, *No Place on Earth*, and Godbold, *Ellen Glasgow and the Woman Within*, for example, consistently refer to Glasgow this way.

22. MacDonald and Inge, *Ellen Glasgow*, 238. "Minor characters" can only mean the supporting casts from *Virginia* and *Life and Gabriella*, two surely "major" novels, which Jones discusses at length.

23. All quotations in text are from annotated references in MacDonald and Inge, *Ellen Glasgow*. On the early feminist dissertation (Judith L. Allsup, "Feminism in the Novels of Ellen Glasgow"), see 214; on the little treatise (Elizabeth Gallup Meyer, *The Social Situation of Women in the Novels of Ellen Glasgow*), see 230; and on the feminist study "lacking in control" (Ekman, *The End of a Legend*), see 231.

24. Monique Parent Frazee, "Ellen Glasgow as Feminist," 185–87 and passim.

25. Patricia Meyer Spacks, *The Female Imagination* (1972; rp. New York: Avon, 1976), 129; Adrienne Rich, "Education of a Novelist." Elizabeth

Ammons's 1991 study of twentieth-century American women writers, *Conflicting Stories*, considers Rich's poem and its assessment of Glasgow's racism (175–76). Though Ammons is certainly correct in seeing Glasgow as short-sighted and even condescending when it comes to race, the issue of Glasgow and race is much more complicated than Rich or Ammons have the space or the desire to deal with. Lucinda H. MacKethan in *Daughters of Time* (1990) also briefly discusses Rich's poem on Glasgow (99–100). For more analysis of my own view of Glasgow and race, see chapter five, below.

26. See Heilbrun, *Writing a Woman's Life*, esp. 130–31, on women's age and courage.

27. Preface to *They Stooped to Folly*, vol. 6 of the Virginia Edition, ix. Subsequent page references to this novel and its Preface are cited parenthetically in text to this edition as *TSF*.

28. Glasgow Papers, box 6, notebook 3. The quote from *Paradise Lost* occurs in book 4, line 299. Glasgow's "disdain" for Milton's sentiment is evident in the context of the other quotations surrounding this copied line. Immediately preceding it are quotes celebrating women's strength; the Milton quote is included amidst others celebrating nineteenth-century ideals of True Womanhood.

29. See Alicia Suskin Ostriker, *Stealing the Language*, for an extended and provocative discussion of women poets' responses to masculine myth-making.

30. Muriel Rukeyser, "Myth," in her *The Collected Poems*, 498.

31. Heilbrun, *Writing a Woman's Life*, 25; Glasgow Papers, box 7.

32. Ellen Moers, *Literary Women*, 90–110.

33. For a few examples, both literary and psychological, among many recent ones, see Bella Brodzki and Celeste Schenck, eds., *Life / Lines*; Shari Benstock, ed., *The Private Self*; Heilbrun, *Writing a Woman's Life*; Sidonie Smith, *A Poetics of Women's Autobiography*, Mary Field Belenky et al., *Women's Ways of Knowing*; Nancy Chodorow, *The Reproduction of Mothering*; Carol Gilligan, *In a Different Voice*; Jean Baker Miller, M.D., *Toward a Psychology of Women*.

34. For example, see Margaret J. M. Ezell, "The Myth of Judith Shakespeare," 590–91, and *Writing Women's Literary History*, 32–33; and Nancy K. Miller, "Writing Fictions."

35. Linda W. Wagner, *Ellen Glasgow*, 41; Ellen Glasgow, *The Miller of Old Church*, vol. 2 of the Virginia Edition, 321; Carroll Smith-Rosenberg, "The Female World of Love and Ritual." Subsequent references to *The Miller of Old Church* are cited parenthetically in the text to *MOC*, with page numbers.

Marcelle Thiébaux briefly discusses female friendships in *Ellen Glasgow* (8–9). Lynette Carpenter provides the fullest exposition of the importance of women in Glasgow's fiction, in "Visions of Female Community in Ellen Glasgow's Short Stories." For another extended discussion, with particular reference to Glasgow's relationship with Anne Virginia Bennett, see Pamela Rae Matthews, "Two Women Blended": Ellen Glasgow and Her Fictions."

36. I recognize the universalist (and essentialist) tendencies of much psychoanalytic feminism, and want to stress that I am following proposed psychological models based on women whose race and class is similar to Glasgow's. Although, as critics have charged, the arguments of theorists such as Chodorow and Gilligan do underemphasize (ignore, even) crucial differences of race, class, and cultural and historical context, I believe nonetheless that their explorations of many women's identity formation remain useful for redirecting our attention to women's relationships with other women. Nancy Chodorow addresses these criticisms—and acknowledges them in her own earlier work—in *Feminism and Psychoanalytic Theory*, especially on pages 3–6.

37. See Belenky et al., *Women's Ways of Knowing*; Chodorow, *The Reproduction of Mothering,*; Gilligan, *In a Different Voice*; and Jean Baker Miller, *Toward a New Psychology,* for example.

38. See Heilbrun, *Writing a Woman's Life,* 16–18, for a discussion of power and the necessity for women to confront it as an issue.

Especially in her autobiography, Glasgow frequently expresses her aversion to conflict, particularly in the context of the two world wars she lived through. At one point she recalls the "*danse macabre* whirling over the battlefields" of France in World War I, which left her with "a poignant disgust, more sickening than pain," and her sleeplessness as she imagines the "horror" of the war. "Even more than the conflict," she says, she "hated" the "intolerance and cruelty" (*WW* 233–34). Later, she writes that she had just finished her first draft of *In This Our Life* "when the second World War broke. I cannot write of this war. I have tried, and I cannot. . . . The cruelty is too near. This cruelty is now in my mind. This agony is now in my nerves" (*WW,* 285).

39. Sandra M. Gilbert and Susan Gubar, *No Man's Land:* vol. 1, *The War of the Words.*

40. Heilbrun, *Writing a Woman's Life,* 37.

Chapter Two

1. Glasgow, "No Valid Reason against Giving Votes to Women" (1913), reprinted in Julius Rowan Raper, ed., *Ellen Glasgow's Reasonable Doubts,* 24. The parenthetical page numbers cited for the quotes that immediately follow in text are from this collection.

2. Glasgow Papers, box 5; Glasgow, "I Believe" (1938), reprinted in Raper, *Ellen Glasgow's Reasonable Doubts,* 244. For similar sentiments, see also "Unidentified Notes by Ellen Glasgow," Glasgow Papers, box 7.

3. Nancy F. Cott, *The Bonds of Womanhood,* and Smith-Rosenberg, "The Female World of Love and Ritual," respectively.

4. See Cott, *The Bonds of Womanhood,* for a thorough discussion of the

origins and implications of the ideology of "separate spheres." I do not intend here to debate the "truth" of the private-public paradigm, but rather to describe Glasgow's encounter with it. In an interesting account, Michelle Z. Rosaldo—who as coeditor of the influential *Woman, Culture, and Society* contributed significantly to the emphasis on separate spheres in feminist thought—rethinks her own earlier formulation in light of Western cultural bias; see Rosaldo, "The Use and Abuse of Anthropology."

5. See, for example, Ammons, *Conflicting Stories;* Josephine Donovan, *New England Local Color* and *After the Fall;* Susan Goodman, *Edith Wharton's Women;* Sarah Way Sherman, *Sarah Orne Jewett;* and Cheryl B. Torsney, *Constance Fenimore Woolson.*

6. See Jones, *Tomorrow Is Another Day,* 10–11, for a helpful summary of historians' views of Southern white male hegemony, gender, and race.

7. See Gilbert and Gubar's now classic *The Madwoman in the Attic* on the "anxiety of authorship" experienced by women writers. Ammons's *Conflicting Stories* discusses the shift in women writers' conceptions of their aesthetic goals from the "domestic" writers earlier in the nineteenth century, who saw themselves as part of the *profession* of writing, to those later women writers—Glasgow's contemporaries and near contemporaries—who conceived of themselves as Artists "with a capital A" (Ammons, quoting Charlotte Perkins Gilman, in *Conflicting Stories,* 170).

8. Carol Gilligan, *In a Different Voice,* 30, 74, 98, 164, and passim; Nancy Chodorow, "Family Structure and Feminine Personality" and *The Reproduction of Mothering.* For more recent applications of Gilligan's theories, see *Making Connections,* in which Gilligan and her coeditors discuss the results of their study of female adolescents at the Emma Willard School. Findings support Gilligan's earlier work; in *Making Connections* they find that in adolescent women, the process of separation and individuation usually seen as a staple feature of the Oedipal stage is complicated by the need and desire to remain attached, specifically to the mother. Hence, as in Gilligan's earlier discussion of morality (see note 13 below), what has often looked like immaturity is, rather, a product of women's different psychological development and makeup. See also Jean Baker Miller, *Toward a New Psychology of Women,* and Belenky et al., *Women's Ways of Knowing.*

See note 35 to chapter one, above, for a brief discussion of the limitations of some psychoanalytic feminism. See Abel et al., eds., *The Voyage In,* especially the Introduction, for an example of heavy reliance on theorists such as Chodorow and Gilligan. More recently, Rita Felski, in *Beyond Feminist Aesthetics,* questions such theories because they are in danger of "minimizing the magnitude of the social, economic, and ideological barriers which have obstructed women's self-realization in the public world" (123).

9. Chodorow, *The Reproduction of Mothering,* 169. Abel's phrasing occurs in her article's title: "(E)merging Identities."

10. See, for example, Godbold, *Ellen Glasgow and the Woman Within;*

Helen Fiddyment Levy, *Fiction of the Home Place;* Julius Rowan Raper, *Without Shelter;* and Wagner, *Ellen Glasgow,* as well as Glasgow's own views in *The Woman Within.*

11. Glasgow, "I Believe," 229–30. The comment in text about her mother's magnunimity also occurs in typed draft of "What I Believe" (1933), in manuscript holdings in the Glasgow Papers, box 5.

12. It is not known when Glasgow began to add her mother's family name, Gholson, to her own and to sign herself Ellen Anderson Gholson Glasgow.

13. See Gilligan's formulation of the differences between a morality of justice, which she sees as more typically masculine, and a morality of responsibility, which for Gilligan is more typically feminine (*In a Different Voice,* 5–23 and passim).

14. Glasgow, "I Believe" (1938), 229.

15. See Lillian Faderman's discussion of nineteenth-century father-daughter relationships in *Surpassing the Love of Men,* 187. See also Adrienne Rich, who, in *Of Woman Born,* reminds us of the responsibility that mothers have to show their daughters the positive possibilities open to women.

16. Elizabeth Ammons, in *Conflicting Stories,* briefly but perceptively discusses Glasgow's antiheterosexuality.

17. On Wharton's relationships with women, see Goodman, *Edith Wharton's Women.*

The importance of linking the personal and the public, evident during the early years of the second wave of feminism in the mid-twentieth century in the slogan "the personal is political," has recently been extended into feminist approaches to scholarly discourse as well. See Jane Tompkins, "Me and My Shadow," and Tompkins's Epilogue to her *West of Everything,* for two examples among many.

18. Though I have emphasized Glasgow's positive attitudes toward Lizzie Jones in order to underscore Jones's place in a nurturing female community significant to Glasgow's self-definition, there is no escaping the fact that those attitudes, however unconsciously on Glasgow's part, originate in racially informed relationships that are asymmetrical. However genuine her affection for Jones, Glasgow participates in and benefits from a tradition of female caregiving that ultimately demeans black women even as it celebrates a sense of nurturing connection. See note 26 to chapter one, and chapter five for additional brief discussions of Glasgow and race.

19. Quoted in Monique Parent, *Ellen Glasgow, Romancière,* 132.

20. See Jones, *Tomorrow Is Another Day,* xi and passim.

21. Glasgow, "A Woman of To-Morrow" (1895), reprinted in Raper, *Ellen Glasgow's Reasonable Doubts,* 4. Subsequent references are to the latter edition and are cited parenthetically in the text to WT, with page numbers.

22. An illustration by Currier & Ives (1869), "The Triumphs of Womans

[*sic*] Rights," particularly appropriate to my argument here, pictures a masculine social worry that women's rights would mean men's defeat and domestication. It is reproduced in John F. Kasson, *Rudeness and Civility*, 137.

Among the many provocative recent discussions of nineteenth-century men's anxiety that women's gains meant their loss, see Gilbert and Gubar, *The War of the Words* (vol. 1 of *No Man's Land*), especially "The Battle of the Sexes: The Men's Case," 3–62; Elaine Showalter, *Sexual Anarchy*, especially "New Women," 38–58; Carroll Smith-Rosenberg, *Disorderly Conduct*, especially "The New Woman as Androgyne," 245–96.

23. Glasgow, *The Descendant*, 74. Subsequent references to this novel are cited parenthetically in the text to *D,* with page numbers.

24. Godbold, *Ellen Glasgow and the Woman Within*, 35, notes the parallel between this and Glasgow's account in *The Woman Within* of her meeting with the agent.

25. Wagner, *Ellen Glasgow*, 24.

26. See Showalter, *Sexual Anarchy*, 29, on Joan of Arc as cultural symbol, particularly for women, in the late nineteenth century. Glasgow herself wrote a juvenile story called "A Modern Joan of Arc," the manuscript of which is in the Glasgow Papers (accession no. 7225-a).

27. See, for example, Heilbrun, *Writing a Woman's Life*.

28. Richard K. Meeker, ed., *The Collected Stories of Ellen Glasgow*, 39.

29. Glasgow, *Phases of an Inferior Planet*, 16, 17. Subsequent references to this novel are cited parenthetically in the text to *PIP,* with page numbers.

30. Rachel Blau DuPlessis, *Writing beyond the Ending*, 94 and chapter six, pages 84–104, discusses at length women writers of *Kunstlerromane* of the nineteenth and twentieth centuries.

31. Glasgow was familiar with Ellis. See note 33 below and chapter six for a fuller discussion of Glasgow and the psychosexual theorists of her time.

32. For a particularly insightful discussion of the turn-of-the-century sexologists and their influential views on "deviant" female behavior, see Smith-Rosenberg, *Disorderly Conduct*, especially "The New Woman as Androgyne," 245–96. Other helpful discussions are in Donovan, *After the Fall*, especially 25–26; Faderman, *Surpassing the Love of Men;* Nancy Sahli, "Smashing"; and Martha Vicinus, "Distance and Desire." See also chapter five, below.

33. Bonnie Zimmerman, "Exiting from Patriarchy," 248; ibid., 349n. See also chapter five, below, for a fuller discussion of Glasgow in relation to cultural attitudes toward women's friendships.

There is no doubt about Glasgow's knowledge of Ellis later: she owned his four-volume *Studies in the Psychology of Sex,* published in 1936. Curiously, it had disappeared from her library by the time her nephew, Carrington C. Tutwiler, Jr., published his catalogue of Glasgow's collection in 1967. Her fascination with the sexologists and particularly with Freud are discussed in chapters five and six, below.

34. Will Brantley, *Feminine Sense in Southern Memoir*, 106. In a recent article in the *Ellen Glasgow Newsletter*, Frances W. Saunders identifies Gerald as William Riggin Travers, a wealthy New York financier whose suicide was reported in the New York *Herald* in September 1905, when Glasgow says she read of Gerald's death there (*WW* 167). But I find the reasons to assume that Travers was Gerald less convincing than the reasons to assume he wasn't. See "Glasgow's Secret Love: 'Gerald B' or 'William T' " (*EGN* no. 31 [Fall 1993]: 1–4).·

35. Glasgow to Elizabeth Patterson, 2 January 1902, in *Letters of Ellen Glasgow*, ed. Blair Rouse, 34. All of Glasgow's letters to Lizzie Patterson (Crutchfield) are in box 28 of the Glasgow Papers, unless otherwise noted; hereafter, dates of the letters will be provided parenthetically in text. This letter (2 January 1902) and the one that follows (22 March 1902) are the only two letters to Patterson published in *Letters* (34). All other citations of correspondence between Glasgow and Patterson are to unpublished letters.

36. *Letters*, 35. Though Rouse says the letter has no date or place, the Richmond postmark carries the date 22 March 1902.

37. Glasgow to Bessie Zaban Jones, 18 April 1938 (*Letters* 238).

38. Glasgow, *The Wheel of Life*, 3. Subsequent references to this novel are cited parenthetically in the text to *WL*, with page numbers.

39. Julius Rowan Raper, *From the Sunken Garden*, 193; see pages 15–35 and 193–207 in Raper for a fuller summary discussion.

40. Glasgow, "The Difference," in Meeker, *Collected Stories*, 170.

41. Jean E. Kennard, *Vera Brittain and Winifred Holtby*, 1–2.

42. Diane Price Herndl, *Invalid Woman*, 175.

43. See Harriette Andreadis, "The Sapphic-Platonics of Katherine Philips, 1632–1664," 34–60, especially 54–55.

44. Glasgow to Mary Johnston, 22 March 1904, Mary Johnston Papers, accession no. 3588, box 2, Alderman Library, University of Virginia; also reprinted in *Letters*, 43–44.

45. The folder in the Johnston Papers containing this letter is dated 1904. However, as Raper in *Without Shelter* also points out (208n. 11), it must be 1905 because of Glasgow's reference to her 6 July voyage to Europe, which was in 1905.

46. The date looks like 19 (or perhaps 14) August 1906. Rawlings dated the Glasgow to Johnston letter "August 15, 1906"; also in Rouse, *Letters*, 54.

47. This letter from Glasgow to Johnston has no date, but is from "Hurricane Lodge"; also in Rouse, *Letters*, 51–52.

48. Glasgow to Johnston, "Sunday midnight," section D, Rawlings Papers.

49. Glasgow to Johnston, 4 (?) July 1908, Johnston Papers, box 2.

50. Glasgow to Johnston, 15 September 1906, Johnston Papers, box 2; in Rouse, *Letters*, 55–56.

51. In Rouse, ed., *Letters*, 55.

52. Rawlings obviously recognized the "-bad" suffix in Glasgow's letter, but did not have the postcard to help her. Her translation is "Bremenbad" (Rawlings Papers, section D).

53. Godbold, *Ellen Glasgow and the Woman Within*, 74; Raper, *Without Shelter*, 209 and 208n. 12.

54. The date of this letter from Glasgow to Johnston appears to be 19, 14, or 15 August 1906.

55. The letters from Glasgow to Louise Chandler Moulton are preserved in the Papers of Louise Chandler Moulton, accession no. MSS 18,869 (reel 5), Library of Congress. All quotations are from this collection. Although this first letter is undated, subsequent ones confirm its date as 1905.

56. Glasgow to Moulton, 5 October 1905; Godbold, *Ellen Glasgow and the Woman Within*, 150 and passim.

57. See Pamela R. Matthews, "Between Ellen and Louise," for a fuller discussion of the Glasgow-Moulton correspondence.

58. Godbold, *Ellen Glasgow and the Woman Within*, 66; Raper, *Without Shelter*, 210–11.

59. Rebe Glasgow to Rawlings, 14 November 1953, Rawlings Papers, folder D. Godbold (*Ellen Glasgow and the Woman Within*, 56) gives as his source only " 'Notes for a Biography of Ellen Glasgow,' in Rawlings Papers," so it is difficult to know what he means by Glasgow's sister having "confirmed" Glasgow's affairs. The Rawlings Papers contain an account of an interview conducted by Rawlings with Roberta Wellford, a close friend of Glasgow's and of her sisters. Rawlings's notes attribute the following statements to Wellford, and possibly Godbold refers to them: "She was always having violent love-affairs. Most of them never went very far. . . . Only two or three of us knew about the men in N.Y." (Rawlings Papers, section B.36).

60. Glasgow, *The Ancient Law*, 482–83.

61. Glasgow, "The Miller of Old Church," in *A Certain Measure* (1943), 129. Slightly revising her 1938 Preface (in the Virginia Edition), Glasgow substitutes "tradition" for the earlier "Great Tradition" (x). Her substitution asks us to think less specifically about a novelistic tradition as later identified by F. R. Leavis in *The Great Tradition* (1948), and more generally about an inclusive notion of "tradition."

62. Wagner, *Ellen Glasgow*, 41.

63. See Sherry B. Ortner, "Is Female to Male as Nature Is to Culture?" 67–87 for a discussion of the gendered cultural associations of nature and culture.

64. Glasgow returns to this theme of the hidden pervasiveness of female friendships in "Some Literary Woman Myths" (1928) and in the Virginia Edition preface (1938) to *They Stooped to Folly*.

65. Todd, *Women's Friendship in Literature*, 413–14.

66. Jean Baker Miller, in *Toward a New Psychology of Women*, discusses the tendency of members of subordinate groups to internalize the dominant

group's standards. See especially chapter one, "Domination-Subordination,"
3–12.

67. Glasgow, "What I Believe," in Raper, *Ellen Glasgow's Reasonable Doubts*, 225.

Chapter Three

1. Glasgow, "Feminism" (1913) reprinted in Raper, ed., *Ellen Glasgow's Reasonable Doubts*, 26–27. Parenthetical references that follow in text are to this edition and are cited to F, with page numbers.

2. For current views of women's friendships that are less specifically grounded in psychological theory, see, Elizabeth Abel, "(E)Merging Identities"; Louise Bernikow, *Among Women;* Cott, *The Bonds of Womanhood;* Todd, *Women's Friendship in Literature;* Faderman, *Surpassing the Love of Men;* and Elizabeth A. Meese, *Crossing the Double-Cross.* Cott, Todd, Faderman, and Meese (esp. pp. 128–30 on Monique Wittig's lesbianism as defiance of patriarchy) also emphasize female friendship as a rejection of men.

3. On "mature dependence," see Chodorow, "Family Structure," 62. Chodorow is quoting Harry Guntrip, *Personality Structure and Human Interaction* (1961).

4. Heilbrun, *Writing a Woman's Life,* 64–65, observes that often it is a "dead" woman who facilitates self-discovery.

5. Glasgow, *The Romance of a Plain Man,* vol. 2 of the Virginia Edition, 98. Subsequent references to this novel are cited parenthetically in text to *RPM,* with page numbers.

6. For the cult of domesticity or the cult of true womanhood, see Cott, *The Bonds of Womanhood,* especially 1–18 and 63–100, and Barbara Welter, "The Cult of True Womanhood." For a provocative recent approach to the question of women's relationships, particularly the idealization of women's friendship and the potential for female conflict as well as community, see Betsy Erkkila, *The Wicked Sisters,* especially the Introduction.

7. It would be possible to argue that Mrs. Chitling's low social status and clear powerlessness work in precisely the opposite way: that through them, Glasgow denounces the complicity required of women under patriarchal rule. But nothing in the novel suggests that we are even to sympathize with Mrs. Chitling, much less take her views seriously.

It is also possible to see Glasgow's unflattering characterization of Mrs. Chitling as racist. Though she is white, her name (which resembles the colloquial pronunciation of a traditional soul food), her language (which often lapses into stereotypical black dialect), and her socially inferior position, all suggest a negative judgment of her, based, in part, on her resemblance to black stereotypes.

8. C. Hugh Holman, "The Tragedy of Self-Entrapment," 158.

9. See Glasgow, *The Woman Within,* 83, for Glasgow's comments on

Cary's aspirations toward authorship. A few manuscripts in the Glasgow Papers have been tentatively attributed to Cary.

10. See Raper, *Without Shelter*, 48–50, for the full account of Walter McCormack's suicide; Godbold, *Ellen Glasgow*, 30, and Glasgow, *The Woman Within*, 100–101, respectively, for Cary's response and Glasgow's moving account of her sister's grief; Glasgow, *The Woman Within*, 101, and Raper, *Without Shelter*, 50, for Cary's reading to prepare for her afterlife with Walter.

11. Gilligan, *In a Different Voice*, 30 and passim, 132.

12. Blair Rouse's edition of the letters contains twenty-seven mentions of Bennett; of those, only four are letters to her, even though over twenty lengthy letters and additional postcards exist. Marcelle Thiébaux's *Ellen Glasgow* treats Bennett only in passing references; neither Raper, *From the Sunken Garden*, nor Wagner, *Ellen Glasgow*, discuss Bennett even briefly.

13. Godbold, *Ellen Glasgow and the Woman Within*, 196.

14. Jones, *Tomorrow Is Another Day*, 203; Elizabeth Ammons, *Conflicting Stories*, 170–71. Joan Foster Santas, in *Ellen Glasgow's American Dream*, is harsher on Virginia than I am, calling her "almost contemptible in her helpless hysteria of despair." But Santas also notes the problematic conclusion of *Virginia*, commenting that "even Ellen Glasgow is not much comforted by the bond between Harry and his mother that precipitates the concluding note of the novel" (95).

15. Glasgow, Preface to *Virginia*, vol. 9 of the Virginia Edition, x. Subsequent references to this Preface will be cited parenthetically in text to *V*—followed by a lowercase roman-numeral page reference.

16. *Virginia* 22; 17. Here and in subsequent parenthetical citations in the text, page references will be to two texts: the first edition of 1913, followed by the Virginia Edition. Discrepancies, as in the case of revision of the latter edition, will be noted.

17. There is a slight revision in the Virginia Edition, quoted in text. The second sentence quoted here appears in the first edition as: "She felt again the great hope which is the challenge that youth flings to destiny."

18. In the Virginia Edition, Glasgow omits the word *involuntarily*.

19. Glasgow omits this sentence in the Virginia Edition, leaving the reader instead with the unanswered question: "Would life yield nothing more to that radiant girl than it had yielded to her or to the other women whom she had known?" (*V* 25; 20). Certainly, such a revision throws more emphasis on the ominous question, forcing the reader to confront that question of a woman's tradition that had yielded precious little to Miss Priscilla. The "sadness" in the earlier version comes close to trivializing the tragic implications Glasgow plays out in the novel.

20. Donovan, *After the Fall*, Fiddyment Levy, *Fiction of the Home Place*, and Linda W. Wagner, "Ellen Glasgow: Daughter as Justified," also discuss the role of mothers from perspectives different from each other and

from mine. Donovan emphasizes the mother as "collaborator" in patriarchal oppression (esp. 140–43). Fiddyment Levy sees mothers in Glasgow's fiction as providing "pitiful examples of victimization" (104). Wagner stresses the "sanctified" mothers' responsibility to curtail the "rebellious daughters" (140). I see these mothers' commitment to their daughters' education in patriarchy as more conflicted than these three critics do.

21. The Virginia Edition omits "traditional" to describe Mrs. Pendleton's "wisdom," and revises the second sentence to read: "it could not struggle against her inherited belief in the Pauline measure of her sex" (153).

22. Glasgow's only revision here for the Virginia Edition is an interesting one. She changes the "immemorial attitude of wom*e*n" to "of wom*a*n," as if to universalize Virginia's imagined experience.

23. The revision in the Virginia Edition changes the girls' "whirling" to "revolving" and omits the commas in the sentence. The omission of the commas grammatically merges the parts of the sentence to parallel the merging of the girls into one another and into "all womanhood."

24. Fiddyment Levy, *Fiction of the Home Place*, 105.

25. Glasgow's only revision here for the Virginia Edition was to omit "monosyllabic."

26. Glasgow made two changes in the Virginia Edition. In the first, "of" is omitted before "sterile imagination." The second occurs in the sentence following. Originally, the sentence read: "By virtue of these limitations and this sterility he had risen out of obscurity." The change omits "and this sterility." Both omissions—the simple "of" and the more substantial one that follows—effectively link Cyrus's "small parts" and "sterile imagination" by not distinguishing between them. "Small parts" and "sterile imagination" become inseparable, and the pun more meaningful.

27. Toni Morrison, *Beloved*, 190.

28. Dorothy M. Scura, "A Knowledge in the Heart," 35, links this image in *Virginia* to the similar "chains" binding the women in Glasgow's suffrage poem, "The Call," published in 1912.

29. In the Virginia Edition revisions, Glasgow substitutes the "changing *desires* of the man she loves" for the "changing *ideals* of the man she loves," selecting the word with the greater negative connotation for the woman whose personality must "adjust."

30. Linda Wagner-Martin, Introduction to *Virginia* (Penguin, 1989), xii.

31. Adrienne Rich, "Heroines," 292–95, 95.

32. Glasgow's New York apartment was on the corner of Fifth Avenue and Eighty-fifth Street, according to Parent in *Ellen Glasgow, Romancière*, 160. Glasgow's letterhead was imprinted "One West Eighty-Fifth."

33. Glasgow, *Life and Gabriella*, vol. 12 of the Virginia Edition: "I can manage," 69; other quotations, 197. Subsequent references to this novel are cited parenthetically in text to *LG*, with page numbers.

34. A letter of 26 March 1918 from Glasgow to her brother Arthur sug-

gests that Bennett left that month; see Rouse, *Letters,* 64–65. A letter dated 9 November 1920 to Horace Walpole clearly indicates Bennett's presence as cohost by that time; see *Letters,* 67.

35. Glasgow, *The Builders,* 13. Subsequent references to this novel are cited parenthetically in the text to *B,* with page numbers. Glasgow did not include *The Builders* in the Virginia Edition, but it is the only novel she first published serially (in *Woman's Home Companion,* October through December 1919).

36. Reliable information about Bennett is hard to come by, particularly when so many sources may have their own reasons for representing Bennett as they do (see Rawlings Papers, section B). Certainly Glasgow saw Bennett as capable, independent, and strong-minded, and her photographs show her to be physically imposing and even rather formidable.

37. See Price Herndl, *Invalid Women,* for a provocative discussion of female invalidism from 1840 to 1940.

38. Charlotte Perkins Gilman's *Women and Economics* addressed the issue of unnecessary conflict among women brought on by competition for male attention, and her feminist utopian novel, *Herland,* satirizes this competition. For recent discussions, see Louise Bernikow, *Among Women,* especially 194–224; Luise Eichenbaum and Susie Orback, *Between Women;* Raymond, *A Passion for Friends.* Todd's *Women's Friendship in Literature* is a more exclusively literary treatment. There are numerous discussions of the angel-demon dichotomy. For examples, see, Nina Auerbach, *Woman and the Demon;* Bernikow, *Among Women;* and Gilbert and Gubar, *The Madwoman in the Attic.*

39. Henry Anderson to Glasgow, 7 September 1916, in Glasgow Papers, University of Virginia. Unless otherwise noted, this letter and those that are quoted in the text that follows are in box 8 of the Glasgow Papers.

40. Godbold, *Ellen Glasgow and the Woman Within,* 112–13.

41. An undated notebook in the Glasgow Papers contains this entry in Glasgow's hand: "Dante 'Beatrice upward gazed—and I on her!'" (box 5, notebook no. 3). Several quotes indicate male attitudes toward women; none of them leave any doubt about Glasgow's ironic attitude toward the statements (such as Milton's "He for God only, she for God in Him"). I'm certain that Henry Anderson took the Dante-Beatrice analogy more seriously than Glasgow did.

42. The folder is labeled "c 1916 1920"; the tone of the letters as well as internal evidence generally corroborates the dates. This letter and (those in the following two paragraphs) are in the Glasgow Papers, box 9.

43. Anderson to Rawlings, Rawlings Papers, section D, "Ellen Glasgow Correspondence."

44. Rawlings Papers, section B, interview on the "day after Thanksgiving," 28 November 1952; Rawlings Papers, section B, 23 February 1953.

45. Rawlings Papers, section B, interview on the "day after Thanksgiving."

Notes

The documents representing Anderson's uneasiness about discussing the supposed "engagement" are fascinating. Rawlings describes Anderson as becoming extremely agitated every time she brought the subject up: he turns "purplish," "coughs" from a "constriction of the chest," begins his typical "alarming breathing," and becomes "snappish" in his answers. Anderson's responses are registered in Rawlings's interview notes (Rawlings Papers, section B.7). See also Rawlings's readily available accounts in letters to Anderson himself, to her husband, and to Norman Berg, Macmillan's southeastern representative, in Gordon E. Bigelow and Laura V. Monti, eds., *Selected Letters of Marjorie Kinnan Rawlings* 381–83, 387–89, 389–90, 392–94, 398–400.

46. As Monique Parent observes in *Ellen Glasgow, Romancière* (195), Glasgow's Corinna also resembles her close lifelong friend and frequent traveling companion Carrie Coleman Duke, who lived in the antique shop she owned at 200 West Franklin Street. Carrie was married in Glasgow's house at One West Main in 1919; Glasgow at times bought antiques from Carrie or elsewhere on Carrie's advice. According to Rawlings's notes from an interview with Blythe Branch, brother-in-law of Glasgow's older brother Arthur, Carrie Duke was "one of the few who have Anne V. to formal luncheons and dinners" (Rawlings Papers, section B.8).

47. Glasgow, *One Man in His Time,* 39. Subsequent references to this work will be cited parenthetically in text to *OMHT,* with page references.

48. Rich, "Snapshots of a Daughter-in-Law," ll. 53–59.

49. Wagner, "Ellen Glasgow," 140. Josephine Donovan observes in *After the Fall* that Corinna treats Patty (to whom Donovan refers as "Polly") as a "kind of daughter protégé," thus reconnecting the "mother-daughter bond" with the "collective green-world sources of matriarchal energy" (147).

50. Anderson to Glasgow, 31 August 1916, Glasgow Papers, box 8.

51. Rawlings Papers, interview with Blythe Branch, section B.8; interview with Carrie Duke, section B.15.

52. Wagner, *Ellen Glasgow,* 9; Godbold, *Ellen Glasgow,* 119n. The scrap with Glasgow's statement about her engagement is dated "Thursday," 19 July 1917. Glasgow Papers, box 9.

53. Rouse, *Letters,* 64–65, 67.

54. For discussions of the Ladies of Llangollen, see Faderman, *Surpassing the Love of Men,* 121–25; Elizabeth Mavor, *The Ladies of Llangollen;* and Todd, *Women's Friendship in Literature,* 360.

55. Rawlings Papers, section D.

56. In her interviews with Bennett, Monique Parent clearly perceived the deeply felt affection Bennett had for Glasgow. In *Ellen Glasgow, Romancière,* Parent reports that Bennett

> had dedicated her life to her; then, she pledged an excessive adoration to her memory. She felt herself the rightful proprietor of Ellen, who was the unique object of her thoughts, the sole subject of her conversations: her beauty, her talent, her sufferings, her generosity, her tenderness toward

animals. Surrounded by Ellen's personal property and familiar objects, she had made of her room a sanctuary where flowers ornamented pictures of Ellen at all ages, as well as those of Jeremy, of Billy, and of Bonnie [their dogs]; yellow roses permanently framed the last photograph of Ellen at age sixty. In losing Ellen, Miss Bennett saw her better half die. The rest of her days she passed quietly in Richmond, not far from One West Main which she never wanted to see again. (196)

In the penultimate sentence, *La moitié d'elle-même* translates literally as "half of herself." In colloquial French, the phrase means "better half," as I have translated it above, and, interestingly, also "wife."

57. Glasgow, "Feminism," in Raper, *Ellen Glasgow's Reasonable Doubts*, 31–32.

Chapter Four

1. Rich, "When We Dead Awaken"; DuPlessis, *Writing beyond the Ending;* and Greene, *Changing the Story,* respectively.

2. Glasgow, "One Way to Write Novels," in Raper, *Ellen Glasgow's Reasonable Doubts,* 156.

3. William Patrick Day, *In the Circles of Fear and Desire,* for example, does not consider *Wuthering Heights* "Gothic," and regrets the loose use of the term.

4. Claire Kahane, "The Gothic Mirror," in Shirley Nelson Garner, Claire Kahane, and Madelon Sprengnether, eds., *The (M)Other Tongue,* 334; Ellen Moers, *Literary Women,* esp. 90–99; DeLamotte, *Perils of the Night,* 13–14. Seeing an "anxiety about boundaries" as the "primary source" of "Gothic terror," DeLamotte argues that the Gothic therefore provides the framework for the "expression of psychological, epistemological, religious, and social anxieties that resolve themselves most fundamentally into a concern about the boundaries of the self" (13–14). See Elaine Showalter, *Sister's Choice,* for a discussion of specifically American versions of the female Gothic (127–44).

5. Day—though he uses the term *Gothic* much more strictly than I do here and does not consider the "female Gothic"—addresses the importance of "subjectivity" as a feature of Gothic fiction. Such a consideration suggests an important connection to the writing of women, long involved with subjectivity as an issue.

6. Moers, *Literary Women,* 90; Juliann E. Fleenor, ed., *The Female Gothic,* 7; Nina Auerbach, *Romantic Imprisonment,* 20; Michelle A. Massé, "Gothic Repetition," 681 n. 4. Susan Wolstenholme, *Gothic (Re)Visions,* discusses many of the same issues as Massé, including hidden secrets, female subjectivity, relation to an other, and repetition, in light of the structure of Gothic fiction. She sees the "problem of representation" (12) in Gothic instances of simultaneous revelation and hiding from view as particularly applicable to the "double role" of a woman who is also a writer.

7. I am indebted to Julius Rowan Raper's extremely helpful article "Ambivalence toward Authority" for noting Glasgow's marking of this passage in Maeterlinck (16).

8. DeLamotte, *Perils of the Night*, 10.

9. Leslie A. Fiedler, *Love and Death in the American Novel*, 109.

10. Massé, "Gothic Repetition," 681–82.

11. Marjorie Kinnan Rawlings Papers, section B.8. The quote is from Rawlings's notes from interviews with Anne Virginia Bennett in 1953. Godbold, *Ellen Glasgow and the Woman Within*, 115, also quotes this passage.

12. Allan Gardner Lloyd-Smith, *Uncanny American Fictions*, 75.

13. See Ferguson, *First Feminists*, and Cathy Davidson, *Revolution and the Word*, for helpful brief discussions of *feme covert*.

14. Eve Kosofsky Sedgwick, *The Coherence of Gothic Conventions*, 5 and chap. 2; Virginia Woolf, "Professions for Women," 58–60.

15. Meeker, Introduction to *Collected Stories*, 8; Godbold, *Ellen Glasgow and the Woman Within*, 115; Meeker, Introduction to *Collected Stories*, 5; Frederick P. W. McDowell, *Ellen Glasgow and the Ironic Art of Fiction*, 144–45; Raper, *From the Sunken Garden*, 60.

16. See, for example, DeLamotte, *Perils of the Night;* Kate Ferguson Ellis, *The Contested Castle;* Fleenor, *The Female Gothic;* and Moers, *Literary Women*.

17. Glasgow, "The Shadowy Third," in Meeker, *Collected Stories*, 52. Subsequent quotations from the short stories are to Meeker's edition, unless otherwise noted, and page numbers are cited parenthetically to *CS* in the text.

18. S. Weir Mitchell, "Rest," 26.

19. See Raper, *From the Sunken Garden*, 68; Thiébaux, *Ellen Glasgow*, 185.

20. Lynette Carpenter, "The Daring Gift in 'Dare's Gift,' " 95. Carpenter also notes Mildred Beckwith's "repressed or misdirected rage" (98).

21. See Gilbert and Gubar, *No Man's Land:* vol. 1, *The War of the Words*, and Elaine Showalter, *Sexual Anarchy*, for discussions of male anxiety over increased female visibility in the public domain.

22. Glasgow frequently associates spring with strangely "erratic behavior," especially sexual desire. See, for example, *Virginia, The Romantic Comedians*, and *The Sheltered Life*.

23. Anderson to Glasgow, 26 August 1920, Glasgow Papers, box 9.

24. Gayle Greene, "Feminist Fiction and the Uses of Memory," 291. See also Greene's *Changing the Story*.

25. Sedgwick, *The Coherence of Gothic Conventions*, 5 and passim.

26. See Kennard, *Vera Brittain and Winifred Holtby*, 1–23 passim.

27. Raper, *From the Sunken Garden*, 53–78.

28. See Donovan, *After the Fall;* Ortner, "Is Female to Male as Nature Is to Culture?"; Annis Pratt et al., *Archetypal Patterns in Women's Fiction;* and Sherman, *Sarah Orne Jewett*, for reflections on the relationship between women and nature.

29. Meeker, Editor's Note to "Whispering Leaves," CS 164.

30. It is obviously appropriate and necessary to examine the issue of race. But Glasgow's attitude toward race is complex—as complicated as one would expect of a well-to-do Southerner raised around black servants and caregivers whom she both loved and exploited because of their position. The scope of the question requires more space than I give it. Adrienne Rich's "Education of a Novelist," a poem first included in *The Fact of a Doorframe,* reveals Rich's anger after reading Glasgow's autobiography, where Glasgow regrets never teaching her own surrogate mother, Lizzie Jones, how to read, and thus failing to fulfill a childhood promise. Elizabeth Ammons's *Conflicting Stories,* 175–76, briefly addresses the issue of Glasgow's attitude toward race but, I think, oversimplifies it, just as I think Rich's anger reflects her own attitudes as much as it does Glasgow's. Though Diane Price Herndl does not focus at length on race in Glasgow's fiction, she does note Glasgow's "ambiguous" attitudes toward race in *Barren Ground* (*Invalid Women,* 240n. 17).

31. See chapter two, note 22, above.

32. Gilbert and Gubar, *The Madwoman in the Attic,* 15.

33. Meeker, Editor's Note to "Jordan's End," *Collected Stories,* 216.

34. See Meeker, Introduction, *Collected Stories,* on the resemblance of Glasgow's stories to Poe's (12–15).

35. See Scura, *Ellen Glasgow,* 227–35, for a helpful sampling of reviews. See also brief quotes from reviews of *The Shadowy Third* in MacDonald and Inge, *Ellen Glasgow,* 60–63.

36. See, for example, Glasgow's frequent criticism of Faulkner and his "school of Raw-Head-and-Bloody-Bones" fiction: "Gothic tales have their place; but, after all, why do all mushrooms have to be toadstools?" (Glasgow to Irita Van Doren, 8 September 1933, in Rouse, *Letters,* 143–44). In a letter to Bessie Zaban Jones of 7 February 1934, she expresses similar sentiments: "I agree with you that the Gothic horrors of William Faulkner are legitimate material for grotesque tales, like the Weird Tales of Hoffmann, but not considered as realism or even as naturalism" (ibid., 150). Quoting from Faulkner's introduction to *Sanctuary,* where he admits that the book was a money-making scheme, she conflates Gothic with literary hack-work and regrets that so much seems to be written with only money in mind. It was the combination of violence and sexuality that she seems to have objected to the most. In a clear evocation of the sensational rape in *Sanctuary,* she refers to the "corncob cavaliers" of Faulkner (Glasgow to Irita Van Doren, 23 May 193, in ibid., 154), yet she takes pains to explain that her objections are motivated by human sympathy, not prudery.

Chapter Five

1. Glasgow, *Barren Ground,* vol. 1 of the Virginia Edition, 451. Subsequent citations to this novel and its Preface are given parenthetically in text to *BG.*

2. For examples of Dorinda's denials, see Glasgow, *Barren Ground*, 158, 195, 202, 211, 214, 262, 287, 403.

3. Glasgow uses the phrase "vehicle of liberation" in her 1933 Preface to the Old Dominion Edition of *Barren Ground*, vii.

4. Rachel Blau DuPlessis, *Writing beyond the Ending*, 5; Frances Cobb quoted in Elizabeth Nestor, *Female Friendships and Communities*, 4.

5. Glasgow owned many of the texts of the so-called new psychologists and probably discussed many of them with her friend Joseph Collins, a neurologist and author in New York. I will address Glasgow's attitudes toward the new psychologists in more detail in chapter six.

6. See Donovan, *After the Fall*, 25–27; Faderman, *Surpassing the Love of Men;* Smith-Rosenberg, especially "The New Woman as Androgyne" in *Disorderly Conduct*, 245–96; Sahli, "Smashing"; Martha Vicinus, "Distance and Desire" and *Independent Women*.

7. See Ammons, *Conflicting Stories*, 169.

8. See Smith-Rosenberg, *Disorderly Conduct*, on the dangers inherent in women's adopting male discourse.

9. Glasgow's relationship with Radclyffe Hall is instructive as an example of Glasgow's clear awareness of the complicated responses of the reading public to female friendships, or what we would now term lesbianism in the case of Hall's *The Well of Loneliness*, published in 1928 and censored in England. A letter from Hall to Glasgow in 1929 indicates that Glasgow had signed the American petition protesting the censorship: "I saw your name on the splendid list of my American supporters, and this made me feel very proud indeed—believe me I was and am deeply gratified" ([14 September?] 1929, Glasgow Papers, box 15). Glasgow's support was more than a generalized show of anticensorship sentiment too: she had earlier refused to sign the petition protesting an attack on Dreiser's *The Genius*. She wrote to H. L. Mencken in 1916 that, though she sympathized in "spirit" with the protest, "A temperamental disinclination to appear to know more about a subject than I really do know keeps me from signing this protest" (Glasgow to H. L. Mencken, 12 December 1916, Dreiser Collection, University of Pennsylvania).

10. As I will discuss in chapter six, Glasgow's autobiography, *The Woman Within*, with its emphasis on romantic relationships with men, has also made it difficult for scholars to see beyond the surface romance or marriage plots, fictional and otherwise.

11. Glasgow, *Life and Gabriella*, vol. 12 of the Virginia Edition, vii. Subsequent citations to this novel and its Preface are given parenthetically in text to *LG*, with page numbers.

12. Rawlings Papers, section B.8.

13. On the mother-daughter relationship in *Barren Ground* and elsewhere in Glasgow, see Donovan, *After the Fall*, 136–37, 140–42; Fiddyment Levy, *Fiction of the Home Place*, 97–130; MacKethan, *Daughters of Time*, 71–72; and Wagner, "Ellen Glasgow: Daughter as Justified" and *Beyond Convention*, 74.

14. Ellen M. Caldwell, "Ellen Glasgow and the Southern Agrarians," argues that Glasgow's sense of tradition in *Barren Ground* is tied to the Southern Agrarians' "traditional values of history and myth" as "bulwarks against the chaos of the modern world" (203). Fiddyment Levy argues in *Fiction of the Home Place* that Glasgow, beginning with *Barren Ground*, depicts women characters who require "the shelter of tradition and the continuity of the generations" in order to "rescue" their "sexuality from male exploitation and failure" (122).

15. MacKethan, *Daughters of Time*, 69; Catherine Rainwater, "Narration as Pragmatism in Ellen Glasgow's *Barren Ground*," 674. See Smith-Rosenberg, *Disorderly Conduct* (especially "Hearing Women's Words"), for a solid discussion of Victorian manipulations of "natural."

16. Joan Foster Santas disagrees in *Ellen Glasgow's American Dream*, arguing that Glasgow increasingly looked to "the 'good people' of the yeoman class and rising representatives of the 'common man' to infuse new energy into her vision" (14).

17. One of Glasgow's favorite criticisms of men is that they love to cut down trees. She associates such destruction with what she sees as men's failure to understand growth and nurturing. Mrs. Burden of *They Stooped to Folly*, for example, thinks: "she could never understand, no woman could understand, how men enjoy cutting down trees" (216).

18. Wagner, *Ellen Glasgow*, 10–11.

19. Godbold, especially, set the tone for readers who complain about Dorinda's coldness and emotional deadness. He accuses Glasgow of using her fiction to assert "her superiority" to men and of inhabiting a "barren plateau" where no one (especially no man) "would wish to go or dare to stay" (*Ellen Glasgow and the Woman Within*, 138).

20. Ibid., 137.

21. Ammons, *Conflicting Stories*, 175. In "Education of a Novelist," Adrienne Rich, it should be noted, implicates herself in Glasgow's racism, and thus recognizes the danger of adopting a critical position of superiority.

22. Elizabeth Schultz, "Out of the Woods and into the World," 71.

23. Ibid., 70–71.

24. In revising this Preface for *A Certain Measure* (1943), Glasgow removed the words "invisible protagonists" (*BG* xiii) from the 1938 Preface and substituted "dominant powers" (158).

25. Raper, *From the Sunken Garden*, 84–88, discusses Glasgow's possible use of Freud in the dreams in *Barren Ground*. In doing so, Glasgow uses a male model (Freudian) of dream analysis (dreams as subconscious desire). Since the dreams of Dorinda and her mother both reveal the desire to undercut patriarchal inheritance, Glasgow thus makes use of a patriarchal structure in order to subvert patriarchal tradition.

26. See Ammons, *Conflicting Stories*, and Donovan, *After the Fall*, for discussions of mother-daughter tensions in the work of women writers around the turn of the twentieth century.

27. Passages such as this one lead both Parent Frazee and Raper to see *Barren Ground* as a revenge drama. See Parent Frazee, "Ellen Glasgow as Feminist," 174–75; and Julius Rowan Raper, "The Landscape of Revenge."

28. Glasgow, "Van Doren on Cabell," New York *Herald-Tribune Books* (1925), 3–4; reprinted in Raper, *Ellen Glasgow's Reasonable Doubts,* 201–4. Subsequent citations are given parenthetically in text to VDC, and page references are to the latter text.

29. Smith-Rosenberg, *Disorderly Conduct,* 281. See also George Chauncey, Jr., "From Sexual Inversion to Homosexuality"; Faderman, *Surpassing the Love of Men;* Sahli, "Smashing."

30. Donovan, *After the Fall,* 25.

31. See Chauncey, "From Sexual Inversion to Homosexuality"; Sahli, "Smashing"; Smith-Rosenberg, *Disorderly Conduct.*

32. Glasgow, "Some Literary Woman Myths," in Julius Rowan Raper, *Ellen Glasgow's Reasonable Doubts,* 36, 37. Subsequent citations, given parenethetically in text to "SLWM," are to this edition.

33. Glasgow's observations about male modernists' female characters implicitly criticize women for accepting the male discourse about female freedom. Glasgow thus lends support to Smith-Rosenberg's argument that the New Women of the twenties, in adopting male discourse and accepting sexual freedom divorced from political and economic power as the goal of female independence, in some ways may have defeated their own cause. See Smith-Rosenberg, *Disorderly Conduct,* especially pp. 282–83.

34. See ibid., 39–40, Gilbert and Gubar, in "Cross Dressing and Re-Dressing," 286–90; *No Man's Land:* vol. 2, *Sex Changes,* 324–76.

35. *They Stooped to Folly* had been published by September 1929; see Glasgow to Carl Van Vechten, 19 September 1929, in Rouse, *Letters,* 98.

36. Glasgow, "The Novel in the South," in Raper, *Ellen Glasgow's Reasonable Doubts,* 71.

37. Ibid., 71. The novel contains several references to "Magdalen," a name associated not only with its obvious biblical prototype but with the institutions devoted to reforming "fallen" women and to such women themselves. See Lynne Vallone, " 'The True Meaning of Dirt.' "

39. See Elaine Showalter, ed., *These Modern Women,* for essays from New Women of the 1920s.

40. Ibid., 15–16.

41. Glasgow to Bennett, 1 June 1937, Glasgow Papers, box 28. The dates of these letters from Glasgow to Bennett, respectively, are 14 August 1927, 7 August 1930, and 1 June 1937, Glasgow Papers, box 28.

42. See note 9 above.

43. Clare Leighton to Glasgow, 5 July 1940; Leighton to Glasgow, 5 July 1940 and 26 November 1940, respectively, all in Glasgow Papers, box 16.

44. Signe Toksvig to Glasgow, 25 March 1945, Glasgow Papers, box 18.

45. Glasgow, Preface to Old Dominion Edition of *Barren Ground,* v, emphasis added. See note 3 above.

46. Glasgow first used the term *evasive idealism* in an interview with Joyce Kilmer, " 'Evasive Idealism' in Literature" in *Literature in the Making* (1917), 229–40.

47. Glasgow, *The Sheltered Life*, vol. 4 of the Virginia Edition, 3. Subsequent citations to this text and its Preface are given parenthetically in text to *SL*, with page numbers.

48. Jenny Blair's resistance to *Little Women*, especially to Jo March, indeed marks her separation from generations of American women who have looked to Jo and her text as models of independent American womanhood. See Showalter's chapter, "*Little Women:* The American Female Myth," in *Sister's Choice*, 42–64.

49. Louisa May Alcott, *Little Women*, 3. Hereafter cited in text as *LW*, followed by page reference. My thanks to Lynne Vallone for calling attention to Jo's use of the word *poky*.

50. See, for example, Ammons, *Conflicting Stories;* Donovan, *After the Fall;* Sherman, *Sarah Orne Jewett;* Smith-Rosenberg, *Disorderly Conduct;* and Torsney, *Constance Fenimore Woolson*.

51. This process of separation-individuation whereby *self* is defined as *not other* is the model that informs object-relations theory, in which "objects" include other people. This passage bears a remarkable similarity to the opening section of Glasgow's autobiography.

52. Glasgow, "The Biography of Manuel," 213. Glasgow's review of James Branch Cabell's eighteen-volume fictional series collectively titled *The Biography of Manuel* (1927–30) was first published in the *Saturday Review of Literature*, 6 (7 June 1930), 1108–9; reprinted in Raper, *Reasonable Doubts*, 205–16. The page reference above is to the reprinted text.

53. I want to emphasize Jenny Blair's learned behavior, and to point out George's responsibility in it. His sexual exploitation of Jenny Blair as she grows up is partially, even largely, responsible for her attitudes.

Chapter Six

1. All photographs mentioned in text are in the Glasgow Papers, box 25, unless noted.

2. Glasgow Papers, box 24. Glasgow's comment is written in her hand on an envelope containing the daguerreotype.

3. One hundred copies of Henry Adams's *Education* were first printed privately in 1907 and distributed among a small circle of friends. It was published in 1918, after Adams's death.

4. Ellen Glasgow to Van Wyck Brooks, 2 September 1939, in Rouse, *Letters*, 254–55.

5. Domna Stanton, "Autogynography," 9; Sidonie Smith, "Self, Subject, and Resistance," 11. See also Smith, *A Poetics of Women's Autobiography;* Benstock, *The Private Self;* Brodzki and Schenck, *Life/Lines*.

6. Smith, *A Poetics of Women's Autobiography,* 53.

7. Fiddyment Levy, *Fiction of the Home Place,* 99–100, discusses these oppositions in *The Woman Within* as a "paradigm of experience" based on Glasgow's parents' personalities as Glasgow represents them.

8. See, for example, Benstock, *The Private Self;* Brodzki and Schenck, *Life/Lines;* Estelle Jelinek, *The Tradition of Women's Autobiography* and *Women's Autobiography;* Smith, *A Poetics of Women's Autobiography.*

9. Barbara Rose, "I'll Tell You No Lies," 110.

10. Will Brantley, *Feminine Sense in Southern Memoir,* also discusses both Glasgow's self-creation and her reliance on Freud; see especially 93–94. For another recent discussion of *The Woman Within* as self-creation, see Nancy A. Walker, "The Romance of Self-Representation."

11. Gilman, *The Man-Made World; or, Our Androcentric Culture* (1911).

12. Carrington C. Tutwiler, Jr., *Ellen Glasgow's Library* (1967), 28, 3; see also Tutwiler, *A Catalogue of the Library of Ellen Glasgow* (1969). The dates Tutwiler listed in parenthesis after volume titles are the publication dates of the copies Ellen Glasgow owned, and so are not necessarily the same as the original publication dates.

13. Raper, *Without Shelter,* 105–6, speculates that Dr. Pearce Bailey might be the "Gerald B—" of Glasgow's autobiography. Raper also briefly discusses Collins (ibid., 104), as does Godbold, *Ellen Glasgow,* 159–61.

14. See Joseph Collins's undated letter to Glasgow (Glasgow Papers, box 13), which, because of the extended reference in the first paragraph to "your amorous judge," must have been written in 1925 or early 1926, during her composition of *The Romantic Comedians.* Collins's books include: *The Doctor Looks at Literature: Psychological Studies in Life and Letters* (1923), which briefly discusses several women writers (including Katherine Mansfield, Dorothy Richardson, Rebecca West, and Virginia Woolf), and *The Doctor Looks at Love and Life* (1926), with its fascinating chapter on Freud and the "New Psychology." Collins's attitude toward Freud often resembles Glasgow's. Collins points out there, for example, that the "weakness of the Oedipus-complex lies in its inability to explain why little girls are its victims" (236), and so joins Glasgow (and many others) in recognizing gender bias in Freud.

15. Collins, *The Doctor Looks at Love and Life,* 205–6. Nathan G. Hale, Jr., points out in "From Berggasse XIX to Central Park West" that since many of Freud's first followers were lay analysts, they needed to "create a willing clientele" if they were to "earn a living treating nervous disorders" (300). Collins's popular books may have functioned partly in this capacity.

16. See chapter five, note 9, above, on Hall and Glasgow.

17. Glasgow describes the humorous scene (she did not realize until afterward that the tea was for her) in a letter to her sister Cary (Ellen Glasgow to Cary Glasgow McCormack, 28 April 1909, Glasgow Papers, box 14).

Godbold, *Ellen Glasgow and the Woman Within*, 88–89, gives a summary of that letter.

18. See Tutwiler, *Catalogue.*

19. Glasgow, "Literary Realism or Nominalism" (1921), in Raper, ed., *Ellen Glasgow's Reasonable Doubts*, 131.

20. Glasgow, "Elder and Younger Brother" (1937), 171; Glasgow, "Some Literary Woman Myths" (1928), 44; Glasgow, "George Santayana Writes a 'Novel,'" (1936), 194; Glasgow, "Some Literary Woman Myths," 37; Glasgow, "Impressions of the Novel" (1928), 143; Glasgow, "One Way to Write Novels" (1934), 161, respectively: all are quoted from Raper, *Ellen Glasgow's Reasonable Doubts.*

21. Susan Goodman, in "Competing Visions of Freud in the Memoirs of Ellen Glasgow and Edith Wharton," sees Glasgow as more accepting of Freud than I do.

22. Glasgow, "Opening Speech of the Southern Writers Conference" (1931), in Raper, *Ellen Glasgow's Reasonable Doubts*, 92.

23. Smith, "Self, Subject, and Resistance," 13.

24. Ibid., 13.

25. See Godbold, *Ellen Glasgow*, 27; Raper, *Without Shelter*, 29; Parent, *Ellen Glasgow, Romancière*, 137n; Wagner, *Ellen Glasgow*, 8.

26. Notes for *The Woman Within*, Glasgow Papers, box 5.

27. Most notably, Chodorow, *The Reproduction of Mothering*; Gilligan, *In a Different Voice*; Gilligan et al., *Making Connections*; and Jean Baker Miller, *Toward a New Psychology*. See also the Introduction to *The Voyage In*, ed. Abel et al., for a helpful overview, and chapter 2, note 8, above.

28. See Marilyn R. Chandler, "Healing the Woman Within," 94–96, on images of "entrapment" in *The Woman Within.*

29. See Gilligan et al., *Making Connections*, on adolescent girls' acceptance of this model; and Gilligan, *In a Different Voice*, on the limitations of psychological studies historically based on this model.

30. Belenky et al., *Women's Ways of Knowing*, 17–20; ibid., 18.

31. Lois Rudnick, "A Feminist American Success Myth," 153.

32. Glasgow, *The Descendant*, 73; Glasgow, *Barren Ground*, 366.

33. Chandler, "Healing the Woman Within," 104. More recently, Will Brantley, *Feminine Sense*, also briefly discusses Glasgow's "fluid" notion of time (92).

34. On the "two things" that "never failed," see Glasgow, "I Believe" (1938), in Raper, *Ellen Glasgow's Reasonable Doubts*, 244 and "Unidentified Notes" in Glasgow Papers, box 7; Glasgow, "Branch Cabell Still Clings to His Unbelief" (1935), in Raper, *Ellen Glasgow's Reasonable Doubts*, 218.

35. Typed draft of *The Woman Within* [n.d.], Glasgow Papers, box 5.

36. Ibid.

37. Both Sahli, "Smashing," and Vicinus, "Distance and Desire," discuss

the customary older-younger pairing in women's friendships around the turn of the twentieth century.

38. For an explanation of Glasgow's will by her attorneys, an informative article in the Richmond *News Leader* on 3 December 1945, and copies of Glasgow's letters of instruction to Anne Virginia Bennett and Rebe Glasgow Tutwiler, see Rawlings Papers, sections A.15 and A.16. Godbold, *Ellen Glasgow and the Woman Within,* 296–97, also describes Glasgow's final wishes.

39. Agnes Reese to Glasgow, 27 December 1941, Glasgow Papers, box 17.

Works Cited

Manuscript Collections

Theodore Dreiser Collection. University of Pennsylvania Library, Philadelphia.
Ellen Glasgow Papers. Accession number 5060. University of Virginia Library, Charlottesville.
Mary Johnston Papers. Accession number 3588. University of Virginia Library, Charlottesville.
Papers of Louise Chandler Moulton. Accession number MSS 18,869 (reel 5). Library of Congress, Washington, D.C.
Marjorie Kinnan Rawlings Papers. Rare Books and Manuscripts. University of Florida, Gainesville.

Works by Ellen Glasgow

The Ancient Law. New York: Doubleday, Page, 1908.
Barren Ground. Garden City, N.Y.: Doubleday, 1925; vol. 1 of Virginia Edition (1938).
" 'The Biography of Manuel.' " *Saturday Review of Literature,* 7 June 1930: 1108–9. Reprinted in *Ellen Glasgow's Reasonable Doubts,* ed. Raper, 205–16.
"Branch Cabell Still Clings to His Unbelief." New York *Herald-Tribune Books,* 6 October 1935: 7. Reprinted in *Ellen Glasgow's Reasonable Doubts,* ed. Raper, 216–18.
The Builders. Garden City, N.Y.: Doubleday, Page, 1919.
A Certain Measure: An Interpretation of Prose Fiction. New York: Harcourt, Brace, 1943.
The Collected Stories of Ellen Glasgow. Ed. Richard K. Meeker. Baton Rouge: Louisiana State University Press, 1963.
"Dare's Gift." In *The Shadowy Third and Other Stories* (1923). Reprinted in *Collected Stories,* ed. Meeker, 90–118.
The Descendant. New York: Harper, 1897.
"Elder and Younger Brother." *Saturday Review of Literature,* 23 January 1937: 3–5. Reprinted in *Ellen Glasgow's Reasonable Doubts,* ed. Raper, 167–74.
Ellen Glasgow's Reasonable Doubts: A Collection of Her Writings. Ed. Julius Rowan Raper. Baton Rouge: Louisiana State University Press, 1988.
" 'Evasive Idealism' in Literature: An Interview by Joyce Kilmer." New York

Works Cited

Times Magazine, 5 March 1916. Reprinted in Kilmer, *Literature in the Making*, and in *Ellen Glasgow's Reasonable Doubts*, ed. Raper, 122–29.

"Feminism." *New York Times Review of Books*, 30 November 1913: 656–57. Reprinted in *Ellen Glasgow's Reasonable Doubts*, ed. Raper, 26–36.

"George Santayana Writes a 'Novel.'" New York *Herald-Tribune Books*, 2 February 1936: 1–2. Reprinted in *Ellen Glasgow's Reasonable Doubts*, ed. Raper, 189–97.

"I Believe." In Clifton Fadiman, ed., *I Believe: The Personal Philosophies of Certain Eminent Men and Women of Our Time*. New York: Simon and Schuster, 1938. Reprinted in *Ellen Glasgow's Reasonable Doubts*, ed. Raper, 228–45.

"Impressions of the Novel." New York *Herald-Tribune Books*, 20 May 1928: 1, 5–6. Reprinted in *Ellen Glasgow's Reasonable Doubts*, ed. Raper, 140–50.

"Jordan's End." In *The Shadowy Third and Other Stories* (1923). Reprinted in *The Collected Stories*, ed. Meeker, 203–16.

Letters of Ellen Glasgow. Ed. Blair Rouse. New York: Harcourt Brace, 1958.

Life and Gabriella. Garden City, N.Y.: Doubleday, 1916; vol. 12 of Virginia Edition (1938).

"Literary Realism or Nominalism: An Imaginary Conversation" (1921). In *Ellen Glasgow's Reasonable Doubts*, ed. Raper, 129–37.

The Miller of Old Church. New York: Doubleday, 1911; vol. 2 of Virginia Edition (1938).

"No Valid Reason against Giving Votes to Women: An Interview." New York *Times*, 23 March 1913: sec. 6, p. 11. Reprinted in *Ellen Glasgow's Reasonable Doubts*, ed. Raper, 19–26.

"The Novel in the South." *Harper's Magazine* 157 (December 1928): 93–100. Reprinted in *Ellen Glasgow's Reasonable Doubts*, ed. Raper, 68–83.

One Man in His Time. Garden City, N.Y.: Doubleday, Page, 1922.

"One Way to Write Novels." *Saturday Review of Literature*, 8 December 1934: 335, 344, 350. Reprinted in *Ellen Glasgow's Reasonable Doubts*, ed. Raper, 150–62.

"Opening Speech of the Southern Writers Conference" (1931). In *Ellen Glasgow's Reasonable Doubts*, ed. Raper, 90–98.

"The Past." In *The Shadowy Third and Other Stories* (1923). Reprinted in *Collected Stories*, ed. Meeker, 119–39.

Phases of an Inferior Planet. New York: Harper, 1898.

The Romance of a Plain Man. New York: Macmillan, 1909, vol. 11 of Virginia Edition (1938).

"The Shadowy Third." In *The Shadowy Third and Other Stories* (1923). Reprinted in *Collected Stories*, ed. Meeker, 52–72.

The Shadowy Third and Other Stories. Garden City, N.Y.: Doubleday, 1923.

The Sheltered Life. Garden City, N.Y.: Doubleday, 1932; vol. 4 of Virginia Edition.

Works Cited

"Some Literary Woman Myths." New York *Herald-Tribune Books*, 27 May 1928: 1, 5–6. Reprinted in *Ellen Glasgow's Reasonable Doubts*, ed. Raper, 36–45.

They Stooped to Folly. Garden City, N.Y.: Doubleday, 1929; vol. 6 of Virginia Edition.

"Van Doren on Cabell." New York *Herald-Tribune Books*, 5 April 1925: 3–4. Reprinted in *Ellen Glasgow's Reasonable Doubts*, ed. Raper, 201–4.

Virginia. New York: Doubleday, 1913; vol. 9 of Virginia Edition.

The Virginia Edition of the Works of Ellen Glasgow. 12 vols. New York: Scribners, 1938.

"What I Believe." *Nation* 36 (12 April 1933): 404–6. Reprinted in *Ellen Glasgow's Reasonable Doubts*, ed. Raper, 219–27.

The Wheel of Life. New York: Doubleday, Page, 1906.

"Whispering Leaves." In *The Shadowy Third and Other Stories* (1923). Reprinted in *Collected Stories*, ed. Meeker, 140–64.

"A Woman of To-morrow." *Short Stories* 29 (May / August 1895): 415–27. Reprinted in *Ellen Glasgow's Reasonable Doubts*, ed. Raper, 1–14.

The Woman Within. New York: Harcourt, Brace, 1954.

Secondary Sources

Abel, Elizabeth. "(E)Merging Identities: The Dynamics of Female Friendship in Contemporary Fiction by Women." *Signs* 6, no. 3 (Spring 1981): 413–35.

Abel, Elizabeth, and Emily K. Abel, eds. *The Signs Reader: Women, Gender and Scholarship*. Chicago: University of Chicago Press, 1983.

Abel, Elizabeth, Marianne Hirsch, and Elizabeth Langland, eds. *The Voyage In: Fictions of Female Development*. Hanover, N.H.: University Press of New England, 1983.

Alcott, Louisa May. *Little Women*. New York: Penguin, 1989.

Allsup, Judith L. "Feminism in the Novels of Ellen Glasgow." Ph.D. diss., Southern Illinois University, 1973.

Ammons, Elizabeth. *Conflicting Stories: American Women Writers at the Turn into the Twentieth Century*. New York: Oxford University Press, 1991.

Andreadis, Harriette. "The Sapphic-Platonics of Katherine Philips, 1632–1664." *Signs: A Journal of Women in Culture and Society* 15, no. 1 (Autumn 1989): 34–60.

Auerbach, Nina. *Romantic Imprisonment: Women and Other Glorious Outcasts*. New York: Columbia University Press, 1985.

———. *Woman and the Demon: The Life of a Victorian Myth*. Cambridge, Mass.: Harvard University Press, 1982.

Beauvoir, Simone de. *The Second Sex*. Translated by H. M. Parshley. New York: Knopf, 1953; reprint (2 vols. in 1) New York: Vintage, 1989. Originally published as *Le deuxième sexe:* vol. 1, *Les faits et les mythes;* vol. 2, *L'éxpérience vécue.* Paris: Librairie Gallimard, 1949.

Belenky, Mary Field, Blythe McVicker Clinchy, Nancy Rule Goldberger, and Jill Mattuck Tarule. *Women's Ways of Knowing: The Development of Self, Voice, and Mind.* New York: Basic Books, 1986.

Benstock, Shari, ed. *The Private Self: Theory and Practice of Women's Autobiographical Writings.* Chapel Hill: University of North Carolina Press, 1988.

Bernikow, Louise. *Among Women.* New York: Crown, 1980.

Berry, J. Bill, ed. *Located Lives: Place and Idea in Southern Autobiography.* Athens: University of Georgia Press, 1990.

Bigelow, Gordon E., and Laura V. Monti, eds. *Selected Letters of Marjorie Kinnan Rawlings.* Gainesville: University Presses of Florida, 1983.

Brantley, Will. *Feminine Sense in Southern Memoir: Smith, Glasgow, Welty, Hellman, Porter, and Hurston.* Jackson: University Press of Mississippi, 1993.

Brodzki, Bella, and Celeste Schenck, eds. *Life / Lines: Theorizing Women's Autobiography.* Ithaca, N.Y.: Cornell University Press, 1988.

"By the Great Unknown." [Review of *The Descendant.*] *Chap-Book* 6 (1 April 1897): 403–4.

Cabell, James Branch. *As I Remember It: Some Epilogues in Recollection.* New York: McBride, 1955.

Caldwell, Ellen M. "Ellen Glasgow and the Southern Agrarians." *American Literature* 56, no. 2 (May 1984): 203–13.

Carpenter, Lynette. "The Daring Gift in 'Dare's Gift.'" *Studies in Short Fiction* 21 (Spring 1984): 95–102.

———. "Visions of Female Community in Ellen Glasgow's Short Stories." In Lynette Carpenter and Wendy K. Kolmar, eds., *Haunting the House of Fiction: Feminist Perspectives on Ghost Stories by American Women,* 117–41. Knoxville: University of Tennessee Press, 1991.

Chandler, Marilyn R. "Healing the Woman Within: Therapeutic Aspects of Ellen Glasgow's Autobiography." In Berry, ed., *Located Lives,* 93–106.

Chauncey, George, Jr. "From Sexual Inversion to Homosexuality: Medicine And The Changing Conceptualization of Female Deviance." *Salmagundi,* no. 58–59 (Fall 1982–Winter 1983): 115–46.

Chodorow, Nancy. "Family Structure and Feminine Personality." In Rosaldo and Lamphere, eds., *Woman, Culture and Society,* 43–66.

———. *Feminism and Psychoanalytic Theory.* New Haven: Yale University Press, 1989.

———. *The Reproduction of Mothering: Psychoanalysis and the Sociology of Gender.* Berkeley: University of California Press, 1978.

Cixous, Hélène. "Difficult Joys." In Helen Wilcox, Keith McWatters, Ann Thompson, and Linda R. Williams, eds., *The Body and the Text: Hélène*

Works Cited

Cixous, Reading and Teaching, 5–30. New York: St. Martin's Press, 1990.

———. "The Laugh of the Medusa." In Abel and Abel, eds., *The Signs Reader,* 279–97.

Collins, Joseph. *The Doctor Looks at Literature: Psychological Studies of Life and Letters.* New York: George H. Doran, 1923.

———. *The Doctor Looks at Love and Life.* New York: George H. Doran, 1926.

Cooper, Frederic Taber. "Inconclusiveness and Some Recent Novels." *Bookman* 37 (July 1913): 536–37.

Cott, Nancy F. *The Bonds of Womanhood: "Woman's Sphere" in New England, 1780–1835.* New Haven: Yale University Press, 1977.

Culley, Margo. "What a Piece of Work is 'Woman'!: An Introduction." In Culley, ed., *American Women's Autobiography: Fea(s)ts of Memory,* 3–31. Madison: University of Wisconsin Press, 1992.

Davidson, Cathy N. *Revolution and the Word: The Rise of the Novel in America.* New York: Oxford University Press, 1986.

Davidson, Cathy N., and E. M. Broner, eds. *The Lost Tradition: Mothers and Daughters in Literature.* New York: Ungar, 1980.

Day, William Patrick. *In the Circles of Fear and Desire: A Study of Gothic Fantasy.* Chicago: University of Chicago Press, 1985.

DeLamotte, Eugenia C. *Perils of the Night: A Feminist Study of Nineteenth-Century Gothic.* New York: Oxford University Press, 1990.

Donovan, Josephine. *After the Fall: The Demeter-Persephone Myth in Wharton, Cather, and Glasgow.* University Park: Pennsylvania State University Press, 1989.

———. *New England Local Color: A Women's Tradition.* New York: Ungar, 1983.

DuPlessis, Rachel Blau. *Writing beyond the Ending: Narrative Strategies of Twentieth-Century Women Writers.* Bloomington: Indiana University Press, 1985.

E[dgett], E[dwin] F[rancis]. "*Virginia:* Ellen Glasgow's Story of Old Fashioned Womanhood." *Boston Evening Transcript,* 19 April 1913: pt. 3, p. 6.

Eichenbaum, Luise, and Susie Orbach. *Between Women: Love, Envy, and Competition in Women's Friendships.* New York: Viking, 1988.

Ekman, Barbro. *The End of a Legend: Ellen Glasgow's History of Southern Women.* Stockholm: Uppsala, 1979.

Ellis, Kate Ferguson. *The Contested Castle: Gothic Novels and the Subversion of Domestic Ideology.* Urbana: University of Illinois Press, 1989.

Erkkila, Betsy. *The Wicked Sisters: Women Poets, Literary History, and Discord.* New York: Oxford University Press, 1992.

Ezell, Margaret J. M. "The Myth of Judith Shakespeare: Creating the Canon of Women's Literature." *New Literary History* 21 (1989–90): 579–92.

————. *Writing Women's Literary History.* Baltimore: Johns Hopkins University Press, 1993.

Faderman, Lillian. *Surpassing the Love of Men: Romantic Friendship and Love Between Women from the Renaissance to the Present.* New York: William Morrow, 1981.

Felski, Rita. *Beyond Feminist Aesthetics: Feminist Literature and Social Change.* Cambridge, Mass.: Harvard University Press, 1989.

Ferguson, Moira, ed. *First Feminists: British Women Writers, 1578–1799.* Bloomington: Indiana University Press, 1985.

Fetterley, Judith. *The Resisting Reader: A Feminist Approach to American Fiction.* Bloomington: Indiana University Press, 1978.

Fiedler, Leslie A. *Love and Death in the American Novel.* New York: Criterion Books, 1960.

Fleenor, Juliann E., ed. *The Female Gothic.* Montreal: Eden Press, 1983.

Friedan, Betty. *The Feminine Mystique.* New York: Dell, 1963.

Gilbert, Sandra M., and Susan Gubar. *The Madwoman in the Attic: The Woman Writer and the Nineteenth-Century Literary Imagination.* New Haven: Yale University Press, 1979.

————. *No Man's Land: The Place of the Woman Writer in the Twentieth Century.* Vol. 1: *The War of the Words.* New Haven: Yale University Press, 1988. Vol. 2: *Sexchanges.* New Haven: Yale University Press, 1989.

Gilligan, Carol. *In A Different Voice: Psychological Theory and Women's Development.* Cambridge, Mass.: Harvard University Press, 1982.

Gilligan, Carol, Nona P. Lyons, and Trudy J. Hammer, eds. *Making Connections: The Relational Worlds of Adolescent Girls at Emma Willard School.* Cambridge, Mass.: Harvard University Press, 1990.

Gilman, Charlotte Perkins. *The Man-Made World; or, Our Androcentric Culture.* New York: Charlton Co., 1911.

Godbold, E. Stanly, Jr. *Ellen Glasgow and the Woman Within.* Baton Rouge: Louisiana State University Press, 1972.

Goodman, Susan. "Competing Visions of Freud in the Memoirs of Ellen Glasgow and Edith Wharton." *Colby Library Quarterly* 25, no. 4 (December 1989): 218–26.

————. *Edith Wharton's Women: Friends and Rivals.* Hanover, N.H.: University Press of New England, 1990.

Greene, Gayle. *Changing the Story: Feminist Fiction and the Tradition.* Bloomington: Indiana University Press, 1991.

————. "Feminist Fiction and the Uses of Memory." *Signs* 16, no. 2 (Winter 1991): 290–321.

Hale, Nathan G., Jr. "From Berggasse XIX to Central Park West: The Americanization of Psychoanalysis, 1919–1940." *Journal of the History of the Behavioral Sciences* 14 (1978): 299–315.

Heilbrun, Carolyn G. "Non-Autobiographies of 'Privileged' Women: England and America." In Brodzki and Schenck, eds., *Life / Lines,* 62–76.

————. *Writing a Woman's Life*. New York: W. W. Norton, 1988.

Herrick, Christine Terhune. "The Author of *The Descendant*." *Critic*, n.s. 27 (5 June 1897): 383.

Holman, C. Hugh. "The Tragedy of Self-Entrapment: Ellen Glasgow's *The Romance of a Plain Man*." In Louis J. Budd, Edwin H. Cady, and Carl L. Anderson, eds., *Toward a New American Literary History: Essays in Honor of Arlin Turner*, 154–63. Durham, N.C.: Duke University Press, 1980.

Howe, Florence. "Introduction: T.S. Eliot, Virginia Woolf, and the Future of 'Tradition.' In Howe, ed., *Tradition and the Talents of Women*, 1–33. Urbana: University of Illinois Press, 1991.

"An Iconoclastic Hero." *New York Times Saturday Review of Books and Art*, 17 April 1897: 7.

Inge, M. Thomas, ed. *Ellen Glasgow: Centennial Essays*. Charlottesville: University Press of Virginia, 1976.

Jelinek, Estelle. *The Tradition of Women's Autobiography from Antiquity to the Present*. Boston: Twayne, 1986.

————, ed. *Women's Autobiography: Essays in Criticism*. Bloomington: Indiana University Press, 1980.

Jones, Anne Goodwyn. *Tomorrow Is Another Day: The Woman Writer in the South, 1859–1936*. Baton Rouge: Louisiana State University Press, 1981.

Kahane, Claire. "The Gothic Mirror." In Shirley Nelson Garner, Claire Kahane, and Madelon Sprengnether, eds., *The (M)Other Tongue: Essays in Feminist Psychoanalytic Interpretation*, 334–51. Ithaca, N.Y.: Cornell University Press, 1985.

Kasson, John F. *Rudeness and Civility: Manners in Nineteenth-Century Urban America*. New York: Hill and Wang, 1990.

Kennard, Jean E. *Vera Brittain and Winifred Holtby: A Working Partnership*. Hanover, N.H.: University Press of New England, 1989.

Kilmer, Joyce. *Literature in the Making*. New York: Harper and Brothers, 1917.

Kolodny, Annette. "A Map for Rereading: Gender and the Interpretation of Literary Texts." In Showalter, ed., *The New Feminist Criticism*, 46–62.

Levy, Helen Fiddyment. *Fiction of the Home Place: Jewett, Cather, Glasgow, Porter, Welty, and Naylor*. Jackson: University Press of Mississippi, 1992.

Lloyd-Smith, Allan Gardner. *Uncanny American Fiction: Medusa's Face*. New York: St. Martin's, 1989.

MacDonald, Edgar E. "An Essay in Bibliography." In Inge, ed. *Ellen Glasgow: Centennial Essays*, 191–224.

MacDonald, Edgar E., and Tonette Bond Inge. *Ellen Glasgow: A Reference Guide*. Boston, Mass.: G. K. Hall, 1986.

McDowell, Frederick P. W. *Ellen Glasgow and the Ironic Art of Fiction*. Madison: University of Wisconsin Press, 1960.

MacKethan, Lucinda H. *Daughters of Time: Creating Woman's Voice in Southern Story.* Athens: University of Georgia Press, 1990.

Marcosson, Isaac F. "*The Voice of the People.*" *Louisville* (Ky.) *Courier-Journal,* 21 April 1900, p. 8.

Massé, Michelle A. "Gothic Repetition: Husbands, Horrors, and Things That Go Bump in the Night." *Signs* 15, no. 4 (1990): 679–709.

Matthews, Pamela R. "Between Ellen and Louise: Female Friendship, Glasgow's Letters to Louise Chandler Moulton, and *The Wheel of Life.*" In Dorothy M. Scura, ed. *Ellen Glasgow: New Perspectives,* Knoxville: University of Tennessee Press, forthcoming.

———. " 'Two Women Blended': Ellen Glasgow and Her Fictions." Ph.D. diss., Duke University, 1988.

Mavor, Elizabeth. *The Ladies of Llangollen.* London: Penguin, 1974.

Meeker, Richard K., ed. *The Collected Stories of Ellen Glasgow.* Baton Rouge: Louisiana State University Press, 1963.

Meese, Elizabeth A. *Crossing the Double-Cross: The Practice of Feminist Criticism.* Chapel Hill: University of North Carolina Press, 1986.

Mencken, H. L. *The Diary of H. L. Mencken.* Ed. Charles A. Fecher. New York: Knopf, 1989.

Meyer, Elizabeth Gallup. *The Social Situation of Women in the Novels of Ellen Glasgow.* Hicksville, N.Y.: Exposition Press, 1978.

Miller, Jean Baker, M.D. *Toward a New Psychology of Women.* Boston: Beacon, 1976.

Miller, Nancy K. *The Heroine's Text: Readings in the French and English Novel, 1722–1782.* New York: Columbia University Press, 1980.

———. *Subject to Change: Reading Feminist Writing.* New York: Columbia University Press, 1988.

———. "Writing Fictions: Women's Autobiography in France." In Brodzki and Schenck, eds., *Life / Lines,* 45–61.

Mitchell, S. Weir. "Rest." In Angela G. Dorenkamp, John F. McCllymer, Mary M. Moynihan, and Arlene C. Vadum, eds., *Images of Women in American Popular Culture,* 24–26. San Diego: Harcourt Brace Jovanovich, 1985.

Moers, Ellen. *Literary Women.* Garden City, N.Y.: Doubleday, 1976.

Moi, Toril. *Sexual / Textual Politics: Feminist Literary Theory.* London: Methuen, 1985. Rpt., London: Routledge, 1988.

Morrison, Toni. *Beloved.* New York: New American Library, 1987.

Nestor, Pauline. *Female Friendships and Communities: Charlotte Brontë, George Eliot, Elizabeth Gaskell.* Oxford: Clarendon Press, 1985.

Ortner, Sherry B. "Is Female to Male as Nature Is to Culture?" In *Woman, Culture and Society,* Rosaldo and Lamphere, eds., 67–87.

Ostriker, Alicia Suskin. *Stealing the Language: The Emergence of Women's Poetry in America.* Boston: Beacon Press, 1986.

————. "The Thieves of Language: Women Poets and Revisionist Mythmaking." In Showalter, ed., *The New Feminist Criticism,* 314–38.

Parent, Monique. *Ellen Glasgow, Romancière.* Paris: A. G. Nizet, 1962.

Parent Frazee, Monique. "Ellen Glasgow as Feminist." In Inge, ed., *Ellen Glasgow: Centennial Essays,* 167–87.

Pratt, Annis. With Barbara White, Andrea Lowenstein, and Mary Wyer. *Archetypal Patterns in Women's Fiction.* Bloomington: Indiana University Press, 1981.

Price Herndl, Diane. *Invalid Women: Figuring Feminine Illness in American Culture, 1840–1940.* Chapel Hill: University of North Carolina Press, 1993.

Rainwater, Catherine. "Narration as Pragmatism in Ellen Glasgow's *Barren Ground.*" *American Literature* 63, no. 4 (December 1991): 664–82.

Raper, Julius Rowan. "Ambivalence toward Authority: A Look at Glasgow's Library, 1890–1906." *Mississippi Quarterly* 31 (1977–78): 5–16.

————. *From the Sunken Garden: The Fiction of Ellen Glasgow, 1916–1945.* Baton Rouge: Louisiana State University Press, 1980.

————. "The Landscape of Revenge: *Barren Ground.*" *Southern Humanities Review* 13, no. 1 (Winter 1979): 63–76.

————. *Without Shelter: The Early Career of Ellen Glasgow.* Baton Rouge: Louisiana State University Press, 1971.

————, ed. *Ellen Glasgow's Reasonable Doubts: A Collection of Her Writings.* Baton Rouge: Louisiana State University Press, 1988.

Raymond, Janice. *A Passion for Friends: Toward a Philosophy of Female Affection.* Boston: Beacon, 1986.

Review of *The Descendant. Bookman,* 5 July 1897: 368–70. Reprinted in Scura, ed., *Ellen Glasgow: The Contemporary Reviews,* 5–6.

Rich, Adrienne. "Education of a Novelist." In her *The Fact of a Doorframe: Poems Selected and New, 1950–1984,* 314–17. New York: W. W. Norton, 1984.

————. "Heroines." In her *The Fact of a Doorframe,* 292–95.

————. *Of Woman Born: Motherhood as Experience and Institution.* 1976; Tenth anniversary edition, New York: W. W. Norton, 1986.

————. "Snapshots of a Daughter-in-Law." In *Adrienne Rich's Poetry and Prose,* selected and edited by Barbara Charlesworth Gelpi and Albert Gelpi, 9–13. New York: W. W. Norton, 1993.

————. "When We Dead Awaken." In *Adrienne Rich's Poetry and Prose,* selected and edited by Barbara Charlesworth Gelpi and Albert Gelpi, 90–98. New York: W. W. Norton, 1993.

Rosaldo, Michelle Z. "The Use and Abuse of Anthropology: Reflections on Feminism and Cross-Cultural Understanding." *Signs: A Journal of Women in Culture and Society* 5 (1980): 389–417.

Rosaldo, Michelle Z., and Louise Lamphere, eds. *Woman, Culture, and Society.* Stanford, Calif.: Stanford University Press, 1974.

Works Cited

Rose, Barbara. "I'll Tell You No Lies: Mary McCarthy's *Memories of a Catholic Girlhood* and the Fictions of Authority." *Tulsa Studies in Women's Literature* 9, no. 1 (Spring 1990): 107–26.

Rouse, Blair, ed. *The Letters of Ellen Glasgow.* New York: Harcourt Brace, 1958.

Rubin, Louis D., Jr. *No Place on Earth: Ellen Glasgow, James Branch Cabell, and Richmond-in-Virginia.* Austin: University of Texas Press, 1959.

Rudnick, Lois. "A Feminist American Success Myth: Jane Addams's *Twenty Years at Hull-House.*" In Howe, ed., *Tradition and the Talents of Women,* 145–67.

Rukeyser, Muriel. *The Collected Poems.* New York: McGraw-Hill, 1978.

Sahli, Nancy. "Smashing: Women's Relationships before the Fall." *Chrysalis* 8 (Summer 1979): 17–27.

Santas, Joan Foster. *Ellen Glasgow's American Dream.* Charlottesville: University Press of Virginia, 1965.

Saunders, Frances W. "Glasgow's Secret Love: 'Gerald B' or 'William T'?" *Ellen Glasgow Newsletter,* no. 31 (Fall 1993): 1, 3–4.

Schultz, Elizabeth. "Out of the Woods and into the World: A Study of Interracial Friendships between Women in American Novels." In Marjorie Pryse and Hortense J. Spillers, eds., *Conjuring: Black Women, Fiction, and Literary Tradition,* 67–85. Bloomington: Indiana University Press, 1985.

Scura, Dorothy M. "A Knowledge in the Heart: Ellen Glasgow, the Women's Movement, and *Virginia.*" *American Literary Realism* 22, no. 2 (Winter 1990): 30–43.

———, ed. *Ellen Glasgow: The Contemporary Reviews.* Cambridge: Cambridge University Press, 1992.

Sedgwick, Eve Kosofsky. *The Coherence of Gothic Conventions.* New York: Arno Press, 1980; rev. and rpt., New York: Methuen, 1986.

Sherman, Sarah Way. *Sarah Orne Jewett: An American Persephone.* Hanover, N.H.: University Press of New England, 1989.

Showalter, Elaine. *Sexual Anarchy: Gender and Culture at the Fin de Siècle.* New York: Viking, 1990.

———. *Sister's Choice: Tradition and Change in American Women's Writings.* Oxford: Clarendon Press, 1991.

———, ed. *These Modern Women: Autobiographical Essays from the Twenties.* New York: Feminist Press, 1989.

Smith, Sidonie. *A Poetics of Women's Autobiography: Marginality and the Fictions of Self-Representation.* Bloomington: Indiana University Press, 1987.

———. "Self, Subject, and Resistance: Marginalities and Twentieth-Century Autobiographical Practice." *Tulsa Studies in Women's Literature* 9, no. 1 (Spring 1990): 11–24.

Works Cited

Smith-Rosenberg, Carroll. *Disorderly Conduct: Visions of Gender in Victorian America*. New York: Knopf, 1985.

———. "The Female World of Love and Ritual: Relations between Women in Nineteenth-Century America." *Signs* 1 (Autumn 1975): 1–29. Reprinted in Abel and Abel, eds. *The Signs Reader*, 27–55.

Spacks, Patricia Meyer. *The Female Imagination*. 1972; rpt. New York: Avon Books, 1976.

Stanton, Domna C. "Autogynography: Is the Subject Different?" In Stanton, ed., *The Female Autograph: Theory and Practice of Autobiography from the Tenth to the Twentieth Century*, 3–20. Chicago: University of Chicago Press, 1987.

Thiébaux, Marcelle. *Ellen Glasgow*. New York: Ungar, 1982.

Todd, Janet. *Women's Friendship in Literature*. New York: Columbia University Press, 1980.

Tompkins, Jane. "Me and My Shadow." In Linda Kauffman, ed., *Gender and Theory: Dialogues on Feminist Criticism*, 121–39. New York: Basil Blackwell, 1989.

———. *West of Everything: The Inner Life of Westerns*. New York: Oxford University Press, 1992.

Torsney, Cheryl B. *Constance Fenimore Woolson: The Grief of Artistry*. Athens: University of Georgia Press, 1989.

Tutwiler, Carrington C., Jr. *A Catalogue of the Library of Ellen Glasgow*. Charlottesville: Bibliographical Society of the University of Virginia, 1969.

———. *Ellen Glasgow's Library*. Charlottesville: Bibliographical Society of the University of Virginia, 1967.

Vallone, Lynne. " 'The True Meaning of Dirt': Putting Good and Bad Girls in Their Place(s)." In Claudia Nelson and Lynne Vallone, eds., *The Girl's Own: Cultural Histories of the Anglo-American Girl, 1830–1915*, 259–283. Athens: University of Georgia Press, 1994.

Vicinus, Martha. "Distance and Desire: English Boarding-School Friendships." *Signs: A Journal of Women in Culture and Society* 9 (Summer 1984): 600–622.

———. *Independent Women: Work and Community for Single Women, 1850–1920*. Chicago: University of Chicago Press, 1985.

"Views and Reviews of Current Fiction." *New York Tribune*, 22 January 1916, 8–9.

Wagner, Linda W. *Ellen Glasgow: Beyond Convention*. Austin: University of Texas Press, 1982.

———. "Ellen Glasgow: Daughter as Justified." In Davidson and Broner, eds., *The Lost Tradition*, 139–46.

Wagner-Martin, Linda. Introduction to Glasgow's *Virginia*. New York: Penguin, 1989.

Walker, Nancy A. "The Romance of Self-Representation: Ellen Glasgow and

Works Cited

The Woman Within." In Dorothy M. Scura, ed. *Ellen Glasgow: New Perspectives,* Knoxville: University of Tennessee Press, forthcoming.

Washington, Mary Helen. *Invented Lives: Narratives of Black Women, 1860–1960.* New York: Anchor Books, 1987.

Wellford, Clarence. "The Author of *The Descendant,*" *Harper's Bazar,* 30 (5 June 1897): 458. Reprinted in Scura, ed., *Ellen Glasgow: The Contemporary Reviews,* 8–10.

Welter, Barbara. "The Cult of True Womanhood." *Arizona Quarterly,* 18 (1966): 151–74.

Wolstenholme, Susan. *Gothic (Re)Visions: Writing Women as Readers.* Albany: State University of New York Press, 1993.

Woolf, Virginia. "Professions for Women." In *Women and Writing,* edited and with an introduction by Michele Barrett, 57–63. New York: Harcourt Brace, 1979.

Yeager, Patricia. *Honey-Mad Women: Emancipatory Strategies in Women's Writing.* New York: Columbia University Press, 1988.

Zimmerman, Bonnie. "Exiting from Patriarchy: The Lesbian Novel of Development." In Abel, Hirsch, and Langland, eds., *The Voyage In,* 244–57.

Index

Index

Index

Moody, Fluvanna (*Barren Ground*), 159–62
Morley, Frank V. (literary executor), 207
Morrison, Toni (*Beloved*), 82
Motherhood, 76, 100, 141–42, 224 n. 20, 227 n. 49, 231 n. 13
Moulton, Louise Chandler, 51–52, 54–55, 206
Musin, Mariana (*Phases of an Inferior Planet*), 33–38, 44

Narrative viewpoint, 124, 145, 147, 171
Nature, 138–39, 157, 165
New Woman, ix, 3, 27, 99, 158, 169
New York City, Glasgow's residence in, 88
"No Valid Reason against Giving Votes to Women" (Glasgow), 17–18

Oakley, Dorinda (*Barren Ground*), 152–65
One Man in His Time (Glasgow), 63, 97–102
One West Main (Glasgow house), 89, 190
Orback, Susie. *See* Eichenbaum, Luise
Ortner, Sherry B., 222 n. 63, 229 n. 28
Ostriker, Alicia Suskin, 214 n. 2, 216 n. 29

Page, Corinna (*One Man in His Time*), 97–100, 227 n. 46
Paradise Lost (Milton), 11
Parent, Monique, 72, 104, 227 n. 56
"Past, The" (Glasgow), 130–36
Patterson, Elizabeth (Mrs. E. M. Crutchfield), 25, 39–40, 45, 48, 104, 206
Pedlar's Mill (*Barren Ground*), 156–59, 161
Pendleton, Lucy (*Virginia*), 76, 78, 83, 85
Pendleton, Virginia (*Virginia*), 73–75, 77–79, 82–87
Phases of an Inferior Planet (Glasgow), 32–38, 40, 42, 187
Poe, Edgar Allan, 147, 230 n. 34
"Point in Morals, A" (Glasgow), 32
Pratt, Annis, 229 n. 28
Price Herndl, Diane, 45, 226 n. 36, 230 n. 30
Psychology: Glasgow's books on, 194–95, 231 n. 5; Glasgow's friendship with Joseph Collins, 235 n. 14; theories of, 9, 20, 26; *see also* Collins, Joseph; Ellis, Havelock; Freud, Sigmund; Krafft-Ebing, Richard
Psychopathia Sexualis (Krafft-Ebing), 37

Psychopathology of Everyday Life, The (Freud), 194
Public / private dichotomy, ix, 7, 13, 19, 26–28, 125; *see also* Separate spheres

Race, 26, 81–82, 161, 184, 208, 230 n. 30
Rainwater, Catherine, 157
Randolph, Margaret ("The Shadowy Third"), 115–24
Raper, Julius Rowan, 44, 50, 53, 113, 134
Rawlings, Marjorie Kinnan: and Henry Anderson, 95–96; and Anne Virginia Bennett, 104; friendship with Glasgow, 155; and notes for Glasgow biography, 54, 72, 102, 111; in *The Woman Within*, 206
Rawlings, Virginia (family friend), 24–25
Raymond, Janice, 226 n. 37
Reese, Agnes (family friend), 208
Rhody, Mammy ("Whispering Leaves"), 137–44
Rich, Adrienne, 1, 8, 87, 97, 161, 213 n. 2; works: "Education of a Novelist," 161, 230 n. 30; "Heroines," 87; *Of Woman Born*, 219 n. 15; "Snapshots of a Daughter-in-Law," 97
Richardson, Samuel, 11; *see also* Harlowe, Clarissa
Richmond, Virginia, 11, 25, 88, 108, 114
Rives Troubetzkoy, Amélie, 2, 51, 155, 177
Romance of a Plain Man, The (Glasgow), 62–68, 69
Romantic Comedians, The (Glasgow), 195
Romney, George, 98
Rosaldo, Michelle Z., 218 n. 4
Rose, Barbara, 194
Rouse, Blair, 7, 50, 224 n. 12
Rubin, Louis D., 5
Rudnick, Lois, 201
Rukeyser, Muriel, 13

Sahli, Nancy, 220 n. 32, 236 n. 37
Santas, Joan Foster, 224 n. 14, 232 n. 15
Saunders, Frances W., 221 n. 34
Schenck, Celeste, 216 n. 33
Schultz, Elizabeth, 161
Scura, Dorothy M., 225 n. 28
Second Sex, The (Beauvoir), 1
Sedgwick, Eve Kosofsky, 112, 132
Self, female, 10
Self-definition, women's, 107
Self-denial, women's: as a consequence of rejecting female affiliation, 60, 69; as imposed by men, 63; in *The Miller*

Feminist Issues: Practice, Politics, Theory
Alison Booth and Ann Lane, Editors

Carol Siegel, *Lawrence among the Women:*
Wavering Boundaries in Women's Literary Traditions

Harriet Blodgett, ed., *Capacious Hold-All:*
An Anthology of Englishwomen's Diary Writings

Joy Wiltenburg, *Disorderly Women and Female Power in the Street*
Literature of Early Modern England and Germany

Diane P. Freedman, *An Alchemy of Genres:*
Cross-Genre Writing by American Feminist Poet-Critics

Jean O'Barr and Mary Wyer, eds., *Engaging Feminism:*
Students Speak Up and Speak Out

Kari Weil, *Androgyny and the Denial of Difference*

Anne Firor Scott, ed., *Unheard Voices:*
The First Historians of Southern Women

Alison Booth, ed., *Famous Last Words:*
Changes in Gender and Narrative Closure

Marilyn May Lombardi, ed., *Elizabeth Bishop:*
The Geography of Gender

Heidi Hutner, ed., *Rereading Aphra Behn:*
History, Theory, and Criticism

Peter J. Burgard, ed., *Nietzsche and Feminism*

Frances Gray, *Women and Laughter*

Nita Kumar, ed., *Women as Subjects: South Asian Histories*

Elizabeth A. Scarlett, *Under Construction: The Body in Spanish Novels*

Pamela R. Matthews, *Ellen Glasgow and a Woman's Traditions*

Mahnaz Afkhami, *Women in Exile*